AMERICA'S
NATIONAL PASTIME

AMERICA'S NATIONAL PASTIME

A Study of Race and Merit in Professional Baseball

BRET L. BILLET
and
LANCE J. FORMWALT

PRAEGER

Westport, Connecticut
London

Library of Congress Cataloging-in-Publication Data

Billet, Bret L.
    America's national pastime : a study of race and merit in
professional baseball / Bret L. Billet and Lance J. Formwalt.
        p.   cm.
    Includes bibliographical references and index.
    ISBN 0–275–95193–6 (alk. paper)
    1. Baseball—United States—History. 2. Discrimination in sports—
United States. 3. United States—Race relations. I. Formwalt,
Lance J. II. Title.
GV863.A1B56   1995
796.357′0973—dc20   95–3331

British Library Cataloguing in Publication Data is available.

Library of Congress Catalog Card Number: 95–3331
ISBN: 0–275–95193–6

First published in 1995

Praeger Publishers, 88 Post Road West, Westport, CT 06881
An imprint of Greenwood Publishing Group, Inc.

Printed in the United States of America

The paper used in this book complies with the
Permanent Paper Standard issued by the National
Information Standards Organization (Z39.48–1984).

10 9 8 7 6 5 4 3 2 1

Contents

Figures and Tables

FIGURES

TABLES

Acknowledgments

I would like to take time to thank a few people for their involvement throughout this project. First, thanks to co-author, professor, and friend, Dr. Bret L. Billet, for guidance and assistance throughout the writing of this book. Without his encouragement, it is unlikely that this project would have come to fruition as I must admit that I was at first skeptical about the feasibility of embarking on and completing what, to an undergraduate student, seemed like such an immense task.

In addition, I would like to thank my parents, Bill and Glennis Formwalt, not only for their encouragement during this project, but also for their many sacrifices and the time they have committed in raising their three boys in the best way possible. Any success that I may have will be attributed to your efforts as parents.

Lance J. Formwalt

It seems to me that in academic life too few chances for collaborative learning occur and that, in actuality, few of these chances are turned into a brief reality. My co-author, and more importantly, friend, has restored in me what was a waning belief that collaboration is not only a learning experience, but one that is also invigorating. The fact that this effort was in association with a pupil is all the more meaningful.

There are several individuals that I would like to thank including my wife Paula, and our son Brandon. Both have continued to exercise great patience with a person who is all too easily distracted and consumed by everyday events. It is with sincere gratitude that I thank them. Moreover, I would like to thank our department secretary, Terri Roose, who assisted throughout the preparation of the manuscript. Although all errors of omission and/or commission rest with us, we are indeed thankful of all who have provided assistance with respect to this project. To all our family, friends, and colleagues, Godspeed.

Bret L. Billet

Abbreviations

A	Assists
AB	At Bats
ALERA	Average Earned Run Average in the American League
ANCH	Adjusted Net Chances
ATPV	Adjusted Total Pitcher's Value
BA	Batting Average
BB	Base on Balls (Walks)
CS	Caught Stealing
E	Errors
ERA	Earned Run Average
FR	Fielding Runs
GP	Games Played
HR	Homeruns
HWS	Hits and Walks given up during a Season
IP	Innings Pitched
MET	Size of Metropolitan Area (Potential Revenue)
NCH	Net Chances
NLERA	Average Earned Run Average in the National League
ORS	Offensive Runs Scored
PO	Putouts
POS	Position of non-pitching player
PPOS	Pitcher Position
PRAL	Pitching Runs American League
PRNL	Pitching Runs National League
PTB	Pitcher's Total Bases
RACE	Racial/Ethnic Background
RAT	Ratio of Hits and Walks per Nine Innings
RBI	Runs Batted In
SA	Slugging Average
SAL89	Total Salary in 1989

SAL90	Total Salary in 1990
SAL91	Total Salary in 1991
SB	Stolen Bases
TB	Total Bases
THV1B	Total Hitter Value for First Base
THV2B	Total Hitter Value for Second Base
THV3B	Total Hitter Value for Third Base
THVOF	Total Hitter Value for Outfielder
THVSS	Total Hitter Value for Shortstop
TPV	Total Pitcher's Value
YRS	Years Experience in Major Leagues

AMERICA'S
NATIONAL PASTIME

Chapter 1

Introduction:
Race and Meritocracy in America

Throughout its history the sport of professional baseball has been regarded as America's national pastime. It is perhaps the most widely regarded sport in the country. It has not only captured the attention of all ages, but has also been incorporated within the fantasies of young and old alike. If anything is a given in American society it is this enduring quality of baseball and the way that families structure their summer activities according to the schedules of games. Not only is it a mainstay, but it is also deeply embedded in the American culture. Ask a youth what it is they plan to do during their summer vacation and they invariably respond that baseball or softball will be a part of it. When desire and age allow they take to the fields for tee-ball, little league, and the like. Those not as young often join adult city leagues or participate in neighborhood and family games. Those for whom their playing days have passed can often be seen taking in a game, whether it is city league or professional.

Those who are exceptional players are heralded as "standouts" and generate for themselves a great deal of attention. Typically, their abilities are not initially well developed. Those who are afforded and have taken the time to develop the potential within, often succeed and progress to levels that the majority who take up the game can only realize in dream. But fair is fair and the development of the necessary skills to play the game better than most is not something that comes easy. The individual effort required is often more than most are either able or willing to invest. The expectation, however, is that individual drive and effort may one day result in the chance to play in the big leagues. Although most do not make it to this level, they remain an integral part of the cultural experience by their continued participation at other levels and their allegiance to viewing those whose skills are superior to their own. Table 1.1 illustrates that home attendance has continued to grow at major league baseball games. It also suggests that although attendance has continually increased at American League

Table 1.1
Average Attendance at Major League Baseball Games, 1980-1991
(in thousands)

	American League	National League	Overall
1991	32,118	24,696	56,814
1990	30,332	24,492	54,824
1989	29,849	25,324	55,173
1988	28,500	24,499	52,999
1987	27,277	24,734	52,011
1986	25,173	22,333	47,506
1985	24,532	22,292	46,824
1984	23,961	20,781	44,742
1983	23,991	21,549	45,540
1982	23,080	21,507	44,587
1981*	14,066	12,478	26,544
1980	21,890	21,124	43,014

* strike year.
Source: Statistical Abstract of the United States, various years.

ballparks, it has remained relatively constant between 1987 and 1991 at National League ballparks. The key conclusion, however, is that baseball is not only alive and well, but has expanded considerably as shown by attendance over both leagues throughout the 1980s and early 1990s.

To summarize, the American League has witnessed an average annual increase in attendance of 3.9% between the years 1980 and 1991 (46.7% increase if 1980 and 1991 are taken alone as "bookend" years). The National League has seen an average annual increase of 1.7% (16.9% increase for the bookend years of 1980 and 1991). Moreover, overall attendance at major league ballparks has grown at an average annual rate of 2.9% (32.1% for the bookend years). It is abundantly clear from this cursory analysis that baseball continues to grow in popularity as perhaps the greatest spectator sport in the United States.[1]

The national pastime has also grown in terms of it being a recreational activity for millions each year. Table 1.2 illustrates the degree to which swinging the bat has become a favorite recreational activity compared to other major sports. It also indicates that the overall number of participants in recreational sports has increased throughout 1986-91 and that this has been the general trend for baseball, basketball, and football in particular. The numbers further indicate that baseball is the largest recreational sport of the three for this time period.[2] Moreover, more people participated in baseball than in football and basketball together in 1986. Whether looking at recreational or spectator sports, the role of baseball continues to be of vital significance and may well justify it being referred to as America's national pastime.

Table 1.2
Participation in Selected Recreational Activities, 1986-1991 (in thousands)

	Baseball	Basketball	Football	Overall
1991	36,194	26,150	13,287	228,756
1990	35,652	26,315	14,451	224,648
1989	37,498	26,182	14,728	222,551
1988	34,043	23,202	12,360	216,837
1987	36,667	25,168	14,970	216,963
1986	34,801	21,267	12,030	214,818

Source: Statistical Abstract of the United States, various years.

Although it is an enjoyable and relaxing pursuit for the majority who take part in it, the national pastime has come under attack. Stated cogently, many believe that baseball has continued to perpetuate the cultural myth that not only are individuals free to develop and refine their skills, but that all have an equal opportunity to progress to the pinnacle of the sport in the United States. Moreover, the myth continues with the notion that, *ceteris paribus*, renumeration for players of similar quality will be comparable. In sum, the crux of the attack is the proposition that America's national pastime has mirrored the larger society with respect to issues of race and meritocracy.

Although plausible, the possibility of the latter is quite disturbing because it suggests that professional baseball is nothing more than a microcosm of the larger society and culture. Moreover, it assumes from the outset that the American culture is characterized by racist behavior. There are obvious implications stemming from this view. Perhaps most noteworthy is the implication that individuals are brought up believing that America is, in reality, for a privileged few and that those few are typically white males. Moreover, it suggests that even if minorities succeed and gain entrance into the big leagues, that they still will not be treated as equals in terms of remuneration. This is irrespective of the assumption that the skills of both groups are comparable.

This viewpoint is one that must be further investigated prior to suggesting that what might only be perception is in reality the fact for the majority who aspire to make it in the big leagues and achieve equality in every sense of the word. This book is an investigation of the relationship between racism and meritocracy in professional baseball. It critically evaluates the role that two important factors in the debate, race and player performance, have in determining the extent to which the sport of professional baseball is indeed a "microcosm" of what is generally regarded as a culture that continues to harbor racist attitudes, beliefs, and practices. To investigate the latter, this analysis will proceed with a brief overview of the current state of racism in American society. Building on this, an inquiry into the current state of racism in professional baseball is undertaken. Finally, these two inquiries are integrated in order to judge, even at this preliminary stage, the degree to which baseball (and the notion of racism) is a "microcosm" of the larger society. To facilitate this, a brief consideration is given to several studies that clarify the relevance of race in professional baseball.

THE CURRENT STATE OF RACE IN THE UNITED STATES

Any discussion regarding racism as part of the dominant culture of a country must begin by establishing what is meant by the concepts racism, racialism, and culture. According to Lachmann (1991: 241) racism is "a belief in racial superiority that leads to discrimination and prejudice toward those races considered inferior. In the United States racism has most frequently taken the form of white antagonism toward blacks, but other groups, such as Asians, have also been victimized." Moreover, Lachmann (1991: 241) indicates that racism is a derivative form of the Doctrine of Racialism, which can be defined as

the attribution of cultural differences to the genetic characteristics of physically distinct populations. . . . The concomitant attempt to construct grades of cultural development, from savagery to civilization, entrenched the alleged connection of biological features with mental, moral, and artistic abilities. This belief caused the darker races to be branded "culturally inferior" and thus provided a so-called scientific justification for European colonial expansion and domination.

Both the concepts racism and racialism lead one to believe that discriminatory and prejudicial practices will follow once the attitude of a superior-inferior relationship is firmly entrenched. Unmistakably, discrimination and prejudice are perhaps the two most notorious means to carry out the practice of racism and the doctrine of racialism. According to Lachmann (1991: 89) discrimination can be defined as the "unfavorable treatment of groups of people on arbitrary grounds, a form of control that keeps the groups socially distant from one another. This separation [segregation] is accomplished through institutionalized practices that attribute inferiority on the basis of notions that frequently have little or nothing to do with the real behavior of those who are discriminated against." Similarly, Lachmann (1991: 227) defines prejudice as

a feeling or attitude, usually unfavorable or hostile, directed toward a person or group. Prejudice is often considered an individual phenomenon originating in various psychological conditions. Although this view is true, prejudice must also be seen as an integral part of the culture that passes it on by means of the socialization process. . . . If an individual is not prejudiced, he is capable of rectifying his faulty judgments when confronted with new evidence. A prejudiced person, however, will become emotional and resistant when entrenched attitudes are threatened.

This exercise on specifically delineating what is meant by many concepts that are routinely utilized but rarely understood is instrumental in assessing the current state of race in the United States. The sociological development of issues of race in this manner leads one to assess the dominant culture in terms of its social heritage (i.e., customs that are developed and handed down through generations) and norms (i.e., prescriptions about what one can and proscriptions about what one cannot do in a given society). The remainder of this section deals with the evolution of culture in the United States in order to shed light not only on what the dominant culture has been, but how race has played an important role therein. Figure 1.1 details in summary fashion the key events in the evolution of race in the United States in order to provide a more orderly dissemination of the information to be discussed below.

Frantzich and Percy (1994: 613) define culture as "those aspects of a society's history, artistic accomplishment, and attitudes toward the world deemed worthy of transmission from one generation to the next." It is safe to maintain that the dominant set of beliefs and attitudes (i.e., culture) at the inception of the republic were characterized by overt racism.[3] With respect to issues of race there was a definite "home-team" advantage for the white male in society. Members of society, if allowed to participate in the game of politics, would have to submit to playing by the rules of the white male. Moreover, being conversant with the rules and accepting them as the foundation for the way that society was to operate was a definite advantage. In essence, if you knew and were accepting of the "playing field" of the white male you would undoubtedly fare better than those playing outside of the rules.

This overt racism made itself manifest in the earliest relations of the new republic. Moreover, institutionalized discrimination was permitted against groups that were not "on an even playing field" with the white male. The most heralded form of this discrimination and prejudice was the enfranchisement (or lack thereof) of individuals not on the playing field. Although individualism and the desire to be part of the game (i.e., participatory) was an important tenet of the dominant political culture, it was reserved for the elite (i.e., constituted by race, gender, and economics).

The new Constitution of 1787 institutionalized a wide array of discriminatory practices that would be carried on through successive generations as the dominant political culture. Among them was the manner by which blacks[4] were counted for purposes of representation and taxation. The three-fifths compromise institutionalized what was to become a norm with respect to the creation of a superior-inferior relationship. Moreover, the Constitution gave acceptance to the slave trade when it was established that Congress could not place limitations on the importation or migration of slaves prior to the year 1808.[5]

The institutionalization of a dominant political culture characterized by overt racist discrimination was indeed handed down as "social heritage" for many decades until the political "zeitgeist" was altered by the Civil War. One must make abundantly clear that what changed at this time was the political culture and not the societal culture. The period of Reconstruction that witnessed many statements related to racist discriminatory acts was less of a societal change and more of a political change instituted from the top down. Indeed, had the societal

Figure 1.1
Key Events in the Evolution of Race in the United States

1787	**New Constitution**
	- discriminatory practices against blacks for purposes of taxation and representation
	- allowances for continuation of the slave trade
1857	**Dred Scott v. Sandford**
	- disallowance of claims to freedom via travel to free lands
1861	**Civil War**
1865	- attempt from the top down to abolish slavery
1865	**Ratification of 13th Amendment**
	- outlawed slavery and/or involuntary servitude
1866	**Civil Rights (C.R.) Act of April 9, 1866**
	- overturned President Johnson veto
	- provision of full equality before the law
	- response to "black codes" by former slave states
1866	**C.R. Acts of April 21, 1866 and March 2, 1867**
1867	- prohibition on kidnapping and peonage
	- establishment of penalties for delivering persons into involuntary servitude
1868	**Ratification of 14th Amendment**
	- provision of citizenry for slaves
	- establishment of equal protection under the law
1870	**C.R. Act of May 31, 1870**
	- known as the "enforcement act"
	- establishment of penalties for interference with suffrage
1870	**Ratification of 15th Amendment**
	- enfranchisement of black male population
1871	**C.R. Act of February 28, 1871**
	- amended the enforcement act
	- provision for election supervisors and deputies
1872	**C.R. Act of April 20, 1872**
	- known as the Ku Klux Act or the Anti-Ku Klux Act
	- established to enforce the 14th amendment
1875	**C.R. Act of March 1, 1875**
	- known as the second Civil Rights Act
1875	**Rapid Industrialization**
1890	- northern industrialists economically motivated
	- brought attitude that individual property rights were more important than individual civil rights

---

Figure 1.1
Key Events in the Evolution of Race in the United States, continued

1876	**United States v. Cruikshank**
	- shrank the effectiveness of the enforcement act
	- held section 3 and 4 of the enforcement act unconstitutional
1876	**United States v. Reese**
	- held that 15th amendment did guarantee all citizens the right to vote
1877	**Reconstruction Era Ends**
	- Radical Republican Reconstructionists lose control of the House of House of Representatives
1877	**The Deconstruction of Reconstruction**
	- period began by northern political leaders abandoning blacks
	- Supreme Court declaring many old laws unconstitutional or interpreted them narrowly so as to curve their effectiveness
1883	**The Civil Rights Cases**
	- cases from Kansas, California, Missouri, New York, and Tennessee
	- ruled that the public accommodations section of the 1875 Civil Rights Act unconstitutional
	- reinforced and allowed continuation of the Jim Crow Laws
	- greater introduction of poll taxes, literacy tests, and grandfather clauses
1890	**Progressive Movement**
1954	- attempt to reform to social, economic, and political affairs
1896	**Plessy v. Ferguson**
	- test of the 14th amendment
	- Court established "separate but equal doctrine"
1898	**Williams v. Mississippi**
	- Court upheld legality of literacy tests
1899	**Cumming v. County Board of Education**
	- Court ignored suggestion that separate schools were in reality not equal
1905	**Niagara Movement**
	- led by W.E.B. DuBois
	- pushed for full equality
	- short lived organization; less than five years
1909	**National Association for the Advancement of Colored People People (NAACP)**
	- founded by W.E.B. DuBois, Jane Addams, and others
	- pushed for full equality

Figure 1.1
Key Events in the Evolution of Race in the United States, continued

---

1938   Missouri ex rel. Gaines v. Canada
- Court ruled that Missouri could not shift its responsibility to provide an equal education onto other states
- Gaines assisted by NAACP

1942   Congress of Racial Equality (CORE)
- establish to improve racial standing in society as well as improve race relations

1947   President's Committee on Civil Rights
- established by President Truman
- investigatory body to determine the status of race in the United States

1947   President's Committee on Civil Rights - Report
- called for national laws prohibiting racially motivated brutality, segregation, and poll taxes, and for guarantee's of voting rights and equal employment opportunity

1947   United States Department of Justice
- began submitting briefs to courts in support of civil rights

1954   Brown v. Topeka Board of Education
- overturned Plessy v. Ferguson (1896) and the separate but equal doctrine
- Supreme Court agreed to hear Brown in 1952 but postponed decision in order to achieve a cross-section of the U. S.
- Brown included four cases: Brown (Kansas); Briggs v. Elliott (South Carolina); Davis v. Prince Edward County (Virginia); Gebhart v. Belton (Delaware)
- Argued Plessy was unconstitutional under 14th Amendment
- that psychological and intellectual damage to blacks could not be considered "equal"

1954   Bolling v. Sharpe
- NAACP presented evidence of the harmful impact of state-imposed racial discrimination
- "Doll Study" by black sociologist Kenneth Clark illustrated that segregation has a negative impact on the self-image of black children

1955   Brown II
- provided for the means by which integration would occur
- Supreme Court ruled that racially segregated systems must be dismantled "with all deliberate speed"

Figure 1.1
Key Events in the Evolution of Race in the United States, continued

1955	**Montgomery Bus Boycott**
	- Rosa Parks refusal to leave her seat on a non-integrated Alabama bus
	- broadened the sphere of integration concerns
	- Martin Luther King, Jr. emerges as stronger leadership figure
1957	**Civil Rights Act of 1957**
	- first civil rights law since reconstruction
	- makes it a federal crime to prevent persons from voting in federal elections
1958	**Cooper v. Aaron**
	- ruled that actions of states (i.e., Georgia) to prohibit integration were in violation of the supremacy clause of the federal Constitution
1964	**Civil Rights Act of 1964**
	- bars discrimination in employment, public accommodations and federally funded programs on the basis of race, color, sex, religion, and/or national origin
1965	**Voting Rights Act**
	- strengthened penalties for those interfering with right to vote
	- appointed federal examiners to register voters in area's using discriminating practices
1968	**Fair Housing Act**
	- prohibits discrimination on the basis of race, color, religion, or national origin in the sale or rental of most housing
1984	**Grove City College v. Bell**
	- began under President Carter
	- small religious college in Pennsylvania that did not accept federal funding although many students received federal student loans
	- Supreme Court held that only programs directly affected by federal funding were bound by federal anti-discrimination provisions
1988	**Civil Rights Restoration Act**
	- overrode President Reagan's veto
	- Congress overturned a 1984 Supreme Court ruling that the 1964 Civil Rights Act and the 1972 Education Act applied only to specific parts of institutions receiving federal funding and not to the entire institution
1991	**Civil Rights Act**
	- Amends the 1866 Civil Rights Act to prohibit other forms of racial discrimination in the workplace (i.e., promotions). Items include "race norming" tests (i.e., setting different cut-off scores for different races) for employment or promotion

culture changed dramatically, the Civil War may not ever have been part of the history that shapes issues of race in the American culture yet today. Perhaps the best known court case that illustrates this point is *Dred Scott v. Sandford*[6] (1857).

The institutionalization of the doctrine of racialism and associated prejudicial beliefs and attitudes resurfaced by 1877 as the era of Reconstruction virtually ended. Moreover, 1877 witnessed the "deconstruction of Reconstruction" with respect to issues of race in the United States. Many of the Civil Rights Acts of the 1860s and 1870s were held unconstitutional as the political culture became synchronized once again with the racist societal culture. The 1883 Civil Rights Cases all but solidified this reversion back to a discriminatory and racist status quo.

Subsequent reforms movements such as the Progressive Movement from 1890 to 1954 are perhaps best viewed as a break from the aforementioned "deconstruction of Reconstruction" era. Although the progressive movement was at times half-hearted in its goals, some positive changes did occur during the latter part of the movement in the mid-1900s. At first, however, there appeared to be little change as *Plessy v. Ferguson* (1896) and subsequent court cases were seemingly bent on maintaining some semblance of racial ordering in American society.

The culture did begin to change, however, as new groups such as the Niagara movement, the National Association for the Advancement of Colored People, and the Urban League emerged in the early 1900s. The movement to revamp the dominant political culture became even more noticeable as several court cases such as *Missouri ex rel. Gaines v. Canada* (1938) challenged different aspects of the Plessy ruling. It is important to mention again that what was being changed was the institutionalization of the doctrine of racialism (and its associated practices of prejudice and discrimination) in the dominant political culture. Moreover, the racist societal culture, much as during the Reconstruction Era, was not in serious jeopardy of being radically altered.

The change of the political culture was spurred on with the formation of the Congress of Racial Equality in 1942 and subsequent attempts by the institutions of government to alter the dominant racist culture. To some extent the court cases (i.e., *1954 Brown I* and *1955 Brown II*), presidential committees (i.e., on Civil Rights in 1947), and Congressional acts (i.e., Civil Rights Acts of the 1950s, 1960s, and 1970s) served to alter the existing political culture. As mentioned, however, they failed to alter the societal cultural beliefs that harbored racist tendencies. Moreover, much like during the early days of the republic, if one wanted to get ahead, one was forced to play by the rules and regulations that the majority race had established.

Racist tendencies in the societal culture are still noticeable in the 1980s and 1990s, as court cases such as *Grove City College v. Bell* (1984) emerged in opposition to the Civil Rights legislation of earlier years. It is important to note that although the societal culture has been checked by political institutions, it remains a dominant force in race relations. For all that is good about the progressive movement and the accompanying attempt by political institutions to make the "playing field" more level for all of society's participants, it must be stated that the dominant culture in the United States is still characterized by the doctrine of racialism, albeit less overtly noticeable than in the past.

There is support for the proposition that societal attitudes are illustrative of this ever present "latent racism." Some refer to this as "symbolic" or "modern" racism (Sears, 1988: 53-84) as well as "aversive" racism (Dovidio, 1993: 51-57). In a nutshell, these new forms of racism refer to a negative societal attitude toward race that cannot be expressed overtly in a blatantly prejudicial manner. "Modern" racism is an outgrowth of the recognition that more "traditional" racism (i.e., that which expresses an overt belief that blacks are innately inferior to whites, etc.) is no longer acceptable and that alternative means to express prejudice must be implemented (Weigel and Howes, 1985: 117-138). Often "symbolic" racism takes the form of simple agreement with phrases such as "blacks who receive welfare could get along without it if they tried" (Sears, 1988: 57).

Aversive racism is in reality a subtype of modern racism. Whereas the latter is concerned with those who would publicly maintain a stance characterized by prejudice and discrimination if it were permissible by society, the former refers to those who believe that they are not prejudiced and/or discriminatory toward minorities. The typical aversive racist is one who maintains that they are not prejudiced, but yet exhibits (albeit unconsciously) racist behaviors. Aversive racists typically endorse egalitarian values and will not discriminate against minorities "in situations in which discrimination would be obvious to others and themselves" (Dovidio, 1993: 53).

THE CURRENT STATE OF RACE IN PROFESSIONAL BASEBALL

Looking throughout the evolution of professional baseball in the United States it is not surprising to find many developments that are parallel with the evolution of a dominant political and societal culture regarding issues of race. Moreover, the historical role of race in professional baseball may simply be a microcosm of the larger culture, an expression of the political and social zeitgeist. It is worth noting that just as issues of race in the larger culture continue to be expressed in a less overt manner, this "method" has also creeped into the national pastime with respect to attitudes pertaining to black participation.

This position is illuminated repeatedly by Zoss and Bowman (1989) in their influential work on the untold history of baseball. From the outset Zoss and Bowman (1989: xi) state that "there is no doubt that the same historical circumstances that are responsible for the shape of America are responsible for the special place baseball occupies in the hearts of Americans." Zoss and Bowman (1989: 87) continue, stating that

Figure 1.2
Key Events in the Evolution of Baseball in the United States

1787	**New Constitution**
	- discriminatory practices against blacks for purposes of taxation and representation
	- allowances for continuation of the slave trade
1845	**Codification of Baseball Rules**
	- Alexander J. Cartwright and the New York Knickerbockers
1845	**First Wave of Baseball Mania**
1860	- new teams in the northeast competing
	- organized leagues emerging
1858	**National Association of Base Ball Players (NABBP)**
	- NABBP attempted to define amateurism and prohibit payments to team players
	- 60 organizations enrolled in NABBP by 1860
1867	**Second Wave of Baseball Mania**
	- spread throughout the midwest
	- over one-third of the 300 NABBP organizations were midwestern
1871	**National Association of Professional Base Ball Players (NAPBBP)**
	- organized in response to the NABBP in March 1870
	- established the first professional (player paid) association
1872	**John W. "Bud" Fowler**
	- first black player known to have been paid while playing for a white professional team
1876	**National League of Professional Base Ball Clubs**
	- organized as response to NAPBBP
	- league dominated by club owners rather than players themselves
	- Albert G. Spalding contracted to supply official balls for league games
1879	**Reserve Clause**
	- NAPBBP owners began the practice of inserting reserve clauses in player contracts
	- extended to all players by 1883
1879	**International Association**
	- demise of International Association as a direct competitor of the NAPBBP
1880s	**Baseball Prosperity**
	- player salaries averaged $2,000
	- prosperity mainly for whites - black players were absent from the major leagues by the end of the 1880s

---

Figure 1.2
Key Events in the Evolution of Baseball in the United States, continued

1882	**American Association**
	- American Association (AA) founded; rivals the NAPBBP
	- NAPBBP recognizes American Association in exchange for universal implementation of the reserve clause and promise to refrain from "roster robbing"
1883	**"Golden Age" for Black Players**
1888	- was a brief era wherein several black players were allowed to play in the white leagues
	- the Walker brothers, "Bud" Fowler, George Stovey, and Frank Grant among others
1883	**Moses Fleetwood "Fleet" Walker**
	- played in the minors with Toledo of the then Northwestern League (NWL)
	- first black player to play in the majors when Toledo joined the American Association in 1884
	- younger brother Weldy Walker also played with Toledo in 1884
1884	**Union Association**
	- arose in opposition to NL and AA
	- sought to rally players who opposed the reserve clause
	- defeated quickly by NL and AA
1885	**Golden Age of Dual League Baseball**
1889	- NL and AA owners prospered economically
	- tensions mounted over NL domination
1887	**International League**
	- oldest minor league; banned blacks on July 14
1887	**League of Colored Base Ball Clubs**
	- professional minor league founded
1887	**Collective Bargaining**
	- the Brotherhood of Professional Baseball Players established by player/lawyer John M. Ward
	- ineffective with owners at first
1890	**Players' National League (PNL) of Baseball Clubs**
	- attempt by Ward to "force" the hand of owners with respect to the reserve clause
	- PNL was ultimately unsuccessful in 1890 and led to the subsequent demise of the AA in 1892

Figure 1.2
Key Events in the Evolution of Baseball in the United States, continued

---

1892	**NL Domination**
1899	- reassignment of PNL players led to dispute between NL and AA which saw the AA collapse after the 1891 season
	- player salaries were capped due to indebtedness of owners, the collapse of the players union, and NL owner monopoly
	- maximum player salary was $2,400
1897	**League of Colored Baseball Clubs**
	- initially accepted into organized baseball
	- short-lived; ended in less than one week
1898	**Black absence from professional baseball**
1947	- no blacks played in professional baseball unless able to convince others that they were either Indian or Cuban
1901	**Charlie "Tokohama"**
	- attempt to sneak black player Charlie Grant into baseball by suggesting he was an Indian
1903	**National Agreement of 1903**
	- established a peace between the NL and the challenging Western League that wished to be recognized as the new American League (AL)
	- reinstalled dual major league baseball
	- National Commission created to settle disputes between the leagues
	- leagues now functioned as "separate, but equal"
1914	**Federal League**
	- mounted opposition to the dual leagues
	- short-lived challenge to monopoly practices of the NL and AL. Supreme Court dismissed the case as baseball was deemed a sport and not subject to interstate commerce laws
1920	**Fall of the National Commission**
	- 1919 Chicago White Sox scandal led to the fall of the National Commission and the appointment of Judge Kenesaw M. Landis
	- Landis given broad sweeping powers by owners
1920	**National Negro Baseball League (NNL)**
	- originated by Rube Foster
	- blacks still not allowed in either the major or minor leagues
	- went out of business in 1931 primarily due to economic hardship associated with the depression
1923	**Eastern Colored League**
	- arose as a challenge to the National Negro Baseball League
	- short-lived; became the American Negro League (ANL) in 1929 and subsequently folded

---

Figure 1.2
Key Events in the Evolution of Baseball in the United States, continued

1924	**Black World Series**
	- black leagues put together the first black world series pitting the NNL against the Eastern League
	- continued to be played yearly through 1927
1930	**Player Salaries**
	- average player salary in 1930 was $7,000
1933	**New Negro National League**
	- the establishment of a new Negro National League took the place of the old Negro National League that folded in 1931
	- new league folded in 1948
1937	**Negro American League (NAL)**
	- new league established to replace that which folded in 1929
	- established when the NNL withdrew from playing in the midwest
	- lasted until 1960
1939	**Cooperstown**
	- opening of Baseball Hall of Fame to commemorate the "beginning" of baseball in 1839 by Abner Doubleday
1942	**Black World Series**
	- reestablishment of the black world series
	- primarily between the midwestern and southern based NAL and the northeastern based NNL
	- played annually until 1948
1943	**Bill Veeck and the Phillies**
	- many teams profitted from imported Latin players during World War II
	- Veeck proposed buying the Phillies and manning the roster with black talent - it was rejected
	- players average salary was $6,400
1944	**Death of Commissioner Landis**
	- Landis opposed racial integration
	- A.B. "Happy" Chandler, Landis' successor, favored racial integration
1945	**World War II ends**
	- end of war brought with it demands for racial equality
1945	**Jackie Robinson**
	- Brooklyn Dodgers contracted Jackie Robinson to their farm team in Montreal on October 23
1947	**Jackie Robinson**
	- joined Brooklyn Dodgers and wins National League Rookie of the Year

Figure 1.2
Key Events in the Evolution of Baseball in the United States, continued

---

1947	**Larry Doby**
	- becomes first black player in the AL
	- Robinson and Doby open the majors for blacks
1953	**Major League Players Association**
	- formed by the players to deal with unionism and salary issues
1953	**Black presence in Major Leagues**
	- an estimated twenty blacks now playing in the majors
1959	**Formal Integration Completed**
	- with the integration of the Boston Red Sox in 1959 all major league teams were integrated
1960	**Demise of Black Leagues**
	- NAL folded in 1960 much like its predecessor, the NNL, did in 1948
1966	**Major League Players Association (MLPA)**
	- labor organizer Marvin Miller chosen to head the MLPA
	- Miller united players in the service of better bargaining arrangements and the introduction of "basic agreements" which would increase salaries and pension benefits
1969	**Playoff Arrangements**
	- introduction of league championship series as well as the world series between the NL and AL
1970	**Player Salaries**
	- average player salary in 1970 was $25,000
1980	**Player Salaries**
	- average player salary in 1980 was $185,000
1987	**Al Campanis Affair**
	- racist remarks made by Los Angeles Dodger vice-president of player personnel
1989	**Player Salaries**
	- average player salary in 1989 was $500,000
1991	**Baseball Hall of Fame**
	- held tribute honoring the "living legends" of the negro leagues
	- 11 negro league players were in the Hall of Fame
1992	**Marge Schott Affair**
	- Cincinatti Reds owner referred to former players derogatory, racist manner
1993	**Expansion Teams**
	- National League adds two expansion teams: the Florida Marlins and the Colorado Rockies

Figure 1.2
Key Events in the Evolution of Baseball in the United States, continued

---

1993	**Divisional Expansion**
	- Major League determines a new arrangement whereby NL and AL are both divided into three divisions
1994	**Georgia Flag Controversy**
	- Confederate State's of America flag (with stars and bars insignia) was protested
	- Georgia state flag was subsequently removed from display at Fulton County Stadium

---

As a manifestation and an exemplar of American values, baseball began to mirror national political and ideological shifts, both good and bad. . . . When the Republican party accepted a disputed presidency in 1876 in return for agreeing to permit states to handle blacks in their own way, thereby closing the door on equality and ushering in the horrid reign of Jim Crow, the national pastime responded by squeezing blacks out of the major leagues and all but out of organized baseball in little more than a decade.

Indeed it may well be the case that the history of professional baseball is one that evinces all that has been bad as well as good throughout the history of the country. To gain further insight into this, however, it is important to trace the important developments within professional baseball (see Figure 1.2) and trace them concurrently with the developments set forth in Figure 1.1.

Although it is a disputed issue, one can roughly pinpoint the origination of baseball in the United States in the late 1830s and early 1840s. Voigt (1993: 3) suggests that the northeast was the foundation of a sport which would be first codified in 1845 by Alexander J. Cartwright, a member of the New York Knickerbocker Club.

Whatever the specific date of origin, it is accurate to maintain that baseball originated in the United States during perhaps the most blatant period of overt (i.e., traditional) racism. The discriminatory practices provided for by the Constitution were still in tact as the dominant political institutions (and the society itself) maintain the virtues of the Doctrine of Racialism. It would be sixteen years before the real battle for racial equality would be fought on the battlefields and later in the three branches of the American polity.

According to Chadwick (1992: 19-20), the Civil War introduced blacks to the game of baseball as blacks and whites in the Union Army would enjoy the pleasure during breaks in the fighting. It is indeed ironic that the war to free the slaves and to provide equality saw baseball as a primary outlet between battles and that it was primarily an integrated game in the Union and not in the Confederacy. The aftermath of the war continued to see baseball flourish (relatively speaking) as integrated teams, black teams, and all white teams began to challenge one another.

The development of race issues in baseball echoed the period of reconstruction following the Civil War. In the wake of the war some black players met with limited success. For example, in 1872 John W. "Bud" Fowler became the first black player to be paid while playing for a white professional team. There was even a brief period known as the Golden Age (1883-88) when several black players (i.e., Fowler, George Stovey, Frank Grant, and the Walker brothers) were allowed to play in the white leagues. The latter, however, did occur within the time period wherein all that had been accomplished during the Reconstruction period was being torn apart by existing political institutions.

All was not grand during this period, however, as the sport of baseball began to echo the sentiments arising from the political backlash to the Reconstruction era. As was indicated in the Zoss and Bowman quote, 1876 marked a turning point in the political and social climate that would be mirrored in baseball as well. Putting the successes of the Golden Age aside, there were new developments that mirrored the deconstruction of reconstruction. By the end of the 1880s, it became clear that major league baseball was fully segregated and that the economic (an average $2,000 yearly salary) and social (prestige accorded by societal members) rewards accrued mainly to white males.

From 1898 to 1947 virtually no blacks played in the white major leagues unless they could dupe the owners, players, and fans into believing that the player was not actually black. This was the technique that several set out to use, with perhaps the most famous manifestation being the Charlie "Tokohama" ploy attempted by manager John McGraw in 1901.

What existed in the wake of the 1896 *Plessy v. Ferguson* ruling was the "separate, but equal" doctrine. In baseball, this was made manifest by the large number of all black teams that could not hope to break the throws of segregated America. In 1920 this discriminatory mentality was further solidified with the founding of the National Negro Baseball League. Although some might construe this as de facto recognition by blacks of the "separate, but equal" doctrine, it is more accurate to state that the founding of this league did not suggest acceptance of the status quo in any way, shape, or form. It only provided for an organized outlet for blacks to participate in baseball while having to operate during a blatantly discriminatory era manifested not only by decision making in political institutions, but by the decisions made by white, major league team owners as well.

Black baseball, although segregated, flourished during the 1920s as the Eastern Colored League (soon to become the American Negro League) came into existence and blacks established a yearly World Series beginning in 1924. These developments were relatively short-lived, however, as the roaring twenties gave way to the Depression years which led to the financial misfortune of the Negro National League in 1929 and the American Negro League in 1931.

A second round of professional black baseball would be started in 1933 as the new Negro National League (NNL) was established. The new Negro American

League would also be born (in 1937) in part due to the NNL withdrawing from the midwest. In 1942, these two leagues reestablished the Black World Series in 1942 which would be played annually until 1948 when the NNL went out of business. It is important to note the degree to which white major league baseball remained opposed to integration. When in 1943 Bill Veeck proposed to buy the Phillies and man the roster with black talent it was flatly rejected. In all fairness, one should point out that Commissioner Landis was still in power at the time and remained forcefully opposed to integration. Indeed, hindsight is twenty-twenty, but one cannot wonder given the changes in the larger political culture at this time if Veeck's proposal would have been accepted if it was made after Commissioner A. B. "Happy" Chandler succeeded Landis.

During this period of time, changes were being made in the larger political culture pertinent to race issues. The Congress of Racial Equality was organized in 1942 to *inter alia* approve race relations. Moreover, 1947 witnessed the introduction of the President's Committee on Civil Rights to investigate the status of race in the United States. It quickly presented a report calling for national laws prohibiting racially motivated brutality, segregation, and the like. The Department of Justice also started to issue briefs in support of civil rights. The President's Committee Report gave rise to the 1954 *Bolling v. Sharpe* decision as well as the Brown I and Brown II decisions in 1954 and 1955, respectively.

Events in baseball paralleled these events with respect to the larger political culture. As World War II came to an end, the practice of (traditional) racism could no longer be tolerated as it was deemed unjustifiable given the reasons for the United States entry into the war. As Zoss and Bowman (1989: 102) suggest, "integration had been in the air just before the war, but it became inevitable principally because of the blatant hypocrisy of an American policy that fought racist ideologies in Europe and the Pacific but maintained racist policies in its national game. . . . lent moral authority to the growing movement to end discriminatory practices in American life." Indeed, by 1945 the pro-integration commissioner of baseball, A. B. "Happy" Chandler, suggested that if blacks were able to perform successfully in World War II, they should be able to perform successfully in professional major league baseball.

Building on the landmark success of Branch Rickey signing Jackie Robinson to the Montreal team and bringing him up to the Brooklyn Dodgers in 1947, Larry Doby would also break the barrier in 1947, but in the American League. These two successes paved the way for the full integration of major league baseball throughout the 1940s and 1950s. The process formally closed in 1959 when the last bastion of segregation in the majors, the Boston Red Sox, submitted to integration.

An unintended consequence of integration during this time was the demise of the black leagues. Although the Negro National League folded promptly in 1948, the Negro American League continued to exist until 1960. These closures were in large part due to the declining attendance and revenues generated in the black leagues due to integration and many of the "best" black players finding positions with recently integrated major league teams.

In the more recent period, the 1980s and 1990s, there has been a continual interest in how baseball continues to develop with respect to issues of race. Earlier it was suggested that in the larger political culture an attitude of "aversive" or "latent" racism may exist. The same can be said for major league baseball in its more recent past. Many minorities advocates continue to press major league baseball on minority hiring policies and keep watch over any aversive or blatantly racist elements that may continue in the sport.

Among the concerns that contemporary activists promote are the apparent positional segregation of players, the lack of minorities in management/owner roles, and the lack of respect accorded to minority players by managers and owners. With respect to the latter the Al Campanis and Marge Schott controversies have received much attention. During the course of an interview with Ted Koppel on *Nightline* in 1987, Campanis made the remark that blacks might lack some of the "necessities" to be managers or hold executive positions in baseball. This was during a broadcast that was to commemorate Jackie Robinson having broken the color barrier. Campanis was promptly fired by the Dodger organization.

In 1992, Schott reportedly referred to former players Eric Davis and Dave Parker as "million-dollar niggers" and said that she would rather "hire a trained monkey than a nigger" to work in her front office.[7] After an investigation by baseballs' executive council (the event happened after Fay Vincent was forced to resign in September) Schott was fined $25,000 and suspended for up to one year. Before the decision, Schott maintained that her behavior was "insensitive" but that she most definitely was not a racist.[8]

The concern over the lack of minorities in managerial and ownership roles has also been of issue. Periodically representatives of major league baseball express concern over the relatively modest strides that blacks have made in these roles.[9] Moreover, there are times when the league is concerned as well about the shrinking number of minority players in professional baseball. Such was the case when in 1992 *Ebony* questioned what was behind the shrinking number of African-American players.[10]

Others have more recently questioned hiring practices of baseball owners. The Reverend Jesse Jackson has repeated his concern that blacks are not making progress if their role has not transcended the playing field. In the wake of the Schott incident, Jackson has more forcefully made his concerns known to the owners. The newly created Rainbow Commission on Fairness in Athletics is the institution by which Jackson seeks to ensure fairness and equality. In his quest to ensure that affirmative action programs are incorporated into major league baseball, Jackson has threatened the use of selective boycotts.[11]

Although it has come under attack for various race-related subjects, it is important to emphasize the great strides that major league baseball has made during the 1980s and 1990s. For example, in 1987 (the year of the Campanis remarks) only 2% of front office personnel were minorities. By 1993 the numbers for all 28 major league teams have risen to 17%.[12]

Other related issues have also surfaced that pertain to the "aversive" racism that may well be carried on in both baseball and the larger political and societal culture. The issue of the Georgia state flag is perhaps most illuminating. In 1956 the "stars and bars" insignia had been added to the state flag to show Georgians opposition to the federal dictate of racial desegregation. On January 30, 1994, the Reverend Jesse Jackson and others demonstrated against its continued display. Subsequently on February 23 the Recreational Authority voted unanimously to remove the display of the Georgia state flag at Fulton County Stadium. The fact that this action went against the findings of a January 28, 1994, poll indicating that 56% of Georgians favored retaining the flag may illustrate more fully the current state of race in the national pastime and in the larger political and societal cultures as well.

EVIDENCE (AND PROBLEMS) FROM RACIAL DISCRIMINATION STUDIES

The analysis of professional baseball for the effects of salary discrimination has been attractive to researchers because of the ease with which performance variables can be objectively quantified. Performance variables in other fields have been less easily quantified. The ease of measurement has led to a plethora of studies on salary discrimination in professional sports. There have been several other angles used in the search for possible racial discrimination in the sport. Among other possibilities, Mogull (1975) identifies the following areas where discrimination may occur: quota systems, higher entry standards, restrictions on position assignments, exclusion from managerial and executive positions, and fewer economic opportunities outside of baseball, such as product endorsements.

Several studies have examined the issue of hiring discrimination. Pascal and Rapping (1972), Scully (1974a), Gwartney and Haworth (1974), Medoff (1975), and Hill and Spellman (1984) have all found that minorities (blacks in particular) generally have higher rates of performance than white players. Gwartney and Haworth (1974) also concluded that a larger proportion of blacks on a baseball team produced higher winning percentages. Although all of these studies identified the benefits of hiring black baseball players, Jiobu (1988) discovered that when controlling for performance, blacks had a higher rate of exit from baseball than whites, suggesting that even though blacks performed better, they have shortened careers as a result of intangibles related to their race.

Other studies have addressed the possibility of "positional segregation." The latter refers to the notion that managers (and owners) segregate whites and blacks according to player position. Generally speaking, the results of these analyses have been similar to the findings of Pattnayak and Leonard (1991) that whites constituted an abnormally high percentage of the total pitchers and catchers (i.e., first tier or primary player positions), whereas minorities (typically blacks) constituted a disproportionate percentage of the outfielders (i.e., third tier or peripheral player positions). Latin Americans were generally found in disproportion to whites and blacks at the second tier or infield player positions. Several hypotheses have been developed regarding the reasons for these results supporting the argument offered by researchers of positional segregation. One of the most prominent has been that by placing blacks in the outfield, they are removed from the leadership positions in the infield and catcher (Pascal and Rapping, 1972). As a corollary to this, it has been argued that because blacks have been robbed of the opportunity to gain these leadership skills, they are consequently prevented from moving into managerial or executive positions following their playing careers. A further argument has been made that blacks have been shepherded into these positions because they are less coaching-intensive, meaning that coaches have to spend less time working closely with outfielders (Pascal and Rapping, 1972). A third argument is based primarily on economic and not racial grounds. This position maintains that players from more impoverished backgrounds do not have the resources to afford equipment (especially in the case of catchers) or the specialized coaching (especially in the case of infielders or pitchers) to develop those particular major league talents. Moreover, since the majority of players in this category are blacks, it would follow that more blacks would become outfielders.

A final area in which the possibility of racial discrimination in baseball has recently been tested involves the dearth of minority managers and executives among major league clubs. As indicated earlier, this has become a resurgent area of concern during the 1990s as the Campanis and Schott affairs provoked increasing awareness. Singell (1991) found that although initially (after the color line was broken in 1947) blacks were less likely to coach, their chances have improved over time and the differences that do exist between blacks and whites are no longer statistically significant. The author concludes, however, by stating that the results indicate that the effects of discrimination are apparently more complex than simply a lower probability of coaching.

Many of the aforementioned studies suggest that the possibility of racial discrimination continues to exist into the 1990s. This may or may not be due in part to the unconscious practice of "aversive" racism. The results from the various salary determination analyses, however, have been thus far inconclusive (based in large part on differences in samples, time period studied, and research designs) and merit further study.

Sample Size and Composition

Salary discrimination studies have varied greatly in the number of players analyzed as well as the type of player. Sample size has ranged from a low of 62 (Medoff, 1975) and 126 (Mogull, 1975) to a high of 523 (Hill and Spellman,

1984). The attention paid to sample size is no small consideration when considering two factors: for whom the results are applicable and how reliable the results are, based on the small number of cases analyzed. It would appear that to gain the most accurate accounting of salary discrimination, one would want to exhaust the total population. This would mean that the actual sample size is identical to the population of players from which it is drawn (i.e., everyone is included in the analysis).

Several studies have only considered certain types of players or aggregated players into one category. For example, Medoff (1975), Christiano (1986, 1988), and Johnson (1992) incorporated only non-pitchers. Pascal and Rapping (1972), Scully (1974b), Mogull (1975), Hill and Spellman (1984), and Sommers (1990) included pitchers in their analyses but failed to take into account the differences that exist in pitching position (i.e., starter, reliever, closer), which can result in dramatic salary differences.[13]

Studies that included non-pitchers rarely broke down the analysis by player position even though offensive and, in particular, defensive expectations vary according to specific positions. Christiano (1986, 1988) does separate non-pitchers into infield and outfield, although expectations within the infield vary by position as well. Johnson (1992) provides the most intrusive examination to date with regard to position analysis as he divides non-pitchers into three categories: outfield, the offensive infield positions of first base and third base (i.e., positions where offensive production is generally of greater importance than defense), and defensive infield positions (i.e., second base, shortstop, and catcher). Johnson's classification is adequate if one is analyzing only offensive performance (as he does). However, if defensive performance is to be included in the analysis, each position should be isolated as the requirements of the positions are distinctly different. In previous analyses, however, defensive performance has not been incorporated as a variable in the analysis, with the exception of Mogull (1975). Even though defensive statistics were utilized, Mogull (1975) did not break down the analysis by player positions, thereby comparing apples to oranges.

The players who constitute the samples in the analyses is also an important consideration. Pascal and Rapping (1972) and Scully (1974b) who did two of the earliest analyses of salary determination in baseball used the same set of players, which consisted of 148 players that were generated by a non-random method. As a consequence of the non-random generation, the players represented the upper end of the salary scale for major league baseball. Thus, testing only this small portion of baseball players still allows for the possibility of racial discrimination by salary to occur among the ranks of the lower paid players. The latter, in reality, has not been investigated in the aforementioned studies. The Christiano (1986) study faces similar problems, although not to the same degree. In this analysis, Christiano examines 212 non-pitchers, a much larger pool than the 93 non-pitchers included in the Pascal and Rapping (1972) and Scully (1974a) studies. However, Christiano only examines the opening-day starters, thus once again not taking into consideration the lower paid players.

Other problems regarding the composition of the samples exist in additional studies. Mogull (1975) only used the salary data for the players who responded to a questionnaire mailed to the players in spring training. Medoff (1975) has a different sort of difficulty when analyzing the 1968 season by utilizing thirty-eight whites and twenty-four blacks (American and Latin American) in his study. The minority population thus constituted 38.7% of the overall sample. However, an analysis by Pascal and Rapping (1972) of 784 players on the preseason rosters of the baseball teams in 1968, found that only 22% of the players in the overall major league baseball population were either American or Latin American blacks. Consequently the proportion of minority to white players in Medoff's sample is much higher than in reality, leading one to question the degree to which the results obtained can be generalized to any population.

Time Period Studied

The majority of the studies involving the impact of race on salary determination of baseball players utilize salary data extracted from the 1968-1977 period, a relatively short span of ten years. Pascal and Rapping (1972), Scully (1974a), and Medoff (1975) all used salaries in 1968 as their dependent variables. Mogull (1975) used salary data from 1971, and Hill and Spellman (1984) and Christiano (1986) employed salary data from 1976 and 1977, respectively. Some of the more recent studies have employed more current salary data, however. Christiano (1988), Sommers (1990), and Johnson (1992) all utilized salary data from 1987.

Analysis of the impact of race on salary determination after 1977 is important because that is when free agency was implemented in major league baseball. Prior to 1977, player contracts contained a reserve clause that effectively prevented that player from switching teams. Each player was signed to a one-year contract and at the end of that year, the player had the option of re-signing with the team or retiring (a player could not play for another team unless he was traded or sold). When the reserve clause was struck down by an arbitrator in 1975, it signaled a dramatic change in the operation of the baseball market. As a consequence, studies of salary determination after this point may also be effected. One such effect involves a change in the stability of salaries. When the reserve clause was in effect large salary raises were unlikely (pay cuts were almost as likely as raises) because players had very little bargaining power (they had only one purchaser for their services), which led to a much more stable salary structure within each team. Furthermore, since only one-year contracts were involved, it could be assumed that performance was the primary determinant (and others, including race, could not really be expected to have an overt impact) of salary. However, with the abolition of the reserve clause, multi-year contracts are frequent, which means that players are locked into a certain salary for the upcoming year regardless of their level of performance. Finally, although only a few analyses have been performed after the ten-year span mentioned above, no studies of salary determination and the possible impact of race were performed prior to Pascal and Rapping (1972). There have been studies (Gwartney and Haworth, 1974; and Medoff, 1975) dating back to 1947, however, that examined the issue of entry barriers to black baseball players as a potential source of racial discrimination.

Research Designs

Different types of statistical analysis have been incorporated into the study of salary determinants of baseball players. Some (Mogull, 1975) have used simple regression in conjunction with a correlation matrix to determine which performance factors were the most important in salary determination for both black and white players. Many studies (Pascal and Rapping, 1972; Scully, 1974a; Medoff, 1975; Hill and Spellman, 1984; Christiano, 1986, 1988; Sommers, 1990; and Johnson, 1992) incorporate multiple regression analysis. Others build on multiple regression by also analyzing wage-differentials via means-coefficient (i.e., decomposition) analysis (Hill and Spellman, 1984).

Dummy variable regression analysis is also popular, although at times problematic. Christiano (1988: 142-44) cited problems with the explanatory value of the dummy race variable he used in his original regressions and later ran regressions for black and white players when they were separated. At this point, he compared the differences in the coefficients of the variables to determine if there were statistically significant differences in the salary determination of black and white players. This is problematic, however, as the comparison of unstandardized coefficients may make relative meaningful comparisons between variables much more difficult.

Data envelopment analysis has also been used to examine the degree to which compensation is proportional to player production (Howard and Miller, 1993). This technique compares efficiency to pay and places each individual on a matrix accordingly (the value given to a player is termed an equity metric). The technique is considerably different from regression analysis in that it works off of extremal points and not measures of central tendency. In other words, within the matrix, an efficiency frontier is established for those with the highest and lowest equity metrics. This differs from regression analysis because regression equations establish a line representing the best fit for the data involved. Although data envelopment analysis cannot include in its testing such factors as experience, race, or additional marketplace factors, it has been suggested that it be used in conjunction with regression analysis. A possible application in the future is that the equity metrics could be regressed on other employee attributes (i.e., experience, race, etc.) to test for racial discrimination.

Comparison of Results

The noted differences in sample size, time period, and methodology have resulted in inconclusive results with respect to determining the degree to which race and performance are key in salary determination. Although Pascal and Rapping (1972) found no evidence of racial discrimination against blacks with regard to salary determination, they did find a significant negative impact against Latin non-pitchers. Scully (1974b), using the same sample, discovered evidence of discrimination against black outfielders and infielders, as well as greater barriers to entry for black infielders.[14] Medoff (1975) used some of the same data as that of the first two studies and found that the race variable was statistically insignificant. Another study, Mogull (1975), which used the simple regression approach, concluded that the same criteria was being used to evaluate white players as black players. The analysis of Hill and Spellman (1984) further suggests that the impact of race is insignificant, whereas Christiano (1986, 1988) found that there was some discrimination against whites (although the impact of race was reduced when he ran the equations when the players were separated by race and compared the unstandardized coefficients). Sommers (1990) concluded that race was insignificant in the determination of salary with regard to both pitchers and non-pitchers. Finally, Johnson (1992) uncovered racial discrimination at the team level, when he factored in the number of blacks on each team as his race variable.

METHODOLOGY AND SUMMARY OUTLINE OF BOOK

This study looks at the variables that impact team owners in the salary determination process of major league baseball players. The sample size nearly parallels the population of major league baseball players on opening day in 1991. In all, 621 players (258 pitchers and 363 non-pitchers) composed the sample for the analysis.[15]

The chapters that follow utilize a methodology that relies primarily on multiple regression analysis with a dummy variable. Multiple regression is utilized to assess the significance of the hypotheses being tested. The analysis is based on a model whereby player salary in 1991 (SAL91) is regressed on independent and control variables including player salary in 1989 (SAL89) and 1990 (SAL90), years experience in the major leagues (YRS), race (RACE), metropolitan area (MET), and four measures of player performance in 1990 including that which includes offensive statistics (ORS), offensive and defensive statistics (THV), and statistics for the performance of pitchers (PRAL/PRNL and TPV).

The significance of independent and control variables is evaluated by the standardized regression coefficients (i.e., beta weights), the t-statistics, and the significance levels associated with the t-statistics.[16] Several checks were performed to ensure data quality. Multicollinearity checks and checks to ensure that violations of the various assumptions associated with regression analysis (i.e., a fully specified model and error terms that are normally distributed, not correlated, have constant variance and are not correlated with independent variables in the analysis) were instituted (Lewis-Beck, 1980: 60-61; and Berry and Feldman, 1985: 43). Cook's D was used to check for outliers (Norusis, 1985: 24-26).

A related area that should be addressed is the role of regression analysis in the courts. If a player charges that race is involved in salary determination and takes the team to court or arbitration it is important that the analysis utilized follow the constraints that the United States legal system has placed on it. Moreover, for the first time, in *Bazemore v. Friday* (1986), the United States Supreme Court explicitly accepted the use of regression analysis in employment discrimination cases.

Barrett and Sansonetti (1988) analyzed twenty-nine court cases in which regression analysis was used in the manner described above. In this analysis, they identified the general view of the court toward certain variables used in regression analysis. According to Barrett and Sansonetti, within an analysis, jobs should not be treated as fungible (i.e., jobs with different functions shouldn't be treated as one). In the ten cases where the court found that jobs had been inappropriately treated as fungible, the defendant won every time. This is important to note because the majority of prior analyses regarding the impact of race in the salary determination of baseball players do not make distinctions regarding positions beyond that of pitcher and non-pitcher. Although distinctions among non-pitchers are not extremely necessary beyond the rudimentary distinction of outfield versus infield (unless defense is also being evaluated, in which case the non-pitchers must be divided by position), it is imperative that pitchers be separated into different categories due to their dramatically different responsibilities and the fact that their salaries mirror these responsibilities.

The courts have also been cautious when it comes to accepting proxy variables (i.e., using age as an indicator of work experience). Usually, the court wants the party using the proxy variable to show that the assumptions made are valid. This can also apply to the analyses discussed previously with regard to experience. The analysis by Pascal and Rapping (1972) used a proxy variable for experience when they assumed that the age of a player will indicate how much experience he has. They did not, however, test this assumption.

Finally, the role of the evaluation of performance variables have been criticized in various employment discrimination cases. Criticism has been forthcoming in particular with regard to suits brought by women, who charge that the work a woman performs is always undervalued because of bias. Consequently, the discrimination will be hidden by the regression analysis within the context of the performance variable. However, this concern does not apply to baseball, as it has objective criteria for evaluating performance that cannot be altered to take into consideration other factors such as race.

In conclusion, as this type of analysis also begins to play a role in legal battles, it must adapt to the constraints placed on it by the court system so that it may be valid both in and of itself and as a tool in the legal process. Primarily, future analyses must be sure to differentiate between player positions in order that the most valid comparisons can be made. The following study attempts to take into consideration all of the above concerns in order to derive the greatest utility possible.

Finally, the time period examined is 1989-91. The level of analysis is the individual major league baseball player, and the unit of analysis is one season. Although the analysis looks primarily at the impact of 1990 data on salary determination in 1991, it is also the case that a two-year lag in previous salary (i.e., salary in 1989) is investigated. The latter is designed to provide a more uniform look into the consistency of the results pertaining to both the race and performance variables.

The purpose of this book is to determine the extent to which race is still a key consideration in baseball. Given the aforementioned, it is undoubtedly the case that baseball could be argued to be a microcosm of the larger political and societal culture. What is not known, however, is the degree to which the "latent" or "aversive" racism that continues to exist in society also exist in baseball. This analysis attempts to answer this by incorporating an analysis of the salary determinants of professional baseball players with an emphasis on race and meritocracy as the key explanatory variables.

This book argues that, based on the statistical evidence from the late 1980s and early 1990s, meritocracy is of greater consideration in salary determination in professional baseball than are issues of race. Although it is plausible that owners and management may harbor "aversive" racist attitudes, they are more concerned with how well players meet expectations with regard to performance. In brief, owners are more concerned with the overarching considerations related to economics and winning than with perpetuating what many view as a culture beset by racism.

Findings that indicate that race is a prevalent feature of salary determination would illustrate more than the existence of "aversive" racism. Moreover, it would suggest that the cultural myth that success in major league baseball is based on the talent (i.e., merit) of players would be groundless. To the degree that baseball is indeed a microcosm of the larger political and societal culture, findings that race as opposed to merit is a prevalent factor in the salary determination of players may well be extended to the greater society.

The remainder of this book is outlined in the following manner. Chapter 2 presents a detailed conceptualization and indication of the measures utilized to assess the quantitative results. Chapters 3 and 4 also present the conceptualization and measurement of variables as is necessitated. Moreover, chapters 2, 3, and 4 present the quantitative results for different categories of players and assesses each with respect to two new hypotheses: the "old man hypothesis" and the "superstar hypothesis." Chapter 2 reviews results for infielders and outfielders. Chapter 3 reviews results for "offensive" oriented players. Chapter 4 reviews results for a intrusive breakdown analysis of pitchers by type of pitcher (i.e., starter versus. reliever versus. closer). Finally, chapter 5 concludes by presenting the main findings and drawing implications for the sport of professional baseball and the larger democratic culture.

NOTES

1. Although Table 1.1 only provides figures for 1980-91 (1991 being the final year in the analysis conducted for this book), the percentages increase throughout the 1993 season as the addition of the Colorado Rockies and Florida Marlins brought a very large increase in average attendance in the National League.

2. The category "baseball" includes those who reported participation in either baseball or softball. Combining both is warranted on the grounds of similarity of the sports and is justified given the fact that "organized" (and thus easier to participate in) leagues are more numerous for softball than for baseball.

3. This is not to mention the overt sexism and discrimination based on economic position (i.e., the landed class) in early American society. These concerns, although no less important than race, are not of primary consideration in this analysis.

4. For purposes of this analysis the word "blacks" will be utilized. This goes with the knowledge that the history of racial labels has continuously gone through a process of adaptive change. For example, the term African-American was utilized as early as the late 1700s in the United States. This changed, however, as the acceptance of labels changed by the black community. Thus the preferred term soon became "Colored." The use of Colored subsided, however, in the 19th and early 20th century as Negro grew to be the more preferred term. This too changed by the 1960s as "black" gained in popularity.

As of 1991, the term "black" was preferred by over 98% of respondents. The use of African-American, however, has increased marginally from the late 1980s to the present. Overwhelmingly, the preferred choice appears to be "black." Finally, one should highlight that this is not a game of semantics within the multicultural playing field. The cultural development of a label for any group of similar constituent makeup is an important way of defining one's position in society as well as heightening self-respect, dignity, and social standing in a society. For more on this see Smith (1992).

5. See Article I, Section 9, of the Constitution of the United States of America.

6. Sanford was incorrectly documented as Sandford. The former is the correct spelling.

7. This was reported by a former employee now working for the Oakland Athletics. For more see, "Baseball's Very Big Problem," *New York Times*, December 3, 1992, p. A24.

8. On this see, "Schott's Statement: `I am not a Racist,'" in the *New York Times*, December 10, 1992, p. B19.

9. Perhaps most of this concern has been expressed by three past commissioners: Ueberroth, Giamatti, and Vincent. For one such statement see the article in the September 28, 1991 edition of the *New York Times* (p. I1) that expressed Vincent and National League President Bill White's concern over the lack of minority hiring.

10. On this see, "What's Behind the Shrinking Number of African-American Players?" Ebony (June, 1992: 112).

11. For more on this see, "Jackson Threatens Action," *New York Times*, January 12, 1993, p. B10; and "Jackson is Setting a Focus on Sports," *New York Times*, January 13, 1993, p. B11.

12. See, "Schott Punished for the Wrong Thing," *New York Times*, February 4, 1993, p. B11.

13. Hill and Spellman (1984) attempted to account for these differences when they included a variable in their regression analysis for innings pitched. However, although this may explain why players who pitch more are paid higher salaries, it does not isolate each pitching position so they can be analyzed separately. Furthermore, although middle relievers and closers pitch on average a similar number of innings, there is a dramatic difference in salary as a result of different functions. This latter problem is not accounted for in the Hill and Spellman analysis.

14. Although Scully used the same sample as Pascal and Rapping, there were differences in the models used that account for their discrepant findings. For example, Scully used a market control variable, whereas Pascal and Rapping did not. Furthermore, the two studies used different measures of experience. Finally, and perhaps most importantly, Scully did not include a dummy variable for Latin American players.

15. Although the salary information obtained for 1991 included the salaries of 707 major league baseball players, a number of players were excluded for a variety of reasons including lack of salary data for 1989 or 1990, playing in Japan, and for being injured, released, or demoted to the minor leagues if it caused the player to miss more than half the year.

Furthermore, three pitchers, Julio Machado, Ron Robinson, and Walt Terrell, pitched for teams in both leagues, which would have necessitated weighting their statistics since production values for pitchers vary by league. Thus, they were excluded from the analysis.

16. The primary concern of this analysis is with whether pattern relationships exist and what the strengths of these relationships are. The strength of the relationship is evaluated primarily by analyzing the adjusted R-squared value and magnitude of the beta weights. This analysis is concerned more with the description of and explanation for existing relationships. It is not concerned with the ability to predict future salary determination based on either race or performance concerns. Thus, the slope of the variables are not reported in this analysis.

Chapter 2

The Experience of Infielders and Outfielders

This chapter focuses on the statistical analysis of all players with offensive and defensive statistics (i.e., first base, second base, third base, shortstop, and outfield). Each player position is analyzed separately via the following framework. First, the overall results for the player position are presented. This is accompanied by plausible explanations for the results and is at times augmented with raw data. Second, on completion of the overall analysis, two specific hypotheses will be investigated to determine the degree to which age and superstardom may impact the overall results.

The first hypothesis may be termed the "old man" hypothesis,[1] which consists of two parts, each of which may help to explain various discrepancies in the overall results. The first part of the hypothesis holds that as players go beyond their prime, not only does individual performance begin to decline, but salaries decline as well. Indeed, this is one area where baseball, and professional athletics in general, differ significantly from other business sectors. In most business operations, the increase in experience generally results in salary increases, which continue until retirement. In contrast, when professional athletes reach a certain stage in their career, performance (i.e., production) may begin to decrease, resulting in lesser salaries. Consequently, older players who choose to continue playing the game, albeit at lesser salaries, may cause the overall salary equation to produce a negative relationship for the years experience variable to be discussed in the next section. This suggests that players with fewer years experience are paid higher salaries, a finding that does not seem plausible within the context of salary determinants of most sectors of the larger business economy.

The second part of the old man hypothesis can be termed the "fading superstar" effect. As stated previously, as players advance in years and their production declines, so too can their salaries. Alternatively, performance (i.e., production) decreases do not always necessitate or result in an immediate and corresponding decrease in an individuals salary. This salary adjustment may not occur for at least two reasons. First, players, and in particular superstars, often sign multi-year contracts. Thus, if a player is 32 and signs a four-year contract based on his performance at age 31, his production may decline in each of the subsequent years of his contract. Moreover, barring renegotiation, this player's salary may not adjust to his production until the player is 36. Second, there tends to be a perception (i.e., hope) in professional sports that an aging superstar who has experienced a couple of "off" years will bounce back and duplicate his performance in earlier years. Although resurgence sometimes occurs,[2] at other times the "off" years are simply a product of age and diminished skills (i.e., natural decline in performance). However, these players are often signed to large contracts not only as rewards for prior performance, but also in the hope that the aging superstar might be able to achieve former levels of production.

In addition to the "old man" hypothesis, the "superstar" hypothesis is analyzed for each player position. The "superstar" hypothesis is incorporated by removing from the analysis all players who have an ORS rating (see the next section for an elaboration of the ORS measure) equal to or greater than six games. There are two reasons for keeping the "superstars" out of the study. First and foremost, it appears that if any racism is to be found, it will be uncovered within the ranks of less memorable players. In this day and age, superstars are highly scrutinized by the press and public, and contract negotiations, in part because of the astronomical numbers involved, are also given close attention. Thus, it would be easily apparent for one to discern any sort of racial bias in the salaries of white and minority superstars. However, it seems more plausible that if racism does remain in the sport that it could be more readily hidden within the ranks of role players (i.e., starters with less than superstar statistics, backup players, etc.), who make up the majority of players, but are given much less publicity. Second, as superstars reach their third year, they become eligible for salary arbitration. Moreover, they become eligible for free agency in their sixth year. Consequently, a player has a chance to experience a substantial increase in salary at both of these points in their careers. This may result in these players being paid more than players of similar skill but who are a few years older. This would appear to allow for a result similar to the old man hypothesis, in that it may contribute to a negative relationship between the years experience measure and the dependent variable in this analysis, 1991 salary.

Finally, at the conclusion of each positional analysis, there is a table identifying the top ten performers for that player position for the THV and ORS measures. Accompanying these lists are the top ten wage earners for that player position. This will allow for comparison to see how strong of a prima facie relationship exist between performance and salary. This analysis tests the relationship between salary determination, performance, race, years of experience, and prior salary levels in order to discern the extent to which such salary determination in 1991 was based on merit versus racial bias.

VARIABLE CONCEPTUALIZATION AND MEASUREMENT

Dependent Variable

A summary of all variables utilized in this analysis can be found in the Appendix. The focus of this chapter is on regressing the 1991 salary of major league baseball players on various independent and control variables to determine primarily the impact that racial bias and/or performance have on salary determination. As such, the dependent variable throughout all analyses conducted in this book is 1991 salary (SAL91).

SAL91 is conceptualized as the total package of renumeration accorded to major league players such as base money, signing bonuses, performance bonuses, other guaranteed money, and the like. In essence, the attempt is to get not only data that is comparable so that comparisons can be made, but data that reflects the fullest measure of "salary."

The empirical measure for SAL91 is the total salary package reported for major league players as of opening day 1991.[3] In brief, SAL91 takes into account base salary, prorated share of signing bonus and other guaranteed money, and bonuses that could be earned during the season from post-season awards. Other studies (Sommers, 1990: 862-63) have also relied on this data as their primary source.

Independent Variables

Two independent variables are utilized in this analysis. To keep in line with the investigation of race versus performance as salary determinants both are utilized throughout all analyses conducted in this book.

Race (RACE) is conceptualized quite clearly as the ethnicity of major league players. Identifying the RACE component of the model was a considerably difficult task. Data collected for RACE was originally organized according to one of five racial classifications: U.S. Black, non-U.S. Black, U.S. Latino, non-U.S. Latino, and White.

The most common means of incorporating race as an independent variable is to insert a dummy variable, coding white as 1 and black as 0 or vice-versa (Medoff, 1975; Sommers, 1990). Christiano (1986, 1988) and Scully (1974b) also used dummy variables, although later they separated the players by race and ran two equations, comparing the unstandardized coefficients. Pascal and Rapping (1972) used dummy variables as well, although they had one variable that measured if a player was black or white and another variable used to measure the effect Latin players had on explaining variance in the dependent variable. Mogull (1975) did not use a dummy variable for race as he used a simple regression model to compare the effects of various performance measures on the determination of salary when blacks and whites were separated.

Others have opted not to utilize a dummy variable for race in the statistical analysis. Hill and Spellman (1984) decided to use a means-coefficient (i.e., decomposition) analysis to study the effects of race instead of employing a dummy variable. Perhaps the most unique approach has been taken by Johnson (1992) who stated that racial discrimination would more likely be found within a team than in an overall analysis. According to his hypothesis, as the number of black players increased on a team, the salaries of the blacks on that team will decline, whereas the salaries of white players will increase. Johnson believes that the owners see a certain value in having some blacks on a team and thus, because of this extra value, a black may initially be paid more than a comparable white player. However, as more blacks join the team, the marginal utility of having black players decreases while that of white players increases. At some point, then, the utility of adding a white player to the roster surpasses the addition of another black player. To test this hypothesis, Johnson measures race in terms of the number of black players on any given team. This would appear to be a valid way of examining the question of the role of race. However, if one is going to examine discrimination on a team-by-team basis, one must also consider differences in overall team performance. This must be done because although players on two different teams are of comparable abilities, the cause in a salary difference may be the result of the number of players on the team who perform at higher levels rather than the number of black players on the team. The Johnson analysis does not take this into account, perhaps serving as a basis for calling his results (based on the measures utilized) into question.

The subsequent determination of ethnicity (i.e., racial background) in this study was quite subjective although objective information was relied on. This is not of major concern, however, given the assumption that if RACE does have an impact in the salary determination process, it is based on management's perception of a player's race, a fairly subjective decision in and of itself. The race of each player was ascertained by reviewing the photos on baseball cards and place of birth. Similar methods have been utilized by other authors and is an accepted practice (see Jiobu, 1988; Singell, 1991).

The empirical measure for RACE was collapsed into a dummy variable that distinguished between the majority race in major league baseball, white, and the totality of non-majority (i.e., minority) players. Consequently, the aforementioned fivefold classification was simplified to distinguish between white and non-white players as well as to ensure a sufficient sample size of minority players. The dummy variable is coded "1" for whites and "0" for any of the aforementioned four classifications of minority players. This follows the practice of several studies (Pascal and Rapping, 1972; Medoff, 1975; Sommers, 1990).

The most complex element in the model involves the quantitative measurement of player performance. Conceptually, when assessing the various player positions in the infield (i.e., first, second, third, and shortstop) and outfield, the best performance indicator would be that which takes into consideration both offensive and defensive performance. In an effort to devise an empirical measure for performance, player statistics for the 1990 season were extracted from *Total Baseball* (Thorn and Palmer, 1991) and used in various formulae measuring offensive and defensive production.

Figure 2.1
Expected Runs versus Actual Runs

Season	Expected Runs	Actual Runs	Difference (%)
1990	17,664	17,919	1.4
1989	17,197	17,405	1.2
1988	17,179	17,380	1.2
1987	19,075	19,883	4.1
1986	18,115	18,545	2.3
Total	89,230	91,132	2.1

To measure the production of the offensive performance of the infield and outfield positions, a measure termed offensive runs scored (ORS) was developed. Although this measure is similar to concepts developed by other baseball sabermetricians (e.g., Bill James, Steve Mann) in that it attempts to measure run production, ORS is different as it is based on the simple premise that four bases generated by an individual player will produce the equivalent of one run.[4] This statement is supported and justifiable by a cursory examination (in Figure 2.1) of the relationship between total bases and runs scored in all major league regular season baseball games from 1986 to 1990. The expected runs (ER) column takes the number of total bases for the season (in both leagues) and divides by four, while actual runs reflects total runs scored during the season. As Figure 2.1 illustrates, the ER formula appears to be an extremely accurate predictor of actual runs scored during a given season, differing an average of only 2.1% during the 1986-1990 seasons. Then, in an effort to reduce the size of the numbers and make the results more tangible, the ER value is divided by 10 to reach the ORS value, an expression of the number of games a player contributes to a team's win total via his offensive production.[5] Therefore, in summary, we have

ORS = (ER/10)
    where *ER* = Expected runs = (TB/4)
        TB = Total bases = B1 + ((B2 * 2) + (B3 * 3) + (HR * 4) + (BB)
                + (SB) - (CS))
           B1 = (Total hits - (B2 + B3 + HR))
           B2 = Number of doubles
           B3 = Number of triples
           HR = Number of homeruns
           BB = Number of bases on balls (i.e., walks)

SB = Number of stolen bases
CS = Number of times caught stealing

Although previous studies regarding salary and performance in major league baseball have used traditional baseball statistics such as total home runs (Christiano, 1986, 1988), batting average (BA) (Mogull, 1975; Christiano, 1986; 1988; and Sommers, 1990), or slugging average (SA) (Scully, 1974b), each measure fails to consider some vital aspects of offensive production. BA, for example, is a measure of the percentage of hits a player gets as part of his total at bats (AB). As such it fails to distinguish between different types of hits, thereby treating a single as the equivalent of a homerun, although the former has the value of one base, whereas the latter is worth four bases. An example where a player may be more highly regarded than another simply because of a higher BA can be found in a comparison of the 1990 National League batting champion Willie McGee (with the St. Louis Cardinals) and Matt Williams of the San Francisco Giants, the 1990 National League runs batted in (RBI) leader.[6] If BA were the sole basis for evaluation of offensive performance, McGee would win the contest easily as he batted .335 to Williams' .277. However, when their ORS values are computed, McGee is found to contribute 8.18 games to his teams victory total, whereas Williams ORS (8.43) suggests that he is slightly more valuable to his team.

Slugging average as used by Scully (1974b), on the other hand, suffers from a different problem. Although SA uses total bases (TB) (it divides total bases into total at bats), it fails to take into consideration other activities which account for a base earned or lost such as bases on ball (BB), stolen bases (SB), and caught stealing (CS), thus providing an incomplete portrayal of overall offensive production.[7] An additional positive aspect of this measurement is that SA is figured in terms of a percentage, whereas ER and ORS provide much more easily understood and applicable numbers.

Another important component of player performance involves defensive ability. This component of production has traditionally been ignored or treated as too difficult to accurately measure.[8] The final production measure utilized in this study, however, does take into consideration defensive ability. An effort was made, however, to prevent defensive ability from attaining the same level of importance as the offensive measure. This was done because players are generally identified by offensive production, whereas defensive ability typically only comes into consideration when it is an extremely positive asset or a severe detriment.

Traditionally, defense has been measured in terms of a negative component such as errors (E). Other relevant defensive statistics, however, are putouts (PO) and assists (A). Any measure of defensive productivity should include all of these as the exclusion of any can lead to a less than precise measure (although as it will be demonstrated later, even consideration of all recorded defensive data may produce an inadequate picture). For example, if one were to look at the error figures, one would notice that Cal Ripken, Jr. committed only three errors while Ozzie Guillen committed seventeen errors, concluding that Ripken is the better player. However, if this is indeed the case, why is Guillen considered by many to be one of the best defensive shortstops in the game? The answer as is obvious in Figure 2.2 is range. Although Ripken committed fourteen fewer errors, few would dispute that Guillen has more range.[9] Consequently, Guillen is able to reach a greater number of balls put into play, thus making a greater number of difficult plays, which can sometimes result in errors. With this in mind, one can see that although Guillen committed more errors, most of these occurred on balls that Ripken perhaps would not have been able to reach, with the result being (at a minimum) a base hit for the opposition.

Figure 2.2
Comparing the Range of Ripken and Guillen

Name	Net Chances (NCH)	Games Played (GP)	NCH per game
Ripken	674	166	4.06
Guillen	709	132	5.37

Once a player's NCH have been computed, it is necessary to compare them to a standard benchmark position. For this analysis, the average number of chances by position were taken from *The Baseball Superstats 1989* (Mann, 1989), which used numbers from the 1987 season and from the 1985 and 1986 *Sporting News Official Baseball Guide* (Sloan, 1985, 1986), which reported defensive statistics from the 1984 and 1985 seasons.[10] Net chances were then normalized (resulting in adjusted net chances or ANCH) for a full season and the resulting figures were used to determine the number of NCH a player had above or below the league average at that position. Furthermore, because each position has a different average net chances figure, any variable that includes defensive values must be broken down by position. Consequently, each time a variable that includes a defensive component is listed, it will inevitably be followed by a position designation (see note 13 for these designations). So, thus far we have the following formula to compute the number of NCH a player has above or below the league average. The formula for first basemen (1B) is used as an example.

NCHAN1B = (ANCH - 1559)
   where $NCHAN1B$ = Net chances above/below average for 1B
      $ANCH$ = Adjusted (normalized) NCH = (1445/IA) * NCH
      1445 = Average number of innings played per team
      IA = Innings played by a given player = (GP * 9)
      GP = Games played[11]

Before the step of attaching a game value to defensive performance can be taken, however, it must be determined whether all net chances are created equal. According to calculations by Mann, each NCH an infielder has above average saves approximately .55 runs, whereas NCH above average for an outfielder will save .75 runs per chance (Mann, 1989). These numbers appear to make sense as most errors committed by infielders result in one base gained by the opposition, whereas errors in the outfield often yield two or three bases. From this point, the numbers are converted into fielding runs (FR) by dividing by 30.[12] Now, the calculation of defensive value is complete, and we have

FR1B = (NCHAN1B * .55)/30
where *FR1B* = Fielding runs for first base

At this point, both the offensive and defensive values for each player has been derived. The final step is to combine the two variables to form the total hitters value (THV). Again the following uses the first base position as an example.

THV1B = (ORS + FR1B)

This THV measure will serve as the basis of evaluation for each non-pitcher position throughout this book. Consequently there will be measures for THV2B, THV3B, THVOF, and THVSS in this chapter and THVDH, THVC, and THVU in the next chapter.

With that, the foundation for evaluating a player's performance has been laid. However, some questions still remain about the defensive evaluation that appear to be insolvable because of the intangibles involved. First, the number of chances a player may have depends in large part on the pitching staff of the team. For example, the New York Mets starting pitchers had four of the top five National League leaders in strikeouts (David Cone, Dwight Gooden, Frank Viola, and Sid Fernandez), which results in a smaller number of balls being put into play (i.e., fewer chances).[13] Indeed, the Mets combined for 1,217 strikeouts while the St. Louis Cardinals struck out only 833, a difference of nearly 400.

Second, although it is almost impossible to measure, few would argue that the type of surface on which a person plays can make a difference in the defensive statistics. On artificial turf, for example, balls travel much faster, meaning that infielders in particular have less time to react to a ball hit in their direction. Thus, a player with less range playing on natural grass may get the same amount of NCH as a player with better range but who plays more of their games on artificial turf. To underscore this point, examine the statistics of Ozzie Smith and Cal Ripken, Jr. Although Smith is regarded by many to be the greatest defensive shortstop of all time and is credited with having excellent range, in 1990, he averaged only 4.18 chances per game, whereas Ripken averaged 4.06. However, Smith plays on artificial turf while Ripken plays on grass.[14]

As has been illustrated, although the numbers may be able to provide some sort of measure of defensive prowess, there are many complicating factors that may serve to render the defensive component of THV inadequate.[15] To compensate for this possibility, this analysis examined each position with ORS first and THV second to determine if any differences exist due primarily to variable measurement.

Control Variables

Several variables have been utilized in the salary determination literature and are incorporated in the present analysis primarily as controls. The first of these considered (and subsequently excluded from the analysis) is the size of the local market (i.e., metropolitan area). Conceptually, the size of the metropolitan area (MET) may have an impact on revenues and consequently on the potential to award larger contracts to players on teams in large markets.

Scully (1974b) and Sommers (1990) use the size of the metropolitan area of the team to account for market factors relating to team location. Christiano (1986, 1988) used the revenues each team received from the sale of its local television and radio broadcast revenues. Medoff (1975) used the percentage increase in attendance for the players team during the past two seasons. Pascal and Rapping (1972), Mogull (1975), Hill and Spellman (1984), and Johnson (1992) did not use any market-oriented variables in their analyses.

Originally, the empirical measure for MET was the population of the metropolitan statistical area in which the team stadium was located. Consequently, both New York teams would be listed in a large market with the consolidated metropolitan statistical area being over 18 million inhabitants. When the original analysis was undertaken it appeared as if MET did not contribute significantly to many (only two of sixteen) of the overall equations.

It was found to be significant and positive for the position of outfield. An analysis of the ten outfielders who received the largest salaries in 1991, moreover, revealed that nine of the ten played for large market teams. This is 80% more than would be normally expected given the percentage of teams that are located in large markets.[16] The consequence makes itself manifest in an uncharacteristic degree of significance. In contrast, the MET variable was found to be significant and negative for an equation involving second basemen. The reason for this relationship is more difficult to identify because seven of the ten highest paid players at this position performed for large market teams, a level 40% higher than the 50% expectation, which would seem to indicate that there should be a slightly positive relationship. On closer examination, however, the significant negative relationship is easily explainable.

First, three of the top five and twelve of the top twenty players based on salary considerations, played for small market teams. Second, all of the four lowest paid players practiced their trades in large markets. Furthermore, on extensive analysis of each of the remaining player positions, it was discovered that of the top ten wage earners, 51.7%, played for large market teams. The latter percentage is extremely close to the expectation of 50% indicating that the MET variable may not be an indispensable component of the model.

Since it appeared that the MET variable did not have much impact or warrant consideration in the model, the equations were run again excluding this control. Generally, there were few changes in the explanatory power of the new, more parsimonious model, as most adjusted R2's moved up or down by no more than one percentage point. In conclusion, because there was very little change in either explanatory power or the direction of relationships among variables, the MET variable was not included in any of the equations throughout the remainder of the analysis. This decision is consistent with the models advanced by Mogull (1975), Hill and Spellman (1984), and Johnson (1992).

The more important control variables were those that considered previous player salaries. Two controls were incorporated including a one-year salary lag (SAL90) and a two-year salary lag (SAL89) in order to control for the impact that previous salary levels may have in determining future renumeration.[17] The empirical measures for both SAL90 and SAL89 are taken from the aforementioned data source for SAL91 and include the same considerations, in terms of what is included in the figures on opening day, as the SAL91 variable.

Another control variable entered into the model is the amount of experience that players have in the major leagues. There is little disagreement in terms of how one measures the experience of a player. Scully (1974b), Hill and Spellman (1984), Christiano (1986, 1988), Sommers (1990), and Johnson (1992) all measure experience of a baseball player in terms of the number of years experience the player has in the major leagues. Sommers (1990) and Johnson (1992) also use variations on the years experience measure in conjunction with the years variable. Sommers uses a quadratic function and Johnson squares the years term in recognition of the possibility that the relationship between salary and experience may be nonlinear as a result of deterioration in skill as one gets older.

In contrast, Pascal and Rapping (1972) use a player's calendar age to measure experience, reasoning that the older a player is, the more years he has played baseball. This may be correct on one level (i.e., the player has most likely played longer once high school, college, and minor league experience are taken into account). It is not logical to assume, however, that because one player is older than another that he has had more major league experience. In fact, some players are still teenagers when they enter the major leagues while other players may be 25 or even 30 years old before they can make it to the "big show." Therefore, the validity of measuring experience in this manner can be questioned.

Finally, Medoff (1975) and Mogull (1975) do not incorporate a years experience variable at all, perhaps severely underspecifying their models given the high impact experience has within other analyses with regards to its explanation of variance in the dependent variable.

Undoubtedly, baseball is a competitive game, one for which greater experience in the "big show" should only accentuate the talent of individual players. Conceptually, one is looking for a measure that looks at the time that players have spent in the majors and how that may translate into differing levels of renumeration. The empirical measure for amount of major league experience is simply the number of years (YRS) that a player has been in the major leagues. The source for this is *Total Baseball* (Thorn and Palmer, 1991), a text that lists the career records and biographical information of all the players in the history of major league baseball.

RESEARCH FINDINGS

Player Position: First Base

This position was first analyzed with the model that utilized THV1B as the player performance indicator for 1990. Two general sets of equations were run. The first incorporated a two-year lag for previous salary (SAL89) while the second included a one-year lag (SAL90). A second set of equations was constructed based on three different measures of player performance (THV, ORS-Small Pool, and ORS-Large Pool).[18] In equation #1 in Table 2.1 it is seen that both SAL89 and THV1B were significant predictors of 1991 salary. This indicates a commonsensical merit-based labor model in which the previous level of salary and performance dictate the following year's salary. However, the results of this equation were slightly unusual in that the years experience variable (YRS) had a negative and significant (at .05) relationship, indicating that players with less experience are being paid more, an anomaly which will be addressed during the discussion of the "superstar" hypothesis results. Although the results from equation #1 appear to be fairly consistent with labor models, the results in equation #2 (that which uses SAL90) yielded different results. First, equation #2 explained 85% of the variation in the dependent variable (1991 salary determination) while equation #1 accounted for only 64%. Second, SAL90 had a larger *t*-statistic than SAL89 indicating that although both were greatly significant (in excess of .001), SAL90 was even more significant. Concurrent with this finding, the performance variable, THV1B, which was significant in equation #1, became insignificant in equation #2. These two findings, however, appear to make sense, as one would expect that a more recent measure of salary level would be more accurate in predicting salary in the year immediately following. Moreover, one would expect that the performance variable (THV1B) would have a greater impact in equation #1 because its measure is based on the 1990 season, a more current measure than the two-year salary lag (SAL89).[19] But although the relationship between the salary variables in both equations #1 and

Table 2.1
SAL91 Regressed on Variables for First Base

VARIABLE	EQ #1	EQ #2	EQ #3	EQ #4	EQ #5	EQ #6
SAL89	1.04****		.98****		.97****	
	(4.20)		(4.35)		(4.46)	
SAL90		.94****		.91****		.88****
		(8.77)		(8.91)		(9.88)
RACE	.22	.18*	.32*	.26**	.29*	.16**
	(1.70)	(2.13)	(2.59)	(2.96)	(2.52)	(2.71)
YRS	-.52*	-.21	-.44	-.16	-.42	-.10
	(-2.09)	(-2.04)	(-1.95)	(-1.52)	(-1.91)	(-1.28)
THV1B	.33*	.15				
	(2.51)	(1.60)				
ORS-SMALL POOL			.43***	.23*		
			(3.41)	(2.36)		
ORS-LARGE POOL					.45****	.23***
					(3.78)	(3.41)
Adjusted R^2	.64	.85	.70	.87	.72	.91
N	23	23	23	23	24	30

* $p < .05$.   ** $p < .01$.   *** $p < .005$.   **** $p < .001$.

Beta weights are reported. N equals sample size. T-statistics are in parentheses. R^2 adjusted for number of independent variables and sample size.

#2 appear normal, equation #2 reveals that the race (RACE) variable was a significant predictor of salary determination for 1991. In equation #2, RACE evinced a significant positive relationship. Remember that race is operationalized as a dummy variable whereby 1 = majority and 0 = minority. Consequently, a positive sign on the beta weight (as is the case in equation #2) indicates the presence of discrimination against minorities. This relationship will be examined more thoroughly later in the analysis.

Following these first two equations, the player position of first base was analyzed again, with ORS incorporated as the performance variable (instead of THV1B). ORS, it should be remembered, measures only offensive production and thereby allows a greater number of players to be analyzed.[20] This model was first run using only those players who also had THV rankings, thus ensuring the same size pool, and although equations #1- 4 were statistically significant, the amount of variance explained in the dependent variable (1991 salary determination) increased from 64% to 70% with a two-year salary lag (equations #1 and #3) and from 85% to 87% with a one-year salary lag incorporated (equations #2 and #4). Moreover, the salary variables maintained their high degree of significance. Particularly noteworthy is that although both SAL89 and SAL90 are significant predictors at the .001 level, SAL90 is the greater predictor since it has a higher t-statistic (4.35 in equation #3 compared to 8.91 in equation #4). This parallels the results found when incorporating THV1B as the performance variable. In brief, a more recent measure of previous salary is a better predictor of future salary. The results of the performance measure, ORS, also paralleled the findings of equations #1 and #2 when THV1B was utilized. However, two items are noteworthy. The statistical power of explanation of ORS when a two-year salary lag was incorporated (equation #3) was considered greater (t = 3.41, p < .005) than the THV1B measure in equation #1 (t = 2.51, p < .05). Second, although the performance measure in equation #2 was insignificant, the use of ORS in equation #4 produced a significant result at the .05 level (t = 2.36). Furthermore, RACE continued to exhibit a positive and significant relationship in both equations #3 and #4, whereas the YRS variable lost its significance.

Equations #5 and #6 incorporate all first basemen with an ORS ranking, including those who may not have had a THV1B ranking for lack of defensive statistics. This resulted in an increase in the number of cases to twenty-four in equation #5 (SAL89) and thirty in equation #6 (SAL90). Both equations remained statistically significant and, generally speaking, the results for each of the independent and control variables remained consistent with the findings of the ORS-small pool. The inclusion of a greater number of players had little impact beyond slightly increasing the explanatory power of the established model (from 70% in equation #3 to 72% in equation #5 and from 87% in equation #4 to 91% in equation #6). One major difference concerning the performance variable in equation #6 is noteworthy. As mentioned, ORS reached statistical significance at .05 in equation #4. In equation #6, the direction of the relationship not only remains positive, but also becomes more significant (t = 3.41, p < .005). The inclusion of seven additional players appears to have resulted not only in the level of explained variance increasing to 91%, but also the suggestion that this was primarily due to the increasing explanatory power of the ORS measure. Moreover, once again, RACE was identified as having a positive and significant relationship in both equations #5 (t = 2.52, p < .05) and #6 (t = 2.71, p < .01), whereas YRS remained insignificant.

The "Old Man" and "Superstar" Hypotheses Exposed

Given the presented results, one must ask whether they accurately depict the situation or whether some of the anomalies may be attributed to various mitigating circumstances. Let us begin with those differences that exist between equations #4 and #6, those that included the small and the large pool of first basemen. The main difference between the two equations was that seven additional first- and second-year players were added to the large pool. Generally speaking, these players fit well into the model that holds that younger players tend to be paid less and produce less. Indeed, first- and second-year players are held to a more rigid salary structure,[21] which allows for a greater correlation between pay and performance than can be found among older players. Figure 2.3 illustrates that although the average performance (ORS) is 2.5 times higher for veterans, salary increases to 12.15 times that of the younger (i.e., first- and second-year) players, which is disproportionate and allows for greater salary deviations. Moreover, when correlations for the two groups were produced, a much higher correlation was discovered between performance of players without a THV rating and their salary in 1991 (.80, $p < .02$) than with the group that did qualify for THV ratings (.40, $p < .03$). Thus, for the younger players, pay more closely mirrors performance, hence resulting in ORS becoming a more significant predictor when the younger players are included.

Figure 2.3
Disproportionate Differences in Salary and Performance

	Avg ORS	Avg SAL91	Correlation	N
Players with THV Rating	6.27	$1,879,290	.40	23
Players without THV Rating	2.53	$154,667	.80	7
Amount of Increase	2.48x	12.15x		

Years experience was also significant in equation #2. If YRS would have had a positive beta weight there would be no cause for concern as generally one would expect salaries to increase as one gains more experience in the major leagues. However, in this case the relationship was negative, suggesting that a player with fewer years would make more money. At first this doesn't seem to make sense, but first base is the home of a large number of superstars, many of whom are fairly young. This leads to the proposition of a "Superstar Effect." As a player reaches a certain level of performance (and maintains it for a couple years), that player will receive a substantial increase in salary regardless of experience, race, and/or metropolitan area. Several examples of this effect can be found within the position of first base and go toward a viable explanation of the negative significance of YRS. Figure 2.4 illustrates the degree to which a superstar effect occurs with respect to first basemen.

Figure 2.4
The Superstar Effect

Player	YRS	SAL91 ($)
Grace, Mark	3	1,200,000
Clark, Will	5	3,750,000
McGriff, Fred	5	2,750,000
Palmeiro, Rafael	5	1,475,000

The next startling result of the equations was the consistent impact of RACE in five of the six equations. As stated previously, this relationship was positive, indicating the presence of discrimination against minorities. One possible explanation for the significant result for race is if several minority players were being underpaid for their level of performance, given that they had more than two years experience. Indeed, there are a couple of players who appear to be underpaid based on their performance. One player is Randy Milligan of the Baltimore Orioles, whose ORS was 6.73, ranking him twelfth out of thirty first basemen. His $330,000 salary in 1991, however, was significantly lower than that of other players with comparable performance levels. It is instructive to compare Milligan's numbers to the averages in Figure 2.3. Milligan's ORS was higher than the average ORS (6.27), but his salary was only 17.6% of the average 1991 salary for veteran players. It should be pointed out, however, that Milligan only had four years experience and at the time played for one of the three stingiest baseball teams (based on 1991 salary figures).

Perhaps a better illustration of a minority player being underpaid is Carlos Quintana of the Boston Red Sox. Although he had only three years experience, thus putting him in a similar position as Milligan, Quintana had an ORS of 6.18, (fourteenth among thirty first basemen), while his THV of 5.58 ranked him as sixth among twenty-three first basemen with THV1B ratings. His salary in 1991, however, was a surprisingly low $285,000 (15.2% of the average 1991 salary for veteran players).

Even though these are two examples where minorities are possibly being underpaid given their performance levels, they are the only players out of thirteen minorities who fall into this category, seemingly not a high enough number to be of real significance. What, then, can help explain the findings of the equations? Another possibility is that the positive and significant relationship of the race variable might be the result of white players who are overpaid. Indeed, there appear to be three players who were considerably overpaid for various reasons. Thus, perhaps the combination of the overpaid players with the undervaluation of Milligan and Quintana, caused the equation to indicate the presence of racism. Keith Hernandez typifies the "Fading Superstar" segment of the old man hypothesis. In 1990, he signed a two-year contract for $1,750,000 per year with the Cleveland Indians. A superstar for many years, Hernandez was playing his seventeenth year and his production had begun to fall off. He still commanded a high salary because of his experience and Cleveland's hope that he would again produce numbers similar to his 1986 season with the New York Mets (in that season, he batted .310 with thirteen HR and eighty-three RBI, while scoring ninety-four runs and winning the Gold Glove, the award given to the best defensive player at each position). Although paid close to the average 1991 salary, his numbers continued to fall and he became injured as well. Thus, for their investment the Indians received an ORS of 1.13 (17.6% of the average ORS) and a THV of 2.55, both ranking near the bottom of the performance ratings for first basemen.

Don Mattingly is another example of how this equation may have been influenced by factors other than racism and led to a high level of significance for the RACE variable. Throughout his career, Mattingly has produced statistics that place him in the superstar category and, consequently, he had been rewarded with a long-term contract that paid him $3,420,000 in 1991 (nearly double the average). However, like Hernandez, Mattingly was injured and played in pain much of the year, causing his numbers to diverge from previous norms - his THV was .47 and he had an ORS rating of 4.03. Unlike Hernandez, however, Mattingly rebounded and has subsequently posted solid statistics.

The third case leading to the negative influence of the RACE variable on salary determination in 1991 is Pete O'Brien. O'Brien, in 1990, was a nine-year veteran who had put up fairly solid numbers throughout his career. Although O'Brien was viewed by many as a quality first baseman, he played for relatively obscure smaller market teams such as Cleveland and Texas and didn't receive a large salary ($700,000 in 1989). But then Seattle, after the 1989 season (in the free agent craze), signed O'Brien to a contract that paid him slightly over $1,000,000 in 1990 and $2,037,000 for 1991, making him one of the highest paid first basemen. Once again, however, the injury bug struck, limiting his season (108 of 162 games) and his production (a THV of 2.5 and ORS of 3.98), resulting in a high-priced, unproductive player.

Figure 2.5
Mean Salary of First Basemen by Race

Race	Mean SAL91 ($)	N
U.S. Black	1,061,125	8
Non-U.S. Black	892,667	3
U.S. Latino	0	0
Non-U.S. Latino	1,921,000	2
White	1,446,333	18
White (less 3 veterans)	1,252,267	15

Figure 2.5 summarizes the mean average 1991 salary for all thirty-one first basemen according to the five categories of race used in this study. If the salaries of the three aforementioned players are removed, the mean salary for white first basemen in 1991 declines nearly $200,000 to $1,252,267, perhaps lending more credence to the proposition that RACE had an undue influence for reasons other than actual racial concerns. Moreover, although the RACE variable appeared to have a greater impact than warranted, it was obvious that the previous year's salary (SAL90) and player performance (THV1B and ORS) were the main contributions to the determination of salary in 1991.

The application of the old man and superstar hypotheses also supports the notion that the results for RACE at the first base position should be discounted.

Table 2.2

SAL91 Regressed on Variables for First Base Incorporating the "Old Man" and "Superstar" Hypotheses

VARIABLE	OLD MAN HYPOTHESIS				SUPERSTAR	
	EQ #1	EQ #2	EQ #3	EQ #4	EQ #1	EQ #2
SAL89	.73***		.76****		.97***	
	(3.88)		(6.10)		(4.85)	
SAL90		.85****		.80****		.93****
		(8.00)		(11.18)		(10.48)
RACE	.12	.13	.17	.11	.09	-.02
	(.78)	(1.33)	(1.68)	(1.95)	(.63)	(-.25)
YRS	-.06	-.03	-.01	.05	-.21	-.02
	(-.09)	(-.24)	(-.05)	(.73)	(-1.04)	(-.66)
THV1B	.40*	.17				
	(2.69)	(1.61)				
ORS			.56***	.24****	.46*	.21**
			(5.60)	(3.95)	(3.03)	(2.91)
Adjusted R^2	.66	.86	.84	.93	.82	.94
N	18	18	19	25	11	16

* $p < .05$.　** $p < .01$.　*** $p < .005$.　**** $p < .001$.

Beta weights are reported. N equals sample size. T-statistics are in parentheses. R^2 adjusted for number of independent variables and sample size.

When the old man hypothesis was tested for both performance variables (THV1B and ORS), significance on the RACE variable disappeared as Table 2.2 indicates.[22] Moreover, a comparison of Table 2.1 and 2.2 indicates the following. First, the level of explained variance when SAL89 and THV are in the equation rose from 64% to 66% with THV and SAL89 remaining as the statistically significant variables. Second, the level of explained variance when SAL90 and THV are in the equation increased from 85% to 86%, with SAL90 remaining statistically significant. Of greater importance here is that the impact of the RACE variable became insignificant.[23] In the remaining ORS equations, RACE had been significant in both the SAL89 and SAL90 versions (equations #3 through #6 in Table 2.1). However, when the old man hypothesis was run, the significance of RACE once again disappeared, whereas the amount of variance explained increased in both instances (from 73% to 84% with SAL89 and from 91% to 93% with SAL90). The results from both of these equations were obtained by eliminating five of the oldest first basemen. Those eliminated included Hernandez (identified previously as a potential source of problems) and Jack Clark, the third highest paid first basemen who, although compiling some decent numbers, did not really produce at the rate needed to justify his

$2,900,000 salary. Interestingly enough, Eddie Murray was also excluded, but his exclusion still didn't prevent the departure of RACE's significance. Murray is a well-paid black first basemen who produced numbers that justify his salary. This appears to suggest that the responsibility for the original significant results of RACE rested with the few white players who were overpaid because of their "fading" superstar status.

A comparison of Tables 2.1 and 2.2 further illustrates that when the superstar hypothesis was run, it resulted in the elimination of the significance of the RACE variable, whereas the SAL89, SAL90, and performance variables remained statistically significant.[24] In addition, the equations also generated higher levels of explained variance. When SAL89 and ORS are in the equation the percent of explained variance rose from 73% to 82%. When SAL90 and ORS were analyzed the percent of explained variance rose from 91% to 94%.[25] These results indicate an apparent lack of racism among the non-superstars. In summary, it appears that the descriptive statistics, old man hypothesis, and superstar hypothesis all support the view that RACE is, in reality, not a significant factor in the salary determination of first basemen and that previous salary level and merit (i.e., performance) are the most significant determinants of 1991 salary. The role of performance in salary determination is illustrated further in Figure 2.6.

Figure 2.6
Top Ten First Basemen by THV, ORS, and SAL91

Rank	THV Rating	ORS Rating	SAL91 ($)
1	8.34 Will Clark	10.70 Fielder	3,750,000 W. Clark
2	7.65 Mark McGwire	9.77 McGriff	3,420,000 Mattingly
3	6.98 Mark Grace	9.38 Murray	2,900,000 Jack Clark
4	6.61 Sid Bream	9.18 McGwire	2,850,000 McGwire
5	6.52 McGriff	8.43 W. Clark	2,750,000 McGriff
6	5.58 C. Quintana	8.00 Palmeiro	2,600,000 Hrbek
7	5.55 Fielder	7.78 Grace	2,562,000 Murray
8	5.55 Galarraga	7.63 Hrbek	2,367,000 Galarraga
9	4.99 Eddie Murray	7.15 Galarraga	2,283,000 Guerrero
10	3.99 Palmeiro	7.08 J. Clark	2,037,000 P. O'Brien

Player Position: Second Base

As was the case with first base, the same three models were run for the second basemen. All three models were statistically significant regardless of whether SAL89 or SAL90 were utilized. The model that used THV2B as its performance variable provided less explanation of variance (48% for equation #1 in Table 2.3 and 56% for equation #2) than the models that incorporated ORS as the production (i.e., performance) measure, perhaps continuing a pattern that should be traced throughout the position analyses.

Within equations #1 and #2, the relationship between SAL89 and SAL90 remained consistent with previous results. Both variables were statistically significant, but SAL90 had a greater level of significance and a higher t-statistic (t = 3.83, p < .001) than SAL89 (t = 3.10, p < .005). Moreover, the THV model yielded similar results in both the first base and second base positions with regard to the statistical significance of the performance variable (THV). Equation #1 for both positions indicated that the performance measure was statistically significant (t = 2.36, p < .05 for THV1B and t = 2.51, p < .05 for THV2B), whereas neither THV1B nor THV2B remained statistically significant in equation #2. Perhaps one reason for this result is that the THV variable has become a negative measure of defensive performance. In other words, it is possible that the average defensive statistics (taken from three previous years)[26] used as norms for defensive production were too high to serve as realistic norms for 1990, thereby creating the impression that the majority of major league players are defensive liabilities. In fact, only two of the first basemen and only seven second basemen were able to use defensive performance to enhance their THV, meaning that most of the players have their performance variable devalued (perhaps unfairly) by the defensive component, potentially resulting in less statistically significant results. Finally, the other two variables included in the analysis, RACE and YRS, did not come close to yielding statistically significant results.

Equations #3 and #4 (which used ORS as the performance variable) produced higher rates of explanation than the equations developed from the THV model. These equations were run with the small pool of players (as explained in the first base position analysis the small pool includes only those players who have also qualified for THV values) and explained 64% of the variance in equation #3 and 70% in equation #4. In addition, equations #5 and #6 (using the ORS performance variable in conjunction with a larger pool of players) produced almost identical results as equation #5 explained the same amount of variance as equation #3,[27] whereas the independent and control variables explained 73% of the variance in 1991 salaries when SAL90 was used in equation #6. Furthermore, the younger players continued to demonstrate that they fit better into the salary and performance model (as argued in the first base section) because of a more rigid salary structure. In comparing equation #4 to equation #6 (which allowed for the inclusion of first- and second-year players), the performance variable, ORS, remained statistically significant at the same level (.005), whereas the large pool equation achieved a slightly higher t-statistic (t = 3.58 in equation #6 compared to t = 3.49 for equation #4). Moreover, SAL90 became a much better predictor when the younger players were included in equation #6 (t = 3.68, p < .001) than in equation #4 (t = 3.00, p < .01). Another item of note involving all three models is that once again the performance variable became much more significant when ORS was used as the performance variable instead of THV, lending further support to the argument that ORS is a better measure than THV.

The THV variable was statistically significant only in equation #1 ($t = 2.51$, $p < .05$). ORS, however, was statistically significant at a higher level (at least $p < .005$ in every case) whenever it was used in an equation (equations #3 - #6). Additionally, as was the case with equations #1 and #2, the RACE and YRS variables were insignificant for equations #3 through #6.

Another important result of the analysis of second basemen is the interesting relationship discovered between the salary and performance variables in the equations that used ORS as the performance variable. Both variables were statistically significant in all of these equations, but, in contrast to the results of the analysis of first basemen, the performance variable appeared to be more significant than the SAL89 variable in equations #3 and #5. This result is not entirely unexpected since, as was argued previously, the performance variable (derived from 1990 statistics) is a more recent and, therefore, more significant measure than SAL89. A more noteworthy item, however, is that in equation #4, when SAL90 was used, the performance variable remained more significant and maintained a higher t-statistic. The results were not as startling in equation #6, as the performance variable was slightly less significant ($p < .001$ for SAL90, $p < .005$ for ORS). However, the t-statistics were nearly identical ($t = 3.68$ for SAL90, $t = 3.58$ for ORS). This is a marked departure from the first base analysis where the t-statistics of the SAL90 variable were 2.5 times higher than the t-statistic of ORS in equation #4 and 4 times greater than the ORS t-statistic in equation #6. These results suggest that ORS (the performance variable) is more of a factor in explaining the variance of SAL91 than is SAL89. In addition, it appears as if ORS is the equivalent of SAL90 in providing explanation for variance in the 1991 salaries.

This occurrence can be explained by examining the individual second basemen. Figure 2.7 isolates some of the second basemen. It can be seen that most of these players had a salary in 1991 that was double or often triple their salary in 1990. As a consequence, there was not an even pattern of increase from salaries in 1990 to salaries in 1991, thus shifting some of the normal explanatory power of SAL90 to the performance variable (ORS).

Closer examination of the player receiving the largest salary increases reveals the reason for this result. The answer can be found by examining the nature of the salary structure in major league baseball. Although there has been much publicity in recent years regarding the skyrocketing salaries of baseball players (and professional athletes in general), it is often forgotten that most players are at the mercy of the owners for the first three years of their career. Once a player has three full years of major league service, he becomes eligible for a process called salary arbitration.[28] This process entitles a player, if he is unsatisfied with the salary offered to him by the team, to submit a salary figure to an arbitrator. The team also submits a salary figure and the arbitrator listens to arguments from both sides before determining the player's salary. The arbitration process in baseball is different than standard arbitration in that the arbitrator must choose one side or the other - there is no middle ground. Thus, if the player is a rising

Figure 2.7
Salary Changes of Second Basemen

Name	SAL91 ($)	SAL90 ($)	YRS	THV	ORS
Alomar, S.	1,250,000	400,000	3	4.62	7.20
Barrett	100,000	1,000,000	9	2.14	1.48
Browne	800,000	310,000	5	4.64	6.70
Deshields	215,000	100,000	1	X	7.05
Doran	2,833,000	934,000	9	3.43	6.70
Duncan	925,000	375,000	5	3.88	5.93
Jefferies	425,000	200,000	4	1.29	7.93
Lind	575,000	270,000	4	6.78	5.45
Ripken, B.	700,000	215,000	4	5.97	4.70
Treadway	770,000	250,000	4	3.91	5.38

star, he often submits a salary figure comparable to that of veteran players at his position who have similar performance characteristics. It follows from this that if the arbitrator rules in favor of the player there will be a huge increase in the player salary. Players remain eligible for arbitration until after their sixth full season, at which time they continue to gain more negotiating leverage when they become eligible for free agency and may sell their services to the club offering the highest salary. As a result of this salary structure, many players in their third, fourth, or fifth years experience large salary increases based more on performance and experience than a previous salary level. Thus, given the regression results and the nature of the major league salary structure, one would expect to see several examples of the arbitration influence in the group of second basemen analyzed. Indeed, seven of the ten players listed as exhibiting the greatest salary increases were in their third, fourth, or fifth year, and often produced fairly significant performance numbers.

The other three cases also contribute to the higher value of performance in explaining the variance of SAL91 but do not fall into the "arbitration influence" discussed previously. Rather they fall into three different categories. First, there is the case of Delino Deshields who in 1990 played his first full year for the Montreal Expos and in the process achieved the seventh highest ORS rating out of 31 second basemen, while finishing second behind David Justice of the Atlanta Braves for the 1990 NL Rookie of the Year award. Because of this extraordinary performance, Deshields was rewarded with a contract that doubled his previous salary to $215,000. Bill Doran of the Cincinnati Reds also contributed to the heavy emphasis on performance. Throughout his nine-year career, he had always been considered one of the top second basemen, but he played on a relatively obscure team, the Houston Astros, never really receiving the amount of publicity many experts felt he deserved (some have stated that he was on a par with Ryne Sandberg). One consequence of this lack of publicity was that his salary remained at relatively low levels. Then, in the heat of the pennant race of 1990 (the last year of Doran's contract), the Cincinnati Reds traded to have him available for the stretch run, knowing that they would have to increase his salary level dramatically in order to retain his services for a subsequent year. They chose to sign him to a contract and his salary tripled to a level comparable to other quality second basemen. Finally, there is the situation of Marty Barrett, a victim of the "Old Man Theory." For a couple years, he was one of the most solid second basemen in the league and his salary was near the one million dollar mark. However, in 1990, his numbers dropped and he was released. He was resigned at the major league minimum of $100,000, representing a 90% pay cut. Although this case represents a downward trend in salary, it still demonstrates how performance (in this case a lack of performance) contributed more to the determination of SAL91 than Barrett's salaries in 1989 or 1990.

The "Old Man" and "Superstar" Hypotheses Exposed

Results of the old man hypothesis appear to support the aforementioned argu-

Table 2.3
SAL91 Regressed on Variables for Second Base

VARIABLE	EQ #1	EQ #2	EQ #3	EQ #4	EQ #5	EQ #6
SAL89	.69***		.45*		.45*	
	(3.10)		(2.26)		(2.26)	
SAL90		.79****		.55**		.62****
		(3.83)		(3.00)		(3.68)
RACE	.02	.12	.04	.10	.04	.11
	(.13)	(.91)	(.31)	(.85)	(.31)	(1.12)
YRS	-.15	-.20	-.01	-.05	-.01	-.08
	(-.67)	(-1.02)	(-.06)	(-.31)	(-.06)	(-.54)
THV2B	.39*	.21				
	(2.51)	(1.30)				
ORS-SMALL POOL			.59****	.49***		
			(4.32)	(3.49)		
ORS-LARGE POOL					.59****	.43***
					(4.32)	(3.58)
Adjusted R^2	.48	.56	.64	.70	.64	.73
N	24	25	24	25	24	28

* $p < .05$.   ** $p < .01$.   *** $p < .005$.   **** $p < .001$.
Beta weights are reported. N equals sample size. T-statistics are in parentheses. R^2 adjusted for number of independent variables and sample size.

Table 2.4

SAL91 Regressed on Variables for Second Base Incorporating the "Old Man" and "Superstar" Hypotheses

VARIABLE	OLD MAN HYPOTHESIS				SUPERSTAR	
	EQ #1	EQ #2	EQ #3	EQ #4	EQ #1	EQ #2
SAL89	.70		.21		.34	
	(2.06)		(.63)		(.85)	
SAL90		.60		.48		.28
		(1.78)		(2.06)		(1.22)
RACE	.02	.05	.07	.07	.23	.18
	(.09)	(.27)	(.43)	(.52)	(.97)	(1.16)
YRS	-.03	.05	.35	.11	-.16	-.09
	(-.08)	(.15)	(1.08)	(.48)	(-.41)	(-.39)
THV2B	.33	.28				
	(1.67)	(1.24)				
ORS			.60**	.45**	.67*	.73****
			(3.14)	(2.96)	(3.07)	(4.57)
Adjusted R^2	.40	.38	.59	.63	.50	.65
N	17	18	17	21	13	16

* $p < .05$.   ** $p < .01$.   *** $p < .005$.   **** $p < .001$.

Beta weights are reported. N equals sample size. T-statistics are in parentheses. R^2 adjusted for number of independent variables and sample size.

ment that the astronomical increases in salary among three- to six-year second basemen have caused performance to become a much more consistent and reliable explanator of SAL91 variance than either SAL89 or SAL90. Equation #1 of Table 2.4, which includes SAL89 and THV2B as variables provided less explanation of variance than equation #1 of Table 2.3 (explanation of variance decreased from 48% to 40%). A corresponding decrease was discovered when equation #2 of Table 2.4 was compared to equation #2 of Table 2.3 (from 56% to 38%).[29] Also, none of the variables were significant, although the equation as a whole was statistically significant. When ORS replaced THV as the performance variable, more insight was provided. Explanation of variance became substantially higher (59% when SAL89 and ORS were used and 63% with SAL90 and ORS), whereas the performance variable in both years were significant at .01. However, although ORS retained a degree of statistical significance, the exclusion of the veterans caused both SAL89 and SAL90 to lose significance, whereas RACE and YRS, consistent with the regular player position analysis, were insignificant as well. The loss of statistical significance within SAL89 and SAL90 can be explained by examining the raw data. When the veterans with ten years or more experience were removed, the majority of players remaining in the analysis had experienced a large increase in salary from 1990 to 1991. In contrast, the veterans generally received fairly steady increases during this period. As a result of this stability, when the veterans are included, the one- and two-year salary lag variables have more explanatory value.

Analysis of the second basemen within the context of the superstar hypothesis provided support for previous findings regarding the role of the salary and performance variables. However, as the results presented in Table 2.4 illustrate, the exclusion of the superstars did not suggest the influence of racial concerns among the leqs productive players.[30] In fact, its results mirrored the conclusions drawn from the old man equations as explanation of variance decreased slightly (to 50% and 65% for the equation using SAL90 and SAL89, respectively), whereas performance was the only variable that remained statistically significant in either equation. Finally, Figure 2.8 illustrates the correlation between performance and 1991 salary within the second base player position. Of the top ten second basemen as ranked by THV, seven also received salaries ranking them in the top ten, whereas six of those found in the ORS rankings are found on the top ten salary list as well. In light of these findings, it seems safe to conclude that with second basemen at least, performance has the most value as a explanator of variance in SAL91 because of the position of the players in baseball's salary structure.

Figure 2.8
Top Ten Second Basemen by THV, ORS, and SAL91

Rank	THV Rating	ORS Rating	SAL91 ($)
1	8.07 Ryne Sandberg	10.30 Sandberg	2,833,000 Doran
2	6.78 Jose Lind	8.43 Franco	2,650,000 Sandberg
3	6.67 Robby Thompson	7.98 Reynolds	2,287,000 Franco
4	6.15 Julio Franco	7.93 G. Jefferies	2,000,000 Whitaker
5	5.97 Billy Ripken	7.20 R. Alomar	1,867,000 Reynolds
6	5.86 Harold Reynolds	7.08 Sax	1,667,000 Sax
7	5.57 Lou Whitaker	7.05 D. Deshields	1,575,000 J. Samuel
8	5.36 Scott Fletcher	6.80 Whitaker	1,500,000 Thompson
9	4.91 Jose Oquendo	6.70 Jerry Browne	1,400,000 Tom Herr
10	4.87 Steve Sax	6.70 Billy Doran	1,300,000 Fletcher

Player Position: Third Base

Analysis of the players at the "hot corner" (as third base is sometimes referred) revealed fewer surprises than the previous two player positions analyzed. Indeed, all three models that were run produced nearly identical results, flagged the same variables as significant, and once again all the regression equations were significant. However, one interesting item of note that came from the descriptive statistics, which will be discussed in greater detail later, is the huge gap among salaries at third base and salaries at other positions given similar levels of production.

Equations #1 and #2 of Table 2.5, which utilized THV3B as the performance variable, explained a greater percentage of variance within this player position than in the second base analysis. When THV3B was used along with SAL89 (equation #1), 63% of the variance was explained, whereas the use of SAL90 with THV3B (equation #2) explained 76% of the variance in 1991 salaries. In addition, both equations, as expected, identified the significant variables as previous salary and THV3B, whereas RACE and YRS did not approach a level close to significance.

Analysis of the results when ORS replaced THV3B as the performance variable revealed a slightly higher explanation of variance. Equations #3 and #4, which maintained the same pool as utilized in the first two equations, explained 62% of the variance when SAL89 was used and provided explanation of 77% of the variance when SAL90 was used. With the addition of the first- and second-year players without THV ratings to the analysis, the large pool equations (equations #5 and #6) explained 64% of the variance when SAL89 was used and 81% with SAL90. Moreover, it is important to note that in each of the three models, the amount of variance explained increased when SAL90 was included in the equation instead of SAL89, once again demonstrating that the more recent salary data is a better predictor. Also, the salary and performance variables were statistically significant in each of the equations when ORS was used. However, RACE and YRS remained insignificant as in the previous equations with THV3B.

Another important point should be made with regard to the results in equation #6. Equation #6 allowed for the inclusion of nine first- or second-year players in the analysis. The addition of these players led to a pronounced increase in the statistical significance of the performance indicator as it increased from .01 in equation #4 (with the small pool) to .001. Furthermore, the increase was accompanied by an increase in the t-statistic of the SAL90 variable from 4.48 to 5.95. Both of these results continue to demonstrate how the younger players contribute to the stabilization of the model because of their position on the salary scale.

The results of the third base player position also indicate a developing pattern that should be explored further. If one examines the results of the various equations (including those within the first and second base player positions), it is noticeable that almost without exception[31] as one goes from the use of a two-year salary lag to a one-year salary lag in any model, two changes occur. First, as noted previously, SAL90 generally increases in statistical significance and t-statistic when compared with the SAL89 variable. However, there is also a rec-

Table 2.5
SAL91 Regressed on Variables for Third Base

VARIABLE	EQ #1	EQ #2	EQ #3	EQ #4	EQ #5	EQ #6
SAL89	.61*		.63*		.68*	
	(2.15)		(2.20)		(2.56)	
SAL90		.70****		.73****		.78****
		(4.06)		(4.48)		(5.95)
RACE	-.02	.07	-.04	.06	.01	.10
	(-.14)	(.58)	(-.25)	(.53)	(.11)	(1.28)
YRS	.08	.08	-.05	-.02	-.14	-.10
	(.28)	(.43)	(-.17)	(-.14)	(-.53)	(-.80)
THV3B	.49***	.32*				
	(3.19)	(2.56)				
ORS-SMALL			.48**	.32**		
POOL			(3.06)	(2.77)		
ORS-LARGE					.45***	.31****
POOL					(3.36)	(3.51)
Adjusted R^2	.63	.76	.62	.77	.64	.81
N	22	24	22	24	24	33

* $p < .05$.   ** $p < .01$.   *** $p < .005$.   **** $p < .001$.

Beta weights are reported. N equals sample size. T-statistics are in parentheses. R^2 adjusted for number of independent variables and sample size.

ognizable pattern with regard to the performance variables and their relationship to the salary variables. Although the salary variable gains statistical significance as the data becomes more recent, the performance variable generally maintains its significance regardless of the salary variable used, but the performance variable usually experiences a relative decrease in t-statistic as one moves from the equation with SAL89 to the equation with SAL90 when compared with the t-statistics of the salary variables. This pattern is illustrated by the results of the equations run for the third base player position. Although there is an absolute decrease in t-statistic in only one of the third base models, the other two models experienced a relative decrease. This is illustrated by a comparison of equations #5 and #6 (the large pool model). Although there is a slight increase in the t-statistic of the ORS variable as one moves from equation #5 to equation #6 (from $t = 3.36$ to $t = 3.51$), the increase in the t-statistic as one moves from SAL89 to SAL90 is much greater (from $t = 2.56$ to $t = 5.95$).

On further examination, there seem to be two reasons for the trend. First, it must be remembered that all THV and ORS ratings are derived from statistics compiled during the 1990 season. Thus, comparatively speaking, it is the most relevant variable in the study when used with SAL89 because it is the most recent variable. In contrast, when it is used in conjunction with SAL90 it is on

Figure 2.9
Large Pay Increases

Name	YRS	SAL90 ($)	SAL91 ($)
K. Caminiti	4	240,000	665,000
C. Hayes	3	150,000	280,000
E. Martinez	4	123,000	350,000
C. Sabo	3	260,000	1,250,000
K. Seitzer	5	1,001,000	1,625,000
M. Sharperson	4	135,000	307,000
G. Sheffield	3	135,000	400,000
M. Williams	4	215,000	600,000

a more level playing field. Second, perhaps another reason for this pattern is the fairly large number of players entering into their third, fourth, or fifth years and whose salaries become subject to the "arbitration influence" discussed in the previous section. This can serve to make SAL89 less significant if a huge raise is granted in 1990, which carries over to SAL91, thereby causing the SAL89 variable to become obsolete in those situations. As Figure 2.9 illustrates, among third basemen, six players in their third, fourth, or fifth years received salary increases of 100% or more between 1990 and 1991, including the astounding increase of Chris Sabo, who with a THV of 7.09 and an ORS of 8.65 received a pay raise from $260,000 to $1,250,000.

The "Old Man" and "Superstar" Hypotheses Exposed

Comparison of Tables 2.5 and 2.6 did not indicate any significant changes when the old man hypothesis was tested.[32] One change occurred as the amount of variance explained by the equations using SAL89 declined regardless of which performance variable was utilized. A probable cause of these results is that the four veterans removed all had fairly constant salaries from 1989 to 1991, which helped to make SAL89 statistically significant in the regular equations. The exclusion of the veterans did not have the same effect on the equations using SAL90 because of an influx of nine young players, which provided stability for the model from the lower rather than the upper end of the salary scale. Not only did this result in the maintenance of the same levels of significance for SAL90 and ORS, but it also increased the amount of variance explained from 81% to 84%. An additional noteworthy development was the increase in the statistical significance and t-statistic of ORS from equation #3 to equation #4 in Table 2.6. Although the rate of increase in the t-statistic of ORS was still outstripped by the increase experienced by the SAL90 variable, the statistical significance increased from .01 to .001. This anomaly appears to have occurred because of the nine first- or second-year players included in the analysis in equation #4 coupled with the exclusion of four veterans who caused the *t*-statistic in equation #3 to decrease from 3.36 in the regular equations to 2.95. Finally, no statistical significance was attached to either the RACE or the YRS variables.

Further examination of Table 2.6, which incorporates the superstar hypothesis, reveals some interesting results.[33] Although no significance was attached to RACE or YRS, there was a dramatic difference in the explained variance between equation #1 (which used SAL89) and equation #2 (which used SAL90). Equation #1 provided only a 61% explanation of variance, whereas SAL89 was the sole variable which registered as statistically significant (at .05). This result most likely occurred for two reasons. First, there were only a small number of players in the case pool (14) which may lead one to question the validity of the results. Second, of the fourteen players, seven had salary increases of 100% or more, perhaps contributing to the lack of explanatory value of the model. For example, Ken Caminiti's salary jumped from $103,000 to $665,000 in the two-year span. When one examines equation #2, however, it is of note that the amount of variance explained increases dramatically to 96%. Moreover, this increase was accompanied by an increase in the statistical significance of the salary variable to .001. Additionally, the performance variable also became statis-

Table 2.6
SAL91 Regressed on Variables for Third Base Incorporating the "Old Man" and "Superstar" Hypotheses

VARIABLE	OLD MAN HYPOTHESIS				SUPERSTAR	
	EQ #1	EQ #2	EQ #3	EQ #4	EQ #1	EQ #2
SAL89	.27		.38		1.49*	
	(.82)		(1.23)		(2.59)	
SAL90		.71***		.80****		.91****
		(3.43)		(6.29)		(13.37)
RACE	-.03	.06	.04	.09	-.20	.00
	(-.20)	(.53)	(.25)	(1.22)	(-1.10)	(.03)
YRS	.43	.10	.14	-.12	-.76	.03
	(1.33)	(.46)	(.48)	(-.97)	(-1.34)	(.43)
THV3B	.57**	.32*				
	(3.06)	(2.21)				
ORS			.48**	.34****	.15	.12*
			(2.95)	(3.87)	(.84)	(2.40)
Adjusted R^2	.58	.76	.57	.84	.61	.96
N	18	20	20	29	14	22

* $p < .05$.   ** $p < .01$.   *** $p < .005$.   **** $p < .001$.

Beta weights are reported. *N* equals sample size. *T*-statistics are in parentheses. R^2 adjusted for number of independent variables and sample size.

tically significant. It appears as if the explanation of this high rate primarily comes from the fact that eight first- or second-year players were added to equation #2. In addition, of the twenty-two cases in this equation, only six received salary increases of 50% or more, contributing to a stable salary environment that manifests itself in the extremely high t-statistic for SAL90 of 13.37. Thus, the results again uphold the stabilizing effects of the younger players on the pay and performance model.

Third Base: The Poor Man's Position?

Although the previous third base player position results appear to generally correspond with those from the previous player position analyses and RACE is not identified as a significant variable in any of the third base equations, a quick glance at Figure 2.10 indicates a large gap in salary between minority players and white players. In fact, white third basemen are earning on average approximately $240,000 more per year than U.S. black third basemen. The salary difference becomes even larger when the other minority third basemen are factored in.

Figure 2.10
Mean Salary at Third Base by Race

Race	SAL91 ($)	N
U.S. Black	565,000	6
Non-U.S. Black	257,500	2
U.S. Latino	0	0
Non-U.S. Latino	102,000	1
White	806,923	26
All Minorities	445,222	9

Figure 2.11
Experience and Performance at Third Base

Race	YRS	THV	ORS
U.S. Black	4.67	3.77	4.61
Non-U.S. Black	2.50	6.04	5.24
Non-U.S. Latin	1.00	NA	.43
White	4.85	4.85	4.68

It appears, however, that these differences can be explained by the data displayed in Figure 2.11. White third basemen average more years of major league experience than any of the minority groups (although U.S. blacks are a close second) and have higher THV and ORS ratings than most of the minority players. Non-U.S. blacks appear to be an exception to this as they averaged higher THV and ORS scores than any of the other groups. This is most likely explained by the fact that there are only two players in that category and one of them is Edgar Martinez, a young rising star with the Seattle Mariners who, in his fourth year, is performing at superstar rates (see Figure 2.13 later), but because of lack of experience, has yet to receive a huge contract.[34]

Another factor in the large salary differences between races is that a majority of the superstars at third base are white. In fact, seven of the top ten performers, as ranked by THV3B, are white, whereas eight of the ten top performers, as measured by ORS, are white. But if this is the case, why is there little difference among the average performance variables? On review, it is discovered that the number of minorities at third base is very small. Overall, minority players comprise 45% of all non-pitchers, but they make up only 26% of the third basemen (only catchers have a smaller percentage). Thus, most of the younger players, who generally have lower performance values than the veterans, are white, thereby reducing the impact the superstars have on the mean performance value.

Finally, another item of note from the descriptive statistics is that third base salaries, when taken together, appear to be exceedingly low compared to other positions. Third basemen average $714,029, whereas the overall 1991 salary average was $949,080. Figure 2.12 illustrates this and compares third basemen to other positions, identifying other factors that may have contributed to this difference.

First, as one can see with the comparison of third base to the positions previously analyzed, not only do first and second basemen draw substantially larger salaries, but they also average more years experience (see Figure 2.13). In this case, experience appears to be a factor since both first and second basemen have an average YRS variable of six or better, the magic number for free agency and skyrocketing salaries. The other factor in the salary differences appears to be performance as measured by ORS. In fact, this is the variable that correlates the best with the salaries as in all cases a higher ORS leads to a higher salary. Additionally, the THV values do not seem to have any effect on salary as the THV values for third basemen are significantly higher than those at other positions, and yet, their salaries are the lowest. This suggests one of two things.

Figure 2.12
Explanation of Salary Variance

Position	Mean SAL91 ($)	Avg. YRS	Avg. ORS	Avg. THV
First Base	1,323,968	6.00	5.29	3.68
Second Base	960,000	6.81	4.90	3.76
Third Base	714,029	4.69	4.58	4.83

Either the THV rating does not adequately measure performance or offensive production is a much greater factor in salary determination then defensive capabilities.[35] In conclusion, after further analysis there does not appear to be anything unusual about the lower salaries of third basemen.

Figure 2.13
Top Ten Third Basemen by THV, ORS, and SAL91

Rank	THV Rating	ORS Rating	SAL91 ($)	
1	8.43 Matt Williams	9.08 Gruber	3,033,000	Gruber
2	8.40 Kelly Gruber	8.65 Boggs	2,700,000	Boggs
3	7.95 Tim Wallach	8.65 Sabo	2,700,000	Gaetti
4	7.09 Chris Sabo	8.43 Williams	1,906,000	Wallach
5	6.44 Gary Gaetti	8.35 Wallach	1,750,000	Pendleton
6	6.36 Charlie Hayes	7.48 Seitzer	1,625,000	Seitzer
7	6.35 Wade Boggs	7.40 Brook Jacoby	1,275,000	Lansford
8	6.11 Gary Sheffield	7.05 Martinez	1,250,000	Sabo
9	6.04 Edgar Martinez	6.60 Sheffield	1,150,000	Jacoby
10	5.58 Kevin Seitzer	6.45 Gaetti	665,000	Caminiti

Player Position: Shortstop

The final player position in the infield to be analyzed is shortstop. Once again, as Table 2.7 indicates, the results achieved were significant for all six different equations run. When one compares the two equations in which THVSS was used (equations #1 and #2) as the performance variable, it is discovered that there is a large jump in explained variance as the SAL89 model (62% explained variance) was replaced by the SAL90 model (89% explained variance). The performance and salary variables remained significant in both equations while the trend between the two salary variables continued to hold as there was a substantial increase in t-statistic from SAL89 ($t = 4.36$) to SAL90 ($t = 10.29$). The statistical significance of both variables was .001. However, the performance variable (THVSS) did not follow the patterns that were established through the first three analyses of player positions. In the case of shortstops, THVSS increased in significance and t-statistic from the SAL89 model to the SAL90 model. This is in contrast to previous results, which typically indicated that the performance variable usually declines in significance and t-statistic since it is being used in conjunction with more recent salary figures (SAL90). Another interesting result of equations #1 and #2 is that although RACE remained statistically insignificant, the YRS variable became significant and negative in equation #2. The results regarding the performance and YRS variables will be addressed later in the analysis.

Equations #3 and #4 were run with ORS in place of THVSS as the perfor-

Table 2.7
SAL91 Regressed on Variables for Shortstop

VARIABLE	EQ #1	EQ #2	EQ #3	EQ #4	EQ #5	EQ #6
SAL89	.74****		.58***		.55***	
	(4.36)		(3.25)		(3.45)	
SAL90		1.05****		1.01****		.97****
		(10.29)		(7.62)		(8.38)
RACE	.05	.06	-.10	-.03	-.10	-.04
	(.35)	(.81)	(-.82)	(-.45)	(-.84)	(-.64)
YRS	-.03	-.30**	-.09	-.32	-.08	-.31***
	(-.20)	(-3.03)	(-.59)	(-2.99)	(-.59)	(-3.16)
THVSS	.34*	.22**				
	(2.56)	(2.93)				
ORS-SMALL			.43**	.18		
POOL			(2.92)	(1.84)		
ORS-LARGE					.50****	.24**
POOL					(3.66)	(2.80)
Adjusted R^2	.62	.89	.64	.86	.70	.89
N	25	26	25	26	27	29

* $p < .05$.   ** $p < .01$.   *** $p < .005$.   **** $p < .001$.

Beta weights are reported. N equals sample size. T-statistics are in parentheses. R^2 adjusted for number of independent variables and sample size.

mance variable, but the same size pool of players remained (i.e., the players with no THVSS rating were excluded). The results of these equations were similar to those of equation #1 and #2 in several respects. First, the amount of variance in SAL91 explained as one moved from the use of SAL89 to SAL90 increased substantially from 64% to 86%. Second, the salary variables remained statistically significant in both equations, whereas use of the SAL90 variable resulted in higher significance (from .005 to .001) and t-statistic ($t = 3.25$ for SAL89, $t = 7.62$ for SAL90). In addition, the RACE variable did not register as significant although YRS exhibited the same significant negative relationship as was found in equation #2. There was a difference, however, in the performance variable (ORS) as it became insignificant in the SAL90 model. This result is in direct contrast with the results when THVSS was utilized as the performance measure, although it is consistent with the results obtained prior to this player position analysis.

The results of the large pool are reported in equations #5 and #6 of Table 2.7.[36] In general, the results of these equations mirrored those of equations #3 and #4 although the addition of the younger players led to an increase in statistical significance in most variables and resulted in a greater explained variance (70% in equation #5, 89% in equation #6). First, the salary variables remained statistically significant and once again there was an increase in significance from SAL89 (t = 3.45, p < .005) to SAL90 (t = 8.38, p < .001). Second, although the results regarding the performance variable in equations #5 and #6 were consistent with equations #3 and #4 in that there was still evidence of a decline in statistical significance, the addition of the first and second year players increased the validity of the measure enough that it also remained significant when SAL90 was used. Finally, YRS also remained negative and significant, and RACE continued to be insignificant.

When the results of the preceding equations are viewed together, it is interesting to note that the equations that used THVSS as the performance variable appeared to hold their own in comparison to the other equations when it came to explanation of variance. Indeed, THVSS appears to have become a better performance variable than ORS in this particular player position. This anomaly will be addressed later in the section.

As mentioned previously, in each of the equations run with SAL90, YRS became both negative and significant. If the relationship were positive there would be little cause for concern as this indicates that as players gain more experience, they are paid higher salaries. However, a negative relationship suggests the opposite; players with fewer years experience earn the highest salaries. Yet when one looks at the pool of shortstops it appears impossible that there could be a negative relationship between YRS and SAL91, especially considering the aging, highly paid superstars who rank among some of the top shortstops (i.e., Cal Ripken, Jr., Alan Trammell, and Ozzie Smith). Indeed, the raw data indicates that the majority of players are young and not paid high salaries compared to those of other positions. For instance, there are seven shortstops who have played more than ten years in the major leagues and five earn more than $1,000,000 per year, while of the remaining twenty-six, only nine have $1,000,000 plus annual contracts.

Figure 2.14
Salary Decline of Veteran Players

Name	YRS	SAL89 ($)	SAL90 ($)	SAL91 ($)
A. Griffin	15	1,000,000	1,000,000	900,000
R. Ramirez	11	1,025,000	1,012,000	1,206,000
C. Ripken	10	2,467,000	1,367,000	2,333,000
O. Smith	13	2,340,000	1,975,000	2,225,000
G. Templeton	15	600,000	650,000	550,000

Perhaps an alternative explanation of the negative sign on YRS can be found by examining the upward or downward trend of salaries of the veteran players. It is possible that even though the veterans earn more money, that they are making less money as they advance in age, thereby leading to the significant negative finding. Indeed, Figure 2.14 indicates that although seven of the shortstops are ten year veterans, five of the seven have experienced a salary decline since 1989. Moreover, four of those players had a 1991 salary level that remained below the 1989 level.[37] Figure 2.15 lends further credence to the theory that salary declines within the ranks of veteran players led to the negative significance of the YRS variable as it contains a comparison with other positions. The other four positions (first base, second base, third base, and outfield) analyzed in this chapter each indicated a lower percentage of ten-year veterans with declining salaries with the exception of third basemen.[38]

Figure 2.15
Salary Decreases among Veterans by Player Position

Position	Salary Decrease	%	Decrease below SAL89	%
Shortstop	5 of 7	71.4	4 of 7	57.1
First Base	1 of 5	20.0	1 of 5	20.0
Second Base	4 of 7	57.1	1 of 7	14.3
Third Base	3 of 4	75.0	2 of 4	50.0
Outfield	4 of 21	19.0	3 of 21	14.3

The "Old Man" and "Superstar" Hypotheses Exposed

The results of the analysis of the shortstop player position with regard to the YRS variable are in line with the old man hypothesis. It appears as if the "fading superstar" problem has occurred within this position. This phenomenon is characterized by a decrease in player salary as the veteran players experience a gradual decline in performance, a situation that fits with the shortstop player position. Thus, this instance provides a perfect time for testing the hypothesis.[39] Indeed, comparison of Tables 2.7 and 2.8 seems to validate the old man hypothesis as the statistical significance of YRS disappears regardless of which performance measure is used. These results demonstrate that the reason for the negative statistical significance of the YRS variable was indeed the ten-year veterans, who, although among some of the higher paid shortstops, had begun to see their salaries decline. Once these players were removed, the relationship between salary and experience became linear.

Other than the results with regard to the YRS variable, most of the other results appear normal. Explanation of variance remained high and as previous results have suggested, use of SAL90 resulted in more explanation than when SAL89 was used (explained variance increased from 59% to 85% between equations #1 and #2 of Table 2.8 and from 74% to 87% between equations #3 and #4). Within equations #1 and #2, only the salary variables were statistically significant, whereas in equation #3 (which used ORS instead of THVSS) the performance variable was significant and SAL89 was not. This situation was re-

Table 2.8

SAL91 Regressed on Variables for Shortstop Incorporating the "Old Man" and "Superstar" Hypotheses

	OLD MAN HYPOTHESIS				SUPERSTAR	
VARIABLE	EQ #1	EQ #2	EQ #3	EQ #4	EQ #1	EQ #2
SAL89	.60*		.41		.94****	
	(2.42)		(2.01)		(4.69)	
SAL90		1.00****		.80****		1.09****
		(6.15)		(5.29)		(7.09)
RACE	-.11	.09	-.17	-.07	.12	-.02
	(-.54)	(.72)	(-1.39)	(-.84)	(.75)	(-.23)
YRS	.16	-.20	.24	-.00	-.39	-.39*
	(.60)	(-1.17)	(1.25)	(-.02)	(-1.82)	(-2.49)
THVSS	.15	.26				
	(.72)	(1.96)				
ORS			.40**	.17	.30	.14
			(2.87)	(1.59)	(1.69)	(1.20)
Adjusted R^2	.59	.85	.74	.87	.68	.82
N	18	19	20	22	20	22

   * $p < .05$.   ** $p < .01$.   *** $p < .005$.   **** $p < .001$.

Beta weights are reported. N equals sample size. T-statistics are in parentheses. R^2 adjusted for number of independent variables and sample size.

versed, however, in equation #4 where SAL90 was significant and ORS was not. A possible reason for the significance of ORS is that once the older players with their steady (albeit slightly declining) salaries were removed, the players with between three and nine years experience, whose performance is often more steady than their salary, caused ORS to become the variable with the best explanatory value. One would think that this line of reasoning would also cause the THVSS variable to become significant in equation #1, but perhaps the lack of this occurrence is another indication of the superiority of ORS as a performance measure. Further examination of Table 2.8, which reports the application of the superstar hypothesis, reveals some interesting results.[40] Although the explained variance remained fairly high and consistent with previous results (68% explanation in equation #1 of Table 2.8 and 82% in equation #2), the YRS variable remained negative and significant. This occurred even though one may have expected the YRS variable to become insignificant since most of the highest paid players (who are usually the top performers) were eliminated. However, the variable did decline in statistical significance from .005 to .05. This resulted from the fact that the removal of the superstars did not eliminate all of the veteran players with declining salaries. Although it did result in the exclusion of four of the veterans, three remained, which explains the continued, albeit reduced, significance of YRS. Beyond the results regarding the YRS variable, the table indicates that only the salary variables were significant while the performance variable became insignificant. Moreover, RACE remains an insignificant factor in salary determination even when those who are not superstars are singled out for analysis.

A Closer Examination of THVSS

Another area of interest with regard to the shortstop player position is the increase in statistical significance of the THVSS variable when SAL90 is used instead of SAL89. As previously noted, generally the opposite result occurs as the performance variable becomes less statistically significant when used in conjunction with the more recent salary data. Perhaps this deviation from the norm can be explained by the seemingly undue influence of defensive statistics on the THVSS ratings as Figures 2.16 and 2.17 would suggest. Although problems with defensive statistics have been mentioned in earlier sections due

Figure 2.16
Differences in THV and ORS

Player Name	THVSS	ORS
Espinoza	8.34	3.38
Fermin	7.17	3.80
Gagne	6.54	4.10
Griffin	4.35	3.73
Guillen	7.15	4.95
Rivera	5.59	3.63
Schofield	5.69	3.58
Spiers	4.88	3.40
Uribe	4.73	3.78
Vizquel	3.65	2.43

Figure 2.17
THV Increases by Position via Defensive Statistics

Player Position	% of Players Increasing THV
First Base	9.5
Second Base	29.2
Third Base	12.5
Shortstop	46.2
Outfield	26.3

to their influence in decreasing THV, in this case the opposite situation exists. In fact, almost half of the shortstops have increased their THV via defensive statistics, many of them quite large increases. Moreover, these large increases in THVSS as the result of defensive statistics have served to justify the large salaries of several shortstops (e.g., Greg Gagne, Ozzie Guillen, and Dick Schofield) who are better known for defensive prowess. Consequently, THVSS is of greater value in explaining the variance in 1991 salary determination than is ORS, thereby explaining its greater statistical significance in this player position when compared with ORS.

Indeed, upon examination of the ranking of the top ten shortstops by THV and ORS in Figure 2.18 one finds that four of the shortstops as ranked by THV disappear from the top ten ORS list and have extremely low ORS totals. Furthermore, although there is a substantial amount of difference between the top THVSS and ORS performers, seven of the top ten players as ranked by THVSS are also among the highest paid. The ORS list, however, placed six players on the highest paid list, once again demonstrating the high impact of defensive statistics on this player position analysis. In conclusion, perhaps the additional impact of defense on this player position is warranted given traditional views about the role of the shortstop. More often than not, the phrase "no hit, good field" (or some other similar version) is used when a manager is referring to a shortstop. Sometimes the only expectation that a manager has of his shortstop is that he play solid defense. Finally, this contention is supported by a comparison of the average batting average's of the shortstop to that of each league. In the American League, the average batting average was .259, whereas shortstops on average batted only .255.[41] Comparison in the National League yielded similar results as the league average was .256 while the average of shortstops was .253.[42]

Figure 2.18
Top Ten Shortstops by THV, ORS, and SAL91

Rank	THV Rating	ORS Rating	SAL91 ($)
1	8.43 Alvaro Espinoza	8.33 Ripken	2,333,000 Ripken
2	7.84 Tony Fernandez	8.30 Fernandez	2,225,000 Smith
3	7.19 Barry Larkin	8.02 Trammell	2,200,000 Trammell
4	7.17 Felix Fermin	7.93 Larkin	2,100,000 Dunston
5	7.15 Ozzie Guillen	7.00 Bell	2,100,000 Fernandez
6	6.67 Cal Ripken, Jr.	6.68 Dunston	2,100,000 Larkin
7	6.60 Shawon Dunston	6.08 Ozzie Smith	1,733,000 Gagne
8	6.54 Greg Gagne	5.93 Dickie Thon	1,600,000 Guillen
9	6.51 Alan Trammell	5.68 Spike Owen	1,483,000 Schofield
10	6.40 Jay Bell	5.38 K. Stillwell	1,333,000 J. Uribe

Player Position: Outfield

The final player position to be analyzed in this chapter is also the last to have defensive statistics included in the analysis. As Table 2.9 illustrates, generally speaking, each of the models exhibited patterns that have been described throughout the analyses thus far. When THVOF was utilized as the performance measure in equation #1 (along with SAL89) and equation #2 (along with SAL90), explained variance increased from 64% to 82%. In addition, both the salary and performance variables were statistically significant at .001 in each equation. Moreover, the variables followed the same patterns of increase and decline found in each of the other player positions. First, when SAL90 was used instead of SAL89, there was an increase in t-statistic (4.36 to 10.29). Second, the t-statistics of the performance variable (THVOF) declined when SAL90 replaced SAL89 ($t = 4.46$ in equation #1 and $t = 3.27$ in equation #2). The RACE and YRS variables were not statistically significant.

ORS replaced THVOF in equations #3 and #4, although the same pool of players was analyzed. The substitution of performance variables resulted in an increase in explained variance to 73% and 84%, respectively. These results are noteworthy as they suggest that ORS serves as a better predictor than THVOF. More important is the difference in explained variance in equations #1 and #3 when SAL89 is used. Use of SAL89 generally causes the performance variable to become the variable with the greatest explanatory value. Thus, when ORS was used in place of THVOF and explained variance increased by nine percentage points, a strong case is made for ORS as being the better measure of performance.

Similar to the first two equations, equations #3 and #4 also identified the salary and performance variables as statistically significant at .001. The same patterns were discovered as well as the t-statistic of the salary variable more than doubled (from 4.43 to 9.79) when SAL90 replaced SAL89. Additionally, the t-statistic of the performance variable declined when SAL90 replaced SAL89 in the equation. Finally, neither RACE nor the YRS variables demonstrated any statistical significance in this model. Perhaps at this point the conclusion could be drawn that the difference in the performance variables has little impact on the other variables in the equations.

When the large pool of players (this led to the addition of five players in equation #5 and twelve players in equation #6) was utilized to analyze the outfield player position, there was little to differentiate the results of these equations from the first four. Perhaps the only noticeable difference was a slight increase in explained variance, which was 74% for equation #5 and 86% for equation #6. Otherwise, the results were almost identical. Both salary and performance variables remained statistically significant at .001 and exhibited the same patterns documented above. Furthermore, once again RACE and YRS were not statistically significant.

Table 2.9
SAL91 Regressed on Variables for Outfield

VARIABLE	EQ #1	EQ #2	EQ #3	EQ #4	EQ #5	EQ #6
SAL89	.60****		.42****		.43****	
	(5.93)		(4.43)		(4.78)	
SAL90		.85****		.72****		.74****
		(12.56)		(9.79)		(11.29)
RACE	-.04	-.04	-.02	-.03	-.03	-.02
	(-.67)	(-.94)	(-.43)	(-.63)	(-.60)	(-.62)
YRS	-.06	-.04	.14	.01	.12	-.00
	(.65)	(-.58)	(1.63)	(.22)	(1.50)	(-.01)
THVOF	.31****	.16****				
	(4.46)	(3.27)				
ORS-SMALL POOL			.48****	.27****		
			(7.25)	(5.02)		
ORS-LARGE POOL					.48****	.26****
					(7.50)	(5.40)
Adjusted R^2	.64	.82	.73	.84	.74	.86
N	85	95	85	95	90	107

* $p < .05$.   ** $p < .01$.   *** $p < .005$.   **** $p < .001$.

Beta weights are reported. N equals sample size. T-statistics are in parentheses. R^2 adjusted for number of independent variables and sample size.

The "Old Man" and "Superstar" Hypotheses Exposed

Comparison of Tables 2.9 and 2.10 illustrate the relatively few changes resulting from the exclusion of veterans with ten years or more of major league experience.[43] The exclusion of the veterans did allow for a slight increase in explained variance by equations #1 and #2 (which used THVOF as the performance measures) as the equations explained 66% and 85% of the variance in 1991 salary, respectively. In addition, the salary and performance variables were statistically significant in both equations although the significance of the THVOF variable diminished slightly from .001 to .005 when SAL90 was inserted in place of SAL89. The t-statistics of the performance variables, however, hardly changed as $t = 3.38$ in equation #1 and $t = 3.30$ in equation #2. Consistent with the other equations in this player position, the t-statistic of the salary variable in equation #2 (when more recent salary data was used) doubled that of the t-statistic in equation #1 (from 6.10 to 12.66). Also, continuing the pattern of the other outfield player position results, neither the RACE or YRS variables were statistically significant.

When ORS replaced THVOF as the performance variable to create equations #3 and #4 of Table 2.10, there was very little difference, with the exception that

Table 2.10

SAL91 Regressed on Variables for Outfield Incorporating the "Old Man" and "Superstar" Hypotheses

	OLD MAN HYPOTHESIS				SUPERSTAR	
VARIABLE	EQ #1	EQ #2	EQ #3	EQ #4	EQ #1	EQ #2
SAL89	.59****		.44****		.28	
	(6.10)		(5.23)		(1.54)	
SAL90		.81****		.73****		.85****
		(12.66)		(12.33)		(12.40)
RACE	-.10	.01	-.08	.00	.00	-.02
	(-1.37)	(.12)	(-1.35)	(.03)	(.02)	(-.52)
YRS	.14	.05	.18*	.06	.40*	.09
	(1.46)	(.91)	(2.34)	(1.16)	(2.21)	(1.36)
THVOF	.27****	.17***				
	(3.38)	(3.30)				
ORS			.43****	.24****	.31***	.07
			(6.25)	(4.97)	(3.09)	(1.51)
Adjusted R^2	.66	.85	.76	.88	.59	.89
N	65	74	70	86	44	58

* $p < .05$.   ** $p < .01$.   *** $p < .005$.   **** $p < .001$.

Beta weights are reported. N equals sample size. T-statistics are in parentheses. R^2 adjusted for number of independent variables and sample size.

ORS maintained statistical significance at .001 in both equations, a further indication of its superiority over THV as a measure of performance. The salary variable remained highly significant as well and continued to demonstrate the marked increase in *t*-statistic from the use of SAL90 instead of SAL89 that has been found in the other models. Although RACE remained statistically insignificant, YRS did exhibit a positive significant relationship in equation #3. The latter indicates that a player with greater years experience will receive a larger salary. This is the type of relationship that would be expected as the veterans are removed from the analysis and the relationship between salary and experience becomes linear. Moreover, if one examines the results of the application of the old man hypothesis (when ORS was the performance variable) for each of the positions analyzed thus far, it will be discovered that although the YRS variable only becomes significant in one of the ten equations, in nine of the ten equations the direction of the relationship is positive. Another item of note pertaining to the YRS variable is that the old man hypothesis has more influence in changing the sign of the relationship when ORS is the performance variable. This appears to be the case because, although the same veterans are excluded regardless of which performance variable is used, the use of ORS enables a larger pool of players to be analyzed. These additional players are all in their first and second year and as argued previously fit in well with the models because their salaries are limited and correlate positively with their experience. Therefore, these players can give a small boost to the statistical significance of the YRS variable, which is absent when THV is used as the performance variable.

When compared with the results of other equations in this player position, the variables in the superstar hypothesis did not achieve the same degree of statistical significance.[44] As Table 2.10 illustrates, the salary variable was significant only when SAL90 was used. In contrast, the performance variable (ORS) achieved significance only when SAL89 was used. These results, however, continue to be consistent with those found in the other equations with regard to the relative significance of salary and performance variables in each of the equations. As has been the case with prior results, the performance variable is generally the most significant variable when SAL89 is used and the salary variable is the most significant when SAL90 is utilized. Moreover, the level of explained variance continued to be high as equation #1 of Table 2.10 explained 59% and equation #2 explained 89%. Finally, RACE was once again insignificant in both equations although YRS became statistically significant and positive in equation #1. This result is easily explained since with the outfield position, the superstar hypothesis acts like the old man hypothesis in terms of its effect on YRS. This occurs because of the twenty-one veterans at the outfield player position, fifteen also qualified as superstars, therefore creating the same linear relationship between salary and experience that previously existed.

The High Rent District of Professional Baseball

Besides fitting in almost perfectly with the trends discussed in the other position analyses, the outfield position is also interesting because in this position, unlike any other, the minority players constitute a numerical majority. In fact, the minority players are also better paid than their white counterparts, as is amply illustrated in Figure 2.19. Moreover, although minority outfielders are paid substantially higher salaries than the white outfielders, the outfield in general appears to outdistance any other position in terms of being the most lucrative. As is illustrated in Figure 2.20, between 1990 and 1991, there was a salary explosion among outfielders as the number of players receiving $2 million to $3 million jumped from eleven to nineteen, whereas players receiving more than $3 million increased from one in 1990 to thirteen in 1991. Additionally, a much greater percentage of outfielders have contracts in the $2 million and $3 million range than their counterparts in the infield. However, according to Figure 2.21, these players are not paid top dollar for nothing, as they produce at substantially higher rates than players at other positions. Thus, in conclusion it appears, at least in the case of outfielders, that there is indeed no racial bias against minorities with respect to 1991 salary determination.[45]

Figure 2.19
Mean Salary of Outfield by Race

Race	Mean SAL91 ($)	N
U.S. Black	1,280,419	62
Non-U.S. Black	905,417	12
U.S. Latino	652,500	2
Non-U.S. Latino	1,356,667	3
White	993,595	37

Figure 2.20
Multimillion Dollar Players by Position

Player Position	SAL91 > $3,000,000		SAL91 $2-3,000,000	
Outfield	11.2%	n=13	16.3%	n=19
Catcher	0.0	n=0	4.8%	n=3
First Base	6.5%	n=2	25.8%	n=8
Second Base	0.0%	n=0	13.3%	n=4
Third Base	2.9%	n=1	5.7%	n=2
Shortstop	0.0%	n=0	18.2%	n=6
Designated Hitter	0.0%	n=0	0.0%	n=0
Utility Players	2.6%	n=1	5.1%	n=2

Figure 2.21
Top Ten Outfielders by THV, ORS, and SAL91

Rank	THV Rating	ORS Rating	SAL91 ($)	
1	10.54 Lenny Dykstra	10.85 Henderson	3,800,000	Strawberry
2	10.40 Barry Bonds	10.65 Bonds	3,750,000	Mitchell
3	9.42 Ricky Henderson	9.43 Dykstra	3,667,000	Joe Carter
4	9.25 Ron Gant	9.43 Gant	3,600,000	Eric Davis
5	9.14 Brett Butler	9.25 Bonilla	3,562,000	McGee
6	8.86 Roberto Kelly	9.02 Butler	3,500,000	Tim Raines
7	8.79 Willie McGee	8.95 Strawberry	3,500,000	Canseco
8	8.57 Robin Yount	8.88 Griff., Jr.	3,300,000	A. Dawson
9	8.01 Billy Hatcher	8.55 Canseco	3,300,000	Winfield
10	7.77 Kirby Puckett	8.50 K. Mitchell	3,250,000	Henderson

NOTES

1. Application of this hypothesis entails removing all players with ten years or more major league experience.

2. The key example here was when Frank Robinson of the Cincinnati Reds won the National League Most Valuable Player award in 1961. In 1965, believing Robinson was too old at the age of 30 to maintain this performance level, the Reds traded Robinson to the Baltimore Orioles where he subsequently won the American League Most Valuable Player award and continued to produce superstar statistics until he was 38.

3. Murray Chass, renowned sports columnist of the *New York Times*, gathers this data yearly and reports it in pre- and post-season columns. Throughout the years, these figures have had a high degree of consistency in terms of the items that account for the total salary of a given player. The opening day salaries for 1991 can be found in the *New York Times* (April 10, 1991): p. B8.

4. Briefly, James (1988) uses a measure entitled runs created, which also uses the total number of bases a player acquires. However, he applies this number within the context of a different formula. Mann (1989), on the other hand, uses a more complex set of ratios and percentages, which are related to total bases generated, in order to form a measure of offensive production that he calls the superstat.

5. The justification for the statement that ten runs equal one win comes from *The Baseball Superstats 1989*, written by Steve Mann. Mann discovered that there was a direct relationship between the number of runs scored by one team as opposed to the runs given up by that team (i.e., the run margin) and the number of games won by a team. Using this relationship, Mann figured that on average, ten runs would add one win to the victory total of an average team (in major league baseball, an average team has an 81-81 won-loss record). For further explanation see Mann (1989).

6. McGee was traded to the Oakland A's late in the 1990 season and since Oakland is a member of the American League, those numbers are not taken into account when figuring his National League batting average.

7. In this context of slugging average, the traditional total base statistic is used and incorporates singles, doubles, triples, and homeruns. However, when total bases are mentioned with regard to this study, it also includes bases gained through bases on balls and stolen bases and subtracting caught stealing.

8. For more discussion of the problematic nature of defensive analysis see Mann (1989).

9. Range may be measured by determining the average number of net chances a player has per game. Net chances (NCH) is the equivalent of adding putouts and assists and subtracting errors. Thus, we have: $NCH = (PO + A) - E$.

10. The average NCH by position used in this analysis are as follows: first base (1B) - 1559, second base (2B) - 853, third base (3B) - 432, shortstop (SS) - 741, and outfield (OF) - 382.

11. For the purpose of defensive statistics, in this study, an alternative method of computing games played is employed. Currently, when a player appears in a game, whether it is for one inning or nine innings, he is given credit for one GP. Thus, in the case of a late inning defensive specialist, a player may be given credit for many more games played than the actual number of full length games (or the equivalent of full length games) in which he participated. A striking example of this is Doug Dascenzo (then of the Chicago Cubs) who, although listed as appearing in 113 games, actually played the

equivalent of only 64 nine-inning games.

To remedy this situation and achieve a more precise measurement, the cumulative totals of plate appearances (PA), which is simply AB and BB added, were used to determine that, on average, in a full nine-inning game, a player would have 4.1 plate appearances. However, since 4.1 is simply an average, there are a few cases in which a player can be listed as appearing in more games than there are in a season, as is the case with Cal Ripken. Not only did he play in all 161 games in which the Baltimore Orioles participated, but he also batted in the fourth position of the batting order. By virtue of the batting order, the players at the top of the lineup are going to average more plate appearances per game than those in the six, seven, eight, or nine spots. As a result, Ripken, in this study, is credited with playing the equivalent of 166 games.

12. The use of 30 as a constant is explained in conjunction with explanation of the constant for the pitching runs measure forthcoming in chapter 4.

13. Strikeouts are recorded as a PO for the catcher, which is why catchers are not evaluated here on defensive ability. A staff such as the New York Mets would make any catcher look like a Hall of Fame defensive player if one were simply looking at total NCH. In addition, catchers serve other defensive functions like calling the pitches and throwing out baserunners, things that serve to further complicate defensive evaluation. Also, utility players are not evaluated defensively, since by definition, they play more than one position, and it becomes exceedingly difficult to measure the exact amount of time a player spent at one position.

14. The previous comparison between Ripken and Guillen remains a valid indicator of range differences though as both players participate on grass. In addition, the pitching staff on Guillen's team (Chicago White Sox) struck out 914 players, whereas the Orioles staff struck out 776. Consequently, Guillen may have averaged even more chances if he had been playing behind Ripken's staff.

15. For more discussion on hindrances to more accurate defensive evaluation see Mann (1989).

16. Large markets are defined as metropolitan areas consisting of more than 4 million people. Nine of the twenty-two markets meet this qualification. In addition, four of those markets, New York, Los Angeles, Chicago, and San Francisco-Oakland, have two teams each, meaning that thirteen of the twenty-six teams can be found in large markets. Moreover, in a perfectly balanced league, one would expect 50% of the players at each salary level to play in large markets.

17. Since many of the first or second year players did not have a salary in 1989, they were excluded from analysis when the two-year salary lag (SAL89) was used. Thus, a smaller number of cases were included in the SAL89 analysis.

18. Each independent variable in the equations in chapters 2, 3, and 4, was regressed on the remaining variables in the equation to determine if multicollinearity posed severe problems. In all of the regression equations throughout this book, extreme cases of multicollinearity (i.e., t-statistic > 2.00 and $R^2 > .90$) were not detected.

19. It is necessary to point out that performance and salary will always be mentioned in conjunction with one another because of the high degree of interrelation between the salary variables. If the salary variables were to be examined in isolation, there would be little difference because of the high correlation between the two values.

20. The statistical source used for this study did not include defensive statistics for players who had played fewer than 100 games at a particular position, thus effectively eliminating many first- and second-year players from THV rankings.

21. Salary for first- and second-year players generally falls between $100,000 (the major league minimum for 1991) and $300,000. Owners have a much stronger position at this point. However, bargaining position becomes more equivalent when the player becomes eligible for salary arbitration in his third year, and the player has the advantage when he becomes a free agent after six years.

22. By applying the old man hypothesis, five first basemen were removed from the pool.

23. The significance of the YRS variable in equation #2 also disappeared with the elimination of veterans who had ten years or more experience. This is to be expected as the reason for the negative relationship was that the highest paid players were those with five to nine years experience. Therefore, when those with over ten years experience were excluded, the highest paid players also became the most experienced, which consequently resulted in the original negative significance of the YRS variable becoming statistically insignificant.

24. When the superstar hypothesis equation was run, it resulted in the exclusion of thirteen players from the equation with SAL89 and fourteen players from the equation with SAL90.

25. Unfortunately, application of the superstar hypothesis to the first base, second base, and designated hitter positions lead to a smaller case pool than one would like to have. However, the results of these equations are similar to the results of the superstar hypothesis when applied to positions with larger pools. One must keep in mind, however, that the results reported in Table 2.2 should be viewed with caution as the number of cases is considerably few.

26. The years 1984, 1985, and 1987 were used based on availability of composite defensive statistics by position for those years.

27. $N = 24$ in both equation #3 and equation #5 (which used SAL89), whereas there was an increase from twenty-five to twenty-eight when SAL90 was utilized in equations #4 and #6. The increase was the result of first- or second-year players being added to the pool. They were not analyzed in previous equations because they did not have THV ratings.

28. In 1990, a change was made and now 17% of second-year players are also eligible.

29. Testing of the old man hypothesis resulted in the removal of seven second basemen from the analysis.

30. Testing of the superstar hypothesis resulted in the removal of eleven second basemen from equation #1 of Table 2.4 and twelve second basemen from equation #2.

31. There is one exception in second base as there was a slight decrease in t-statistic from the SAL89 to SAL90 variable in the THV model.

32. Testing of the old man hypothesis resulted in the removal of four third basemen from the analysis.

33. Testing of the superstar hypothesis resulted in the removal of ten third basemen from equation #1 of Table 2.6 and eleven third basemen from equation #2.

34. Although Martinez' salary figure may not appear large, as Figure 2.9 indicates, his salary nearly tripled from 1990 to 1991.

35. The reader may be wondering how it is possible for third basemen to have a lower average ORS than THV when only three third basemen were able to enhance their ORS through THV. This unusual situation occurred because there are eleven third basemen who were not assigned a THV value because of lack of experience (hence no defensive

statistics) and since the rookies or second-year players tend to have lower ORS values, this served to decrease the ORS average below the THV average.

36. The large pool adds players who did not have a THVSS rating to the analysis. Within the shortstop player position, this resulted in the addition of two players in equation #5 and three players in equation #6.

37. Rafael Ramirez experienced a decline in his salary from 1989 to 1990 but received an increase in 1991 which pushed his salary above the 1989 level.

38. Although third basemen did have a lesser percentage of players whose salary had declined from SAL89 and remained below that level through SAL91.

39. Testing of the old man hypothesis led to the exclusion of seven veterans in each of the equations.

40. Testing of the superstar hypothesis led to the exclusion of seven players from each of the equations.

41. Although Tony Fernandez is listed as a member of the San Diego Padres, a National League team, he actually played for the Toronto Blue Jays in 1990. Following the season he was traded, along with Fred McGriff, to the Padres in exchange for Roberto Alomar and Joe Carter. Consequently, Fernandez' batting statistics are included in the American League averages.

42. In reality, shortstops in the National League probably have a lower batting average in comparison to the other position players than the numbers indicate. The overall league average is undervalued as a measure of the productiveness of the position players because it also includes the at bats of the pitchers, who are notoriously poor hitters (pitchers only bat in the National League; the American League utilized the designated hitter rule). Thus, if they were excluded, the National League average would rise significantly. However, the statistics utilized did not allow for the effect of the pitchers to be removed.

43. Testing of the old man hypothesis resulted in the exclusion of twenty outfielders from equations #1 and #3 and 21 outfielders from equations #2 and #4.

44. Testing of the superstar hypothesis resulted in the exclusion of forty-six players from equation #1 and forty-nine players from equation #2.

45. There have been cases made that the high percentage of blacks in the outfield is a result of positional segregation, designed to keep blacks out of leadership positions. This topic does not belong in this section, but will be discussed further in the conclusion.

Chapter 3

The Experience of Offensively Tracked Players

This chapter focuses on the statistical analysis for the three player positions considered in this study that are primarily tracked by their offensive statistics (i.e., catchers, designated hitters, and utility players). Since these player positions do not have defensive statistics, the THV variable and the small pool/large pool distinctions used when ORS replaces THV as the performance variable (as in the last chapter) are rendered useless. Therefore, only the model which uses ORS as the performance variable and includes all possible players at that position will be analyzed. Moreover, the old man and superstar hypotheses are included in the analysis.

Defensive statistics, although available in some instances, are not utilized for varying reasons. Catchers, the first of the player positions to be examined, have statistics available, but unlike the players at the other positions, are almost wholly dependent on the pitching staff for their statistics. One example can be found in the rules for recording putouts, one of the main components for the defensive evaluation. Catchers do not record most of their putouts as a result of balls that are hit to them. Rather, the majority of their putouts are due to strikeouts. As long as they hold onto the ball on the pitch that is the third strike, they are credited with a putout.

Thus, as is apparent, if a catcher plays on a team with several pitchers who have high strikeout totals, it will appear as if he has much better defensive statistics than other catchers, although it was largely a result of the pitching staff, and not his ability. Catchers are valuable in other areas as well, but those are also difficult to measure. One possible method of evaluation is a comparison of percentages of potential base stealers thrown out. This would be a good measure except for the fact that throwing out a runner is as much due to the ability of the pitcher as the catcher. Depending on how fast the pitcher delivers the ball to the catcher or how closely the pitcher holds the runner at first base, a catcher may have little or no chance of throwing out a would-be base stealer. Finally, a third way of evaluating catchers is by how well they "handle" the pitching staff (i.e., is their pitch selection good, can they calm down the pitchers, etc.). However, this is a fairly subjective measure[1] and cannot be readily factored into a study such as this.

The designated hitter and utility positions cannot be evaluated for other reasons. For the designated hitter, the answer is clear: they do not play defense, hence no defensive statistics. Designated hitters only play in the American League where there is a rule which states that managers may use a regular hitter in place of the pitcher in the batting order. In contrast, utility players are difficult to evaluate defensively because they play in more than one position. Although it may be possible to evaluate these players defensively, it could become exceedingly difficult as one attempts to determine how many games the player participated in at each of the four different positions. Going to this extreme may also be called into question given the results of previous player position analyses, which indicate that offense is a much more sound predictor of salary than a combination of the defensive statistics with the offensive statistics.

VARIABLE CONCEPTUALIZATION AND MEASUREMENT

Dependent Variable

The dependent variable utilized in the analyses in this chapter (SAL91) is conceptualized and measured in a manner similar to that in chapter 2. The focus of this chapter is on regressing SAL91 on various independent and control variables to determine the impact that racial bias and/or performance have on salary determination with respect to the positions of catcher, designated hitter, and utility players.

Independent Variables

The independent variables utilized in this chapter are conceptualized and empirically derived in a somewhat different fashion than in the last chapter. Given that this chapter is concerned with catchers, designated hitter's, and utility players (primarily "offensively tracked" positions), the performance measure for each position is the player's ORS score (refer back to chapter 2 for the derivation of the ORS measure). RACE is measured in dummy variable form whereby "1" = white and "0" = non-white players.

Control Variables

The control variables utilized in this chapter (YRS, SAL89, and SAL90) are conceptualized and empirically derived in a fashion similar to that exercised in chapter 2. Moreover, as per the discussion as to the utility of the MET variable, it was dropped from all of the analyses in this chapter.

RESEARCH FINDINGS

Player Position: Catcher

Regression results for this player position as reported in Table 3.1, differ from those of other player positions and consequently raise some questions. First, the rates of explanation (although still quite high) for this position are less than those found at every other position as only 54% of the variance in SAL91 was explained when the two-year salary lag (SAL89) was used in equation #1. Equation #2, using a one-year salary lag (SAL90), explained 66% of the variance. Second, in equation #1, two interesting things occurred with respect to the independent and control variables. Although the performance variable (ORS) was once again statistically significant ($t = 6.12$, $p < .001$) and had the most explanatory value, SAL89 did not register as statistically significant. Moreover, although the YRS variable did not become statistically significant, RACE was significant at .05. These anomalies will be addressed later in the analysis.

Equation #2 produced results that followed previous patterns more closely as both the one-year salary lag and the performance variable were statistically significant at .001, whereas neither RACE nor YRS were statistically significant. These results are consistent in that the t-score (5.02) of SAL90 increased to a level much higher than when the older salary data was used in equation #1 ($t = 1.79$). Furthermore, although the ORS variable was significant at .001 in both equations #1 and #2, its t-score declined when SAL90 was used. In equation #1, ORS had the highest (6.12) in the equation, but fell below (3.47) the t-score of SAL90 in equation #2.

The fact that ORS is statistically significant in equation #1 while SAL89 is not remains consistent with previous findings and should not be a cause for concern. Generally speaking, performance, when used in conjunction with the two-year salary lag, is a better predictor than SAL89. Thus, even though SAL89 did not reach a level of statistical significance in equation #1, it still fit previous patterns. The results are somewhat unusual, however, in that SAL89 does not register as statistically significant at even the .05 level, a level it reaches in every other equation except one.[2]

Perhaps the reason for this could be discovered by examining the salary data in Figure 3.1 to determine if an inordinate number of catchers received large pay increases between 1989 and 1991 when compared with other positions. A finding

Table 3.1
SAL91 Regressed on Variables for Catcher Incorporating the "Old Man"
and "Superstar" Hypotheses

	OVERALL		OLD MAN		SUPERSTAR	
VARIABLE	EQ #1	EQ #2	EQ #1	EQ #2	EQ #1	EQ #2
SAL89	.24		.20		.22	
	(1.79)		(1.01)		(1.65)	
SAL90		.67****		.67****		.70****
		(5.02)		(6.30)		(6.13)
RACE	-.23*	-.07	-.13	.03	-.29**	-.07
	(-2.29)	(-.17)	(-1.07)	(.34)	(-2.73)	(-.87)
YRS	.05	-.17	.28	.14	.01	-.17
	(.40)	(-1.38)	(1.42)	(1.32)	(.10)	(-1.66)
ORS	.62****	.35****	.62****	.36****	.61****	.35****
	(6.12)	(3.47)	(4.90)	(3.67)	(5.62)	(3.66)
Adjusted R^2	.54	.66	.51	.77	.55	.70
N	49	53	35	39	43	47

* $p < .05$.   ** $p < .01$.   *** $p < .005$.   **** $p < .001$.

Beta weights are reported. N equals sample size. T-statistics are in parentheses.
R^2 adjusted for number of independent variables and sample size.

along these lines would indicate that the two-year salary lag would have even
less impact as a predictor SAL91 than in other player position analyses.

As the data in Figure 3.1 illustrates, the percentage of catchers with two-year
salary increases of 100% or more falls almost exactly in the middle when
compared with the other player positions analyzed. Thus, this finding would
appear to discount the theory that SAL89 is not statistically significant because

Figure 3.1
Large Pay Increases by Position

Position	Salary Increases > 100%	Percentage
Catcher	26 of 49	53.1
First Base	14 of 22	63.6
Second Base	14 of 24	58.3
Third Base	12 of 24	50.0
Shortstop	15 of 27	55.6
Outfield	62 of 90	68.9
Designated Hitter	3 of 12	25.0
Utility	17 of 34	50.0

of a large amount of variance between the salary data in 1989 and 1991. However, when one examines the magnitude of salary increases among the most highly paid catchers, this player position does seem to set itself apart and provide at least some explanation for the lack of significance of SAL89. Indeed, as Figure 3.2 demonstrates, five of the top eight catchers (62.5%) received salary increases that raised their salaries in 1991 to a level from 3.75 to 8.5 times higher than salaries in 1989. In fact, 20% more of the highest paid players at this position were given substantial salary increases from 1989 to 1991 than the next closest position.[3]

Figure 3.2
Size of Salary Increases

Player	SAL89 ($)	SAL91 ($)	Multiplier
Darren Daulton	225,000	1,917,000	8.50
Benito Santiago	345,000	1,650,000	4.80
Mickey Tettleton	300,000	1,600,000	5.30
B.J. Surhoff	180,000	1,085,000	6.03
Terry Steinbach	280,000	1,050,000	3.75

The most intriguing results for the position analysis of catchers is the fact that RACE registered as significant in equation #1. However, unlike the statistical significance of RACE in the first base player position, in this case there is a negative sign on the RACE coefficient. Since white players are coded as "1" and minorities are coded as "0," a relationship with a negative sign indicates that although race is a factor, it is of benefit to the minorities. One potential cause of this result is that minority catchers are paid at higher rates than their white counterparts. On examination of the salary rankings, there appears to be some validity in the argument as two of the top five salaries and six out of the top thirty-six salaries belong to minorities. These players account for all but one of the minority catchers, meaning that there appears to be some degree of disproportion in salary distribution contributing to the higher salaries of minority catchers.

Perhaps an even more convincing argument comes from Figure 3.3, which is a compilation of the mean salaries broken down by race within the catcher player position. The data demonstrates that minority catchers are paid at significantly higher levels than white catchers. Indeed, the combined mean salary of all minority catchers is on average $308,000 higher than those of white catchers.

When one moves to equation #2, however, RACE loses its significance (although the direction of the relationship remains negative), whereas SAL90 becomes significant at the .001 level and ORS also remains significant at the .001 level. It is possible that RACE loses significance simply because as one moves to a more recent year, salary levels become better predictors and conse-

Figure 3.3
Mean Salaries of Catchers by Race

Race	Mean SAL91 ($)	N
U.S. Black	123,000	1
Non-U.S. Black	815,000	3
U.S. Latino	667,000	1
Non-U.S. Latino	1,291,000	2
All Minorities	831,000	7
White	523,000	55

quently replaces RACE as a factor. With regard to the catchers, salary increases from 1990 to 1991, as one might expect, were not nearly as volatile as the cumulative change from 1989 to 1991, meaning that the model could depend more on an external factor (i.e., salary data). This is illustrated by the marked increase in the amount of variance explained as well as the increase in the statistical significance of the salary variable. Moreover, within the SAL89 equation, RACE was significant at the .05 level, while SAL90 is much stronger, at the .001 level of significance. Therefore, perhaps it is possible that the influence of the one-year lag simply "masked" the impact of the RACE variable.

The "Old Man" and "Superstar" Hypotheses Exposed

Table 3.1 also presents the results for the explanatory models when incorporating the "old man hypothesis." A quick comparison within Table 3.1 yields support for the aforementioned argument that RACE gained statistical significance because of the higher pay of a disproportionate number of minority catchers.[4] In equation #1 of Table 3.1, which used the two-year salary lag, the performance variable (ORS) continued to be significant at .001, whereas RACE was no longer statistically significant. Moreover, the amount of variance explained decreased from equation #1 of the overall analysis of catchers in Table 3.1 (from 54% to 51%). The effect that the exclusion of the veterans had on equation #1 will be examined in more detail later in the analysis.

Although equation #1 exhibited a few differences from the original model (which included the veterans) in its results, equation #2 of the old man hypothesis was nearly identical to equation #2 of Table 3.1 with the exception that explained variance increased from 66% to 77%. In this equation, both the salary and performance variables were significant at the .001 level. Furthermore, consistent with the previous results, the t-score of the salary variable increased from equation #1 to #2 (t = 1.01 to t = 6.30). Also, the t-score of the performance variable declined from equation #1 to equation #2 (t = 4.90 to t = 3.67). Finally, the years experience variable was not found to be statistically significant in either equation.

The lack of statistical significance for the RACE variable in equation #1 can be explained by the players who were removed from the pool when testing the old man hypothesis. Only one of the fourteen veterans excluded belonged to a minority. As a result, the most plausible explanation regarding the lack of statistical significance in the RACE variable would appear to be that the white "old men" withheld from the model increased the mean salary. Indeed, many had salaries below the mean, but the net result of the exclusion of the white catchers was a reduction in the mean salary, the opposite of what was expected. Because of this result, it appears that the exclusion of the lone minority player caused the change in results. Although it doesn't seem as if one player could cause much difference in mean salary, in this case the player excluded was Tony Pena, the second highest paid catcher overall. So although the exclusion of the white veteran catchers lowered the mean salary, Pena's salary exclusion resulted in a much greater mean salary decline for the minority catchers, as Figure 3.4 indicates. Thus, by making the mean salary differences much smaller, the salary advantage held by the minority catchers diminished to the extent that it was no longer statistically significant.

Figure 3.4
Difference in Mean Salaries

Race	Mean SAL91 ($)	N	Mean SAL91 ($)	N
	(Excludes Veterans)		(All Catchers)	
Minority	586,166	6	831,000	7
White	442,953	42	523,346	55
Salary Difference	143,213		307,654	

When the superstar hypothesis was tested, the results indicated the opposite of what had originally been hypothesized. It was originally hypothesized that if any evidence of racism against minorities was to be discovered, it would occur in the tiers of players below the superstars. However, once the superstars were removed from the analysis, not only did RACE become statistically significant and negative once again in equation #1 of the superstar hypothesis in Table 3.1, but the statistical significance increased to a higher level (from .05 to .01) than in the original model in Table 3.1.[5] ORS was the only other variable statistically significant in equation #1 ($t = 5.62$, $p < .001$), whereas the amount of variance explained (55%) remained similar to the other equations within this player position when the two-year salary lag was incorporated.

Similar to past results, the use of the one-year salary lag in equation #2 produced statistical significance at the .001 level for both the SAL90 ($t = 6.13$) and the ORS ($t = 3.66$) variables. Also consistent with previous results, the amount of variance in SAL91 explained by equation #2 was higher at 70% than the amount of variance explained by equation #1.

In an effort to explain why RACE once again became statistically significant and the reasons for this significance, one must examine the players excluded from the analysis when the superstar hypothesis was tested. Closer examination reveals that all six of the catchers excluded were white. Furthermore, according to Figure 3.5, four of these players (Tettleton, Fisk, Daulton, and Parrish) also had salaries that ranked in the top seven. Thus, by withdrawing the highest paid white catchers and leaving all of the minority players in the study, the mean salary advantage enjoyed by the minority catchers increased further, causing the statistical significance of RACE to rise to a higher level.

Figure 3.5
Top Ten Catchers by THV, ORS, and SAL91

Rank	ORS Rating		SAL91 ($)	
1	6.83	Mickey Tettleton	2,417,000	Parrish
2	6.75	Carlton Fisk	2,300,000	Pena
3	6.73	Darren Daulton	2,183,000	Scioscia
4	6.55	Todd Zeile	1,917,000	Daulton
5	6.50	Craig Biggio	1,650,000	B. Santiago
6	6.45	Lance Parrish	1,600,000	Tettleton
7	5.85	Mike Scioscia	1,250,000	Fisk
8	5.75	B.J. Surhoff	1,085,000	B.J. Surhoff
9	5.68	Brian Harper	1,050,000	T. Steinbach
10	5.40	Tony Pena	950,000	Mike Heath

This result raises some questions, however. Since most of the top performers are white (nine of ten), why are the minorities being paid more money on average (refer back to Figure 3.4). Perhaps the answer can be found in Figure 3.6, which indicates that even though the top catchers are white, on average the minority catchers produce at higher rates than the white catchers. Since whites represent such a large majority of catchers, most of the poorest performing catchers are also white, causing a decline in average performance. Thus, in the end, the high productivity of the top white catchers is more than adequately offset by the low productivity of the other white catchers, providing minority catchers with a slight edge in productivity.

Figure 3.6
Mean Production

Race	Mean Production (ORS)	N
Minority	3.22	7
White	2.91	55

Player Position: Designated Hitter

Before presenting the results of the designated hitter (DH) player position analysis, a word of caution is necessary. Since the DH rule is only in effect in the American League, the number of players in the analysis is necessarily halved, which results in a very low number of subjects. The consequences of such low numbers are that the results may not be as accurate as hoped for and, as will be pointed out later, allows for outliers to play a significant role since there are not a large number of subjects to "hide" them.[6]

The only variable found to be statistically significant in equation #1 of Table 3.2 is the performance variable (ORS), which is consistent with the findings of previous analyses in that when SAL89 is used instead of SAL90, performance has a greater explanatory value. Equation #2, however, produced some interesting results as none of the variables in the equation were statistically significant, including the one-year salary lag, which had been statistically significant in each of the other player position analyses. Even though no variables were found to be statistically significant, the results of equation #2 are not completely inconsistent with previous findings. In fact, although the salary and performance variables were not statistically significant, each of them almost reached a level of significance, and, as with the other player position analysis, the t-score of the SAL90 variable ($t = 2.10$) was higher than that of the performance variable ($t = 1.91$).[7]

Also consistent with previous analyses was the discovery that the t-score of the salary variable increased from equation #1 to #2, whereas the t-score of the performance variable (ORS) nosedived from $t = 4.22$ to $t = 1.91$. Another noteworthy item is that the designated hitter player position analysis is the only one where the variance was explained at a higher level when the two-year salary lag was used instead of the one-year salary lag. Explained variance in equation #1 was 81% compared to 74% in equation #2. Finally, the YRS and RACE variables were not statistically significant in either of the two equations.

The reasons for these unusual results are unclear and are most likely the result of the small number of players analyzed. Indeed, on examination of the raw data it appears as if the designated hitter player position has a better correlation between salary and performance than any of the other positions. Figure 3.1 in the previous player position analysis isolates by position how many players experienced salary increases of 100% or more between the years 1989 and 1991 and DH was the position with the lowest percentage as only three of twelve players (25%) experienced such an increase. From this data, one can conclude that salaries for designated hitters have not been increasing at the dizzying pace found in other player positions. As a consequence, it would seem as if the salary data should be statistically significant in the equations. However, this is a case where the small number of players in the pool is apparently a factor. In 1989, for instance, Dave Parker received the fifth highest salary of the twelve designated hitters in this study, while in 1990 he produced the highest ORS rating.

Table 3.2
SAL91 Regressed on Variables for Designated Hitter Incorporating the "Old Man" and "Superstar" Hypotheses

	OVERALL		OLD MAN		SUPERSTAR	
VARIABLE	EQ #1	EQ #2	EQ #1	EQ #2	EQ #1	EQ #2
SAL89	.13		.59		.84*	
	(.56)		(.81)		(6.04)	
SAL90		.63		.43		.76*
		(2.10)		(2.14)		(3.15)
RACE	-.43	-.10	.23	.16	-.04	.02
	(-2.30)	(-.66)	(.26)	(1.33)	(-.37)	(.11)
YRS	-.07	-.08	.25	.40*	-.18	.09
	(-.44)	(-.38)	(.35)	(2.59)	(-1.89)	(.46)
ORS	.70***	.37	.63	.45*	.34	.29
	(4.22)	(1.91)	(1.09)	(2.87)	(3.41)	(1.85)
Adjusted R^2	.81	.74	.68	.90	.98	.84
N	12	16	6	10	7	11

* $p < .05$.   ** $p < .01$.   *** $p < .005$.   **** $p < .001$.

Beta weights are reported. N equals sample size. T-statistics are in parentheses. R^2 adjusted for number of independent variables and sample size.

Although this discrepancy between salary and performance does not appear to be substantial, the difference is magnified by the small number of players in the analysis. For example, if this situation occurred in the outfield player position, Parker would be ranked forty-eighth (of 116) in salary. Thus, not only is the discrepancy large, but it is also magnified by the lack of players in the analysis. If this discrepancy would have occurred in a player position with a larger number of players, its effect would, generally speaking, be hidden. The cumulative effect of this situation is that performance became a much more important predictor of variance than SAL89 (Parker's salary had adjusted to his performance by 1991 when he was the highest paid designated hitter).

Scenarios similar to the one involving Parker above are also most likely responsible for the lack of statistical significance of the other variables as well. This is illustrated by Figure 3.7 which indicates that pay in 1991 generally mirrored performance. In fact, seven of the eight highest paid players were also the seven top run producers. However, as pointed out previously, these numbers are misleading as the phrase "eight highest paid players" represents one half of the designated hitters analyzed. Therefore, even an apparently slight difference between salary and performance as is the case with Chili Davis (third in salary

Figure 3.7
Top Ten Designated Hitters by ORS, and SAL91

Rank	ORS Rating	SAL91 ($)	
1	7.83 Dave Parker	1,825,000	Parker
2	7.38 Alvin Davis	1,725,000	Alvin Davis
3	6.65 Chris James	1,700,000	Chili Davis
4	6.18 Harold Baines	1,367,000	James
5	6.00 Dwight Evans	1,333,000	Baines
6	5.60 Chili Davis	1,167,000	Perry
7	5.50 Gerald Perry	1,100,000	Mel Hall
8	5.23 John Olerud	860,000	Evans
9	5.03 Gene Larkin	800,000	Pasqua
10	4.95 Dan Pasqua	725,000	Larkin

and sixth in performance) can reduce the high correlation presumed when stating that seven of the eight highest paid players were also the top run producers.

The "Old Man" and "Superstar" Hypotheses Exposed

The results from the testing of the old man hypothesis that are also presented in Table 3.2 reveal that this model produced the only insignificant equation throughout the analysis of the non-pitchers.[8] Equation #1 was most likely statistically insignificant because only six players were involved in the analysis. When equation #2 was run the results were statistically significant as a whole and explained 90% of the variance in SAL91. In addition, both the YRS and ORS variables became statistically significant at .05 although SAL90 did not become statistically significant (SAL90 almost reached a level of statistical significance as $t = 2.14$). RACE was not statistically significant either.

The factor responsible for the difference in the two equations was the addition of four rookies to equation #2. Generally, the rookies produced at lower rates[9] and were the four lowest paid DHs. As a result, the rookies served to provide stability to the salary structure as the players who were the lowest paid were also the least experienced and the least productive. This undoubtedly led to the positive statistical significance of the YRS and ORS variables.

The results from the testing of the superstar hypothesis (also reported in Table 3.2) returned a degree of normalcy to the equations as the salary variables became statistically significant for the first time within the DH position.[10] In equation #1 SAL89 was the only variable to achieve statistical significance ($t = 6.04$, $p < .05$), and 98% of the variance in SAL91 was explained. The results of this equation were unusual in the sense that, although ORS was not statistically significant, it had a relatively high t-score ($t = 3.41$). This is unusual because as a rule, when the t-score reaches 2.00, a statistical significance at .05 is generally achieved. When SAL90 replaced SAL89 as the salary variable in equation #2, the results were similar. Once again, the salary variable was significant at .05, although the t-score decreased to 3.15, a departure from previous trends. The other three variables (RACE, YRS, and ORS) were not statistically significant. In addition, equation #2 explained 84% of the variance.

Perhaps the salary variables have become statistically significant in this model because the superstars excluded have thrown off the explanatory value of the salary variables in the previous equations. However, on further examination, this does not appear plausible as the salaries of the other designated hitters have varied at similar rates. For example, the problem could have been with Chris James who saw his salary increase 3.42 times from $400,000 in 1989 to $1,367,000 in 1991. But this doesn't make sense since Dan Pasqua and Gene Larkin experienced similar increases (of 3.33 and 5.00 times, respectively) and were included in the superstar model (refer to Figure 3.7). Perhaps these results once again point to the low number of players that are included in the analysis as the source of the problems. Finally, to once again document the problems with the DH analysis, in equation #1, a 98% explanation rate was achieved where $n = 7$. In contrast, equation #2 saw a decrease in the amount of variance explained (adjusted $R^2 = 84\%$). This occurred despite the fact that the four rookies added to the analysis in equation #2 were the same ones who were added to equation #2 of the old man model. Even though the results of the old man model suggest that the rookies promoted stability, they were added to the superstar model with apparently very little effect. Thus, in conclusion, it appears as if the results of the DH analysis, unlike those of the other positions, are mixed and ambiguous at best.

Player Position: Utility

Utility players are the last non-pitcher player position to be analyzed. As is readily apparent in Table 3.3, equation #1 explained 80% of the variance in SAL91. Moreover, both SAL89 and the performance variable (ORS) reached statistical significance at .001. Results from equation #2 are similar as both the salary and performance variables are significant at .001. Also, like the findings of most of the previous analyses, the amount of variance explained rose (87%) when the more recent salary data was used. The trends regarding the salary and performance variable proved to be accurate as well. The t-score of the salary variable increased from $t = 5.31$ when SAL89 was used to $t = 8.00$ when SAL90 was utilized in equation #2, reaffirming the conclusion that the recent salary data is a better predictor of SAL91 variance. ORS also followed the established patterns as its t-score declined from equation #1 to #2 ($t = 4.52$ to $t = 4.11$). Finally, as has been the case in most of the player position analyses, neither the RACE nor the YRS variables were statistically significant in either equation.

Table 3.3
SAL91 Regressed on Variables for Utility Incorporating the "Old Man" and "Superstar" Hypotheses

VARIABLE	OVERALL		OLD MAN		SUPERSTAR	
	EQ #1	EQ #2	EQ #1	EQ #2	EQ #1	EQ #2
SAL89	.72****		.43***		.98***	
	(5.31)		(3.62)		(6.92)	
SAL90		.73****		.45****		.78****
		(8.00)		(4.22)		(7.35)
RACE	-.11	-.06	-.11	-.08	-.29*	-.03
	(-1.23)	(-.99)	(-1.30)	(-1.16)	(-2.46)	(-.34)
YRS	-.11	.04	.13	.19	-.17	.19
	(-.92)	(.48)	(1.17)	(2.01)	(-1.19)	(1.77)
ORS	.53****	.31****	.64****	.55****	.08	.15
	(4.42)	(4.11)	(7.18)	(6.30)	(.71)	(1.51)
Adjusted R^2	.80	.87	.85	.87	.75	.76
N	34	36	26	28	26	28

* $p < .05$.   ** $p < .01$.   *** $p < .005$.   **** $p < .001$.

Beta weights are reported. N equals sample size. T-statistics are in parentheses. R^2 adjusted for number of independent variables and sample size.

In searching for explanations for the results, it is important to note that the utility player position is not so much a position as a category. Utility is a catch-all section, drawing from several positions. Although utility players are generally thought of as role players, who simply serve as substitutes whenever there is an injury or when someone needs a day off, there are a few players who qualified as utility players in this study because they spent time at more than one player position although they had full-time status. Players in this category are really everyday players, but for one reason or another, ended up at two positions. For example, a player may have started the season at one player position, but during the course of the season, was forced to substitute extensively at another player position as the result of injuries. Another example is the situation of Howard Johnson, where there was simply indecision about whether to play him at third base or shortstop; he ended up spending quite a bit of time at each position. At any rate, the inclusion of two distinct groups in this analysis has most likely been the predominant cause of the high statistical significance of the results with respect to the salary and performance variables.

As Figure 3.8 indicates, there is a definite dividing line between the two groups. On average, the "everyday players" had 340 more at bats during the season than did the utility players. In fact, all of the players with 400 or more at bats composed the top ten performers as measured by ORS. Furthermore, as Figure 3.9 illustrates, eight of the top ten performers were also the most highly paid.[11] The difference in the performance of these eight from the rest of the group is also significant. Of the top eight, Paul Molitor of the Brewers had the lowest ORS rating at 6.15. From this point there is a gap until the number nine and ten performers who had ORS ratings of 4.88 and 4.50. The utility players are even less productive, with ORS ratings beginning at 3.70 and declining. Therefore, simply by looking at these statistics, one can see that the performance variable (ORS) appears to have had a substantial influence on 1991 salaries.

Figure 3.8
Everyday versus Utility Players

Player Category	Avg. At Bats	Player Category Avg.	SAL91 ($)	N
Everyday Players	501.1	Top Eight	1,719,875	8
Utility	161.6	Others	435,903	31

Figure 3.9
Top Ten Utility Players by ORS, and SAL91

Rank	ORS Rating		SAL91 ($)	
1	8.77	Howard Johnson	3,233,000	Molitor
2	8.58	George Brett	2,167,000	Johnson
3	8.25	Bip Roberts	2,075,000	Brett
4	7.75	Tony Phillips	1,867,000	Stubbs
5	7.70	Jody Reed	1,567,000	Phillips
6	6.85	Franklin Stubbs	1,300,000	Mike Marshall
7	6.63	John Kruk	1,175,000	Kruk
8	6.15	Paul Molitor	925,000	Carmelo Martinez
9	4.88	Lenny Harris	875,000	Roberts
10	4.50	Luis Salazar	800,000	Reed

The "Old Man" and "Superstar" Hypotheses Exposed

Comparison within Table 3.3 illustrates that there were few differences in results when the old man model was tested.[12] Although the RACE and YRS variables did not achieve levels of statistical significance in either equation, the salary and performance variables (SAL89 and ORS) were once again significant in equation #1 of the old man hypothesis in Table 3.3. However, although the level of statistical significance for ORS remained at .001, the statistical significance of SAL89 fell to .005. This change is probably due to the fact that the veterans excluded from this analysis had remarkably stable salaries when compared with the others. Moreover, the t-score of the performance variable in equation #1 was higher than that of the two-year salary lag ($t = 7.18$ for ORS and $t = 3.62$ for SAL89), suggesting that the performance data is a better predictor of variance than the older salary data. Equation #2 of Table 3.3 exhibited similar characteristics although when the one-year salary lag was used, both the salary and performance variables achieved significance at .001.

Furthermore, the patterns from the previous analyses with regard to the relative explanatory value of the salary and performance variables continue to hold true. When SAL90 was used instead of SAL89 the t-score for the salary variable increased from 3.62 to 4.22. In contrast, the t-score of ORS in equation #2 ($t = 6.30$) represented a decrease from the t-score of 7.18 in equation #1. However, these results are interesting in that the t-score of the performance variable remained higher than the salary variable even when the one-year salary lag was in place. It was stated previously that the salaries of the veterans were fairly stable. Apparently, once these salaries were removed from the analysis, most of the players remaining had experienced large salary increases, resulting in a greater dependence on the ORS variable for explanation of variance. Another item to note is that the amount of variance explained in equation #2 represented a slight increase from equation #1 (an increase from 85% to 87%).

The "fading superstar" aspect of the old man hypothesis is not a real factor within this position either. Two players who may have qualified by virtue of their salaries, Paul Molitor and George Brett, with the number one and three rankings on the salary scale, respectively, also remain top-notch performers. Brett actually outperformed his salary ranking as his ORS placed him as the second best utility player. Molitor, on the other hand, dropped to eighth place, although this is not a large enough fall to be significant (refer to Figure 3.9). The other veterans did not fit into this category either. None of them qualified as superstars and all of them, with the exception of Mike Marshall, had a salary of less than $1 million. Additionally, their salaries were on the decline or holding steady (including Marshall). Thus, in this respect they do fit the other part of the old man hypothesis, which holds that as performance begins to deteriorate, salary levels off and then declines. However, the effect must not have been as significant as in other instances since YRS was not significant either negatively in the first model or positively in this model.

Finally, when one looks at Figure 3.10 and sees the groups (utility or everyday) from which the veterans were drawn, it appears plausible that very little change would take place as they were excluded proportionately.

Figure 3.10
Distribution of Veterans

Category	N	Total Utility Players	Percentage
Veterans	8	39	20.5
Top Ten Veterans (ORS)	2	10	20.0
Other Veterans	6	29	20.7

When the superstar hypothesis was tested, results different than the other two models were discovered, as Table 3.3 further indicates.[13] First, in equation #1, SAL89 retained its statistical significance (t = 6.92, p <.001), whereas the performance variable was no longer statistically significant. Second, although YRS was not significant, RACE was negative and statistically significant, signaling, as was the case with the catcher player position, that racial considerations were working to the benefit of minorities. In equation #2, SAL90 was once again statistically significant (t = 7.35, p <.001), whereas RACE lost its statistical significance. The YRS and performance variables were also found to be statistically insignificant. The decline of performance as a statistically significant variable within the superstar model is perhaps the result of the fact that while the top eight performers (and eight of the top ten salaries) were excluded, two players who ranked in the top ten in salaries remained (Carmelo Martinez and Mike Marshall), both of whom produced at fairly low levels. Thus, salary became a much more useful predictor of SAL91. In addition, apparently because of the decline in ORS, explained variance also decreased to .75 and .76 in equations #1 and #2 of Table 3.3, respectively.

The negative relationship and statistical significance of RACE is harder to explain. Figure 3.11 compares the mean salaries of the players before and after the superstars were removed, and although the numbers demonstrate that the salary gap between the white and the minority players narrowed by nearly $100,000 when the superstars were excluded, the minorities still lag behind the white players (although $428,500 and $440,579 are very comparable salaries).

Figure 3.11
Mean Salary of Utility Players by Race

Race	Mean SAL91 ($)	N	Mean SAL91 ($) Without Superstars	N	Mean SAL89 ($)	N
Minority	630,067	15	428,500	12	257,889	9
White	742,542	24	440,579	19	357,058	17

Figure 3.12
Mean Performance by Race

Race	Mean Performance (ORS)	N
Minority	2.25	12
White	1.87	19

Since the salary comparisons do not really shed any light on the results, Figure 3.12 was compiled in an effort to determine whether whites outperformed minority players.[14] A result such as this would indicate that perhaps minority players were being overpaid, thus resulting in the negative sign on RACE. However, this was not the case as the minority players held a significant edge in performance.

The question of why RACE became significant in equation #1 still remained, and in an effort to answer it, salaries for 1989 were examined in hopes of finding that since 1989, minority players had closed the salary gap. The results from this inquiry were positive (see Figure 3.11). It appears that since 1989, minority players who did not qualify as superstars have narrowed the salary gap from $100,000 on average to $12,000. In conclusion, perhaps the negative sign on the RACE variable can be explained by the dramatic narrowing of the salary gap as demonstrated in Figure 3.11.

NOTES

1. One way of evaluating a catcher's "handling" ability that is fairly objective is to compare the ERAs of the pitching staff when one catcher or the other is playing. However, this method is only effective for catchers on the same team, so it is limited in scope.

2. SAL89 is also insignificant for the designated hitter position.

3. The comparisons with other positions were derived by taking the fact that eight catchers out of the total of sixty-two, represented roughly 13% of all catchers and applying it to each position. Thus, the top 13% of each position were isolated and analyzed to determine how many had salary increases that resulted in 1991 salaries 3.75 times or greater than their 1989 salary. The next closest position were the utility players, of whom 40% (two of five) received large increases.

4. Testing of the old man hypothesis resulted in the exclusion of fourteen veterans from the analysis.

5. Testing of the superstar hypothesis resulted in the exclusion of six catchers from the analysis.

6. The decision to run the analysis with such a low number of subjects rather than incorporate a dummy variable that would place the designated hitters against the entire pool of "other players" was made on the basis of wanting to maintain a certain level of comparability across player positions. The trade-off, however, is that the results for the designated hitter position analysis are specious given the low number of cases.

7. SAL90 was at the .059 level and ORS at the .08 level.

8. Testing of the old man hypothesis led to the exclusion of six veterans from the designated hitter analysis. The reason that such a high proportion of the designated hitters have more than ten years experience can be found in the duties of the position. Many players, as they get older, lose some of their footspeed and agility, consequently causing their defensive skills to deteriorate. However, if they are still good hitters, many players become designated hitters as a way of prolonging their careers.

9. This is true with the exception of John Olerud and Carmen Castillo. In a more perfect situation, these two would have switched salaries as Olerud's ORS (5.23) was superior to Castillo's (.90).

10. Testing of the superstar hypothesis resulted in the exclusion of five players from the analysis.

11. The other two players, who ranked nine and ten in performance were Luis Salazar and Lenny Harris. Salazar is generally considered a veteran journeyman, but spent most of 1990 at third base for the Cubs because of a lack of other candidates. Harris just completed his third year and therefore is only a year or two away from joining the others in the millionaire category.

12. Testing of the old man hypothesis led to the exclusion of eight veterans from both equations #1 and #2.

13. Testing of the superstar hypothesis led to the exclusion of eight utility players from the analysis.

14. Figure 3.12 does not include the superstars.

Chapter 4

The Experience of Pitchers

This chapter focuses on the statistical analysis of all players who are classified as pitchers. Because of the different functions assigned to pitchers, this player position is broken down into three separate pitching positions (i.e., starters, relievers, and closers) and analyzed. Pitchers are categorized as starters if they had started more than half of the games in which they appeared. On the other hand, a pitcher qualified as a closer if he saved more than fifteen games. Pitchers who did not fall into either category are classified as relievers.[1] Conceptually, this classification scheme makes sense since there are three distinct functions for pitchers and their statistics should parallel these functions. The assumption is that remuneration will be based in like manner (i.e., pay based on function and importance of the various type of pitcher). The models used to attempt to explain the variance in 1991 salaries are the same as used in chapters 2 and 3 when non-pitching positions were analyzed. Moreover, the old man and superstar hypotheses are included in the analysis.

VARIABLE CONCEPTUALIZATION AND MEASUREMENT

Dependent Variable

The dependent variable utilized in the analyses in this chapter (SAL91) is conceptualized and measured in a manner similar to that in chapter 2. The focus of this chapter is on regressing SAL91 on various independent and control variables to determine the impact that racial bias and/or performance have on salary determination with respect to the pitching positions of starter, reliever, and closer in both the American and National Leagues.

Independent Variables

The independent variables utilized in this chapter are conceptualized and empirically derived in a bit different fashion than in either chapter 2 or 3. RACE continues to be measured in dummy variable form whereby "1" = white and "0" = non-white (i.e., minority) players. Because this chapter is concerned with the position of pitcher, however, the conceptualization and empirical measures of performance are a bit different than the performance measures utilized in other chapters.

A variety of performance indicators are also used to evaluate the pitchers. It should be noted, however, that none of the previous analyses combined indicators in order to gain better insight into the significance of pitching performance on salary determination. In all fairness, several studies do use more than one pitching performance indicator in their studies, but do not incorporate an aggregate measure. For example, Pascal and Rapping (1972) utilize a variety of measures including games won, innings pitched, and differences between the career average victory total and the most recent seasons victory total. Scully (1974b) and Sommers (1990) on the other hand, use a measure entitled the "strikeout to walk ratio." This measure is of little value, however, since conceptually strikeouts and walks have little or nothing to do with one another. There are many other ways in which a pitcher can get an out (the pitcher's goal) besides a strikeout. Moreover, a strikeout has little value over any other type of out.[2]

As a quick example of this, Jim Palmer and Bob Feller are both Hall of Fame pitchers. Palmer, however, was not known for strikeouts and Feller was, which suggests that the number of strikeouts is not necessarily a prerequisite of success. In contrast, Nolan Ryan holds the record for most career strikeouts and, although he is undoubtedly a future Hall of Famer, his record is only a few games above .500, in part because he has also walked the most batters in a career. Consequently, a measure better than this would simply be the number of walks given up by a pitcher.

The earned run average (ERA) is another measure used in a couple of the studies. Both Hill and Spellman (1984) and Sommers (1990) use career ERA as their performance variable for pitchers. Finally, once again Mogull (1975) uses almost every individual pitching statistic possible in his simple regression analysis.

Other variables that do not fall neatly into the categories described can also be found within some of the studies, mostly in the form of dummy variables. A few of these variables attempted to test the hypothesis that the better a team as a whole performed, the higher a salary the individual player would receive. Medoff (1975) tested this when he included a CHAMP variable, thus separating out the players who had played on the championship team. Christiano (1988) used a similar variable and gave players credit when their teams qualified for the playoffs. Christiano (1986, 1988) also used a dummy variable to identify left-handed batters, reasoning that this versatility may make them more attractive as a player. Sommers (1990) incorporated a measure taken from James (1989) that recognizes a player for receiving votes in the Most Valuable Player and Cy Young award contests, the annual awards that are given to the best non-pitcher and pitcher, respectively. Defensive performance is also measured via a dummy variable within the analysis by Johnson (1992) when he identifies those players who have received a Gold Glove, the award given to the best defensive player at each position.

In this analysis of the salary determinants of pitchers, two methods of evaluating pitcher production are employed. The first utilizes one of the standard means of measuring pitcher performance, the ERA. Although perhaps the most accurate of the standard measures, use of this measure in and of itself precludes a comparison across leagues because of differences between the league earned run averages. Therefore, a second measure, with total bases as its foundation, is utilized. In brief, this measure is computed by calculating the number of total bases a pitcher surrenders. Following this, the total base figure is converted into runs and, ultimately, the value of the pitcher in terms of games. This is essentially the same method used to compute ORS. The utilization of this method creates a situation whereby, regardless of league pitching statistics are comparable, allowing for cross league comparison.

The first method alluded to above is separated by league and is denoted as pitching runs American League (PRAL) and pitching runs National League (PRNL). These measures are based on ERA and since significant differences exist between average ERAs of the leagues (3.79 in the NL and 3.91 in the AL), the most accurate method of evaluation with regard to the measurement of this performance indicator is through comparison of pitchers in the same league only.

PRAL and PRNL are calculated by figuring how many earned runs (ER) were given up by an individual and then subtracting this number from the average number of runs given up by an average pitcher who pitched the same amount of innings in that particular league. In this manner, one can determine how many runs a pitcher gave up above or below the league average. This number is then divided by 15 to derive the number of games a pitcher contributed above or below the league average.[3] Thus, we have the following formula for the computation of PRAL and PRNL:

PRAL = $(((IP/9) * (ALERA)) - ((IP/9) * (ERA)))/15$
     where IP = Innings pitched
           $ALERA$ = 3.91
           ERA = Earned run average

PRNL = $(((IP/9) * (NLERA)) - ((IP/9) * (ERA)))/15$
     where IP = Innings pitched
           $NLERA$ = 3.79
           ERA = Earned run average

For example, Dave Stewart (Oakland A's) had a PRAL of 2.67 for the 1990 season, meaning that if he were to join an average team, his skills would directly contribute 2.67 wins to the team. In major league baseball, an average team (.500 winning percentage) would finish with eighty-one wins and eighty-one losses, so with Stewart on the team, the win total would increase to either eighty-three or eighty-four.

Although ERA can be an effective basis for the evaluation of pitchers, it does have some flaws. First, ERA is expressed as the number of earned runs a pitcher gives up per nine innings pitched (i.e., a complete game). However, only ER are included in this figure. Unearned runs are not included. Roughly speaking, runs in this category are runs that are scored as a result of a defensive miscue (i.e., an error).[4] On closer examination, however, this is not a large concern as unearned runs only make up approximately 10% of total runs, leaving the bulk of the runs scored to be included in the ERA.[5] Another problem also exists that demonstrates the necessity of placing the pitchers into three categories. For example, if Roger Clemens (Boston Red Sox) were pitching, let us suppose that the bases are loaded, and the manager comes to the mound and replaces Clemens with middle reliever Tony Fossas. Fossas faces the first batter and gives up a grand slam home run, allowing all four runs to score. For ERA purposes, Clemens, although he has been pulled from the game, remains responsible for the runs scored as the result of the home run. Thus, in the statistics, Clemens is credited with surrendering three runs, whereas according to the records Fossas only gave up one run. It is this type of situation which serves to inflate the ERAs of starters while deflating ERAs of relievers and closers, making it more sensible to compare starters to starters and not, for example starters to relievers. Consequently, comparison occurs not between categories (i.e., starters to relievers), but purely within any one of the three defined categories for pitcher position.[6]

The other measure utilized in this study is called the total pitchers value (TPV) and allows for comparison across leagues. This measure uses ratio (RAT) as its basic statistical unit. RAT is a concrete measure of the number of hits and bases on balls a pitcher allows per nine innings. The number of hits and walks a pitcher gave up for the season can be calculated from this number and the number of innings pitched (IP). Using the same logic as is employed with the offensive measures of performance, this measure presumes that 4 bases = 1 run, so the next step in determining TPV is to compute on average how many bases

Figure 4.1
Total Bases per Hit or Walk

	National League	American League
Total Bases (TB)	31,478	37,398
Hits and Walks (HWS)	23,138	27,531
TB/HWS	1.36	1.36

are the equivalent of 1 hit or walk given up. As is illustrated in Figure 4.1, in each league, in 1990, 1.36 bases were surrendered per hit or walk.

Once TB is determined for each pitcher, the rest of the equation is derived in a manner similar to ORS. Simply divide the total bases by 4 to arrive at the total number of runs given up and then divide by 15 to determine total games lost by the pitcher. Following this, the TPV is adjusted according to how many innings a pitcher worked compared to the average number of innings pitched at that pitcher position (PPOS). Thus, the final measure is entitled adjusted total pitchers value (ATPV). In summary, this measure is computed as follows:

TPV = ((PTB/4)/15) * -1
   where *PTB* = Pitchers total bases = (HWS * 1.36)
        HWS = Hits and walks given up in a season
             = ((IP/9) * RAT)

   where *IP* = Innings pitched
        RAT = Ratio of hits and walks per nine innings

TPV is adjusted in the following manner:

ATPV = ((AVGIP/IP) * (TPV))
   where *AVGIP* = Average innings pitched
                = 159.02 if PPOS = 1
                = 74.36 if PPOS = 2
                = 74.12 if PPOS = 3

   where *PPOS* = Pitcher position (1 = Starter, 2 = Reliever, and 3 = Closer)

The only major difference between ATPV and ORS is that ATPV is expressed in negative terms. Since pitchers only give up runs, their final number must be expressed in terms of games lost. Thus, in this case, the lower an ATPV a pitcher achieves the more valuable (statistically speaking) he is. In the end, although PRAL and PRNL cannot be used in cross-league comparisons and ATPV must be expressed in negative terms, both methods of evaluation, when taken together, should provide a more accurate indicator of pitcher performance than performance measures utilized in previous studies.

Although ATPV was used to analyze the pitchers by league as well, these results will not be reported for two reasons. First, when compared together, the explanatory power of the PRAL and PRNL variables was generally greater than the ATPV variable. When PRAL and PRNL were used as the performance measure the average amount of variance explained was 60.9%, whereas use of ATPV in league-specific analyses produced an average of 55.3%. The *t*-statistics for each of these measures were also averaged and compared. ATPV had an average *t*-statistic of 1.36 when it was used as the performance variable. However, the replacement of ATPV with either PRAL or PRNL in the same equations led to an average *t*-statistic of 2.39, a significant increase.

Second, correlations run between the two performance measures were extremely tight and highly significant. This finding might suggest that the variables are measuring the same type of performance. Furthermore, an examination of the data reveals that where there are differences found regarding the effect of the performance variable they are only of magnitude and not of direction of relationship. Thus, since the two variables measure the same type of performance and one substantially outperforms the other, PRAL and PRNL are utilized in place of ATPV in the league-specific analyses.[7]

Each pitcher position is analyzed via a similar framework, with the exception of the closers who are analyzed in a slightly different matter, which will be discussed later. First, the results for the models that utilize PRAL and PRNL as the performance variables are presented and analyzed. Then, the results of the ATPV model, which compares players across leagues, are presented. This format is also used to present the results when the old man and superstar hypotheses are tested. The old man hypothesis, when applied to the pitchers, will continue to exclude all players with ten years or more of major league experience. The criteria for determining the superstars deviates slightly from the criteria used for the non-pitching positions because of inherent differences between the positions.

Although one figure (an ORS rating of 6.00) was utilized for all of the non-pitching positions to determine if a player was to be excluded, this was possible only because non-pitching positions do not involve a distinction in offensive performance. This is not the case for pitchers. For example, one of the main distinctions between the pitching positions is the number of innings pitched. Although the most overworked relievers and closers rarely pitch more than 100 innings in a season, a healthy starter will rarely pitch fewer than 175 innings. This problem does not exist for the offensive players, since theoretically, each of them can have the same number of opportunities (i.e., plate appearances) as the other non-pitchers. As a consequence of this difference, the top 20% of each pitcher position (as measured by ATPV or PRAL/PRNL) were excluded from the testing of the superstar hypothesis. Thus, even though the percentage excluded from each analysis was identical, the cutoff point for superstar status varied substantially.

Because of the elite nature of the closer position (generally, a team only has one closer on the roster), there are only twenty-five pitchers who qualified as closers. As a result of this small number, it renders an analysis of the closers by league unproductive for two reasons. First, when the closers are divided by league, it leaves only fourteen pitchers in the American League and eleven in the National League. The small number of participants can lead to inaccurate and ambiguous results as has been pointed out previously in the analysis of the designated hitter player position. In fact, although all of the equations involving the American League closers were statistically significant, ten of the twelve equations including the National League closers were insignificant.

Second, the main reason for this analysis is to test for the presence of race as a salary determinant. However, none of the American League closers are minorities, thus precluding the use of RACE as a variable in the analysis. Nevertheless, although the closers will not be broken down by league (thereby eliminating use of PRAL and PRNL as performance variables), they will be analyzed as one group with ATPV being used as the performance variable. Finally, the old man and superstar hypotheses are also tested in this manner for the closers.

Another distinction between the pitcher and non-pitcher analysis which the astute reader may have identified, is that one of the performance variables (ATPV) for the pitcher is adjusted to take into account the number of innings pitched, whereas the performance variables for the non-pitchers are not adjusted. As will become obvious later when the empirical measure for ATPV is derived, this measure is, out of necessity, expressed as a negative number. Consequently, a pitcher who hurls more innings will be penalized because the measure, prior to adjustment, is based on the cumulative bases surrendered by the pitcher. Thus, if the ATPV ratings were not adjusted, the highest ranking players would consist of mostly rookies who were called up from the minor leagues at some point during the season to replace an injured player for a few games. As a result, salary and performance would not correlate at all. This situation is in contrast to that of a non-pitcher, who benefits by playing more games. Therefore, the best way to measure the overall contribution of a non-pitcher is to incorporate the unadjusted measure.

An example of the necessity of the adjusted TPV measure can be found in a comparison of Scott Lewis of the California Angels and Roger Clemens of the Boston Red Sox. Although Clemens was perhaps the top pitcher in 1990 (a record of 21-6, ERA of 1.93, and his PRAL of 3.34 was more than one full game higher than his closest competitor), his TPV of -5.74 placed him 84th of 131 starting pitchers. Lewis, on the other, hand, was playing in his first season, pitched only 16 innings, and compiled a record of one win and one loss. Furthermore, his PRAL was .20, ranking him 27th of 73 American League starters. However, because of the small number of innings pitched, Lewis was ranked first in TPV with -.27. Once the adjustments were made, some of the unfairness in the measure was reduced as the ATPV rating of Clemens was boosted to -4.00, which placed him 10th, while Lewis' ATPV plummeted to -2.64. Although this still kept Lewis in the number one position, it greatly reduced the difference (i.e., bias). Unfortunately, even when this measure is adjusted there appears to remain a bias toward pitchers with fewer innings, not allowing for as accurate an indicator of performance as one would like. Finally, it must be noted that this difficulty with the younger players and ATPV is generally confined to the starter pitching position. This is the case because starters experience a much greater variance in the number of innings pitched. As

Figure 4.4 illustrates later, five of the top ten pitchers (as ranked by ATPV) are players who pitched fewer than eighty innings during the 1990 season.

This problem is greatly reduced as one moves to the relievers, because on average, relievers only pitch seventy-five innings per season, a number less than half of the average innings of starters. Thus, the amount of variance between pitchers is reduced. Later, Figure 4.7 demonstrates the effect of fewer innings pitched as only two of the top ten relievers as ranked by ATPV had pitched less than fifty innings. Furthermore, the closers are not influenced by the aforementioned problem at all since qualification for the closer pitching position is based on earning a fixed number of saves, therefore ensuring that each closer had pitched extensively in that role.

Since PRAL/PRNL also allows for the possibility of a negative rating, one may speculate that this measure should be adjusted as well. Indeed, Scott Lewis again appears to pose a problem (but not to the same extent as in the previous situation) because although he pitched only sixteen innings, his PRAL was .20, ranking him twenty-seventh out of seventy-three American League starters. Although this may seem like an injustice, one must examine the basis of this measure more carefully. This variable measures the value of the pitcher over and above that of the average pitcher in the league based on the number of earned runs given up. Thus, in certain situations, a pitcher who played the whole year and had a bad year performancewise, may be rated lower than a pitcher like Scott Lewis.

One could argue that the pitcher with more innings was more valuable because he had more playing time. However, if this is argued, then the variable should measure time played, although most would agree that quantity (as opposed to quality) is not exactly the best measure of performance. Although one may agree that innings pitched is the greater factor in determining performance value, it may also be argued that even though Lewis pitched very few innings, the fact remains that he gave up less runs on average than the other pitcher. Finally, even though the above example discusses a player who is harmed statistically by pitching more innings, this measure is different from ATPV in that if a pitcher is giving up fewer runs than average, his PRAL/PRNL rating will rise as he pitches more innings. Therefore, by playing more innings, one can either help or hinder their ratings which serves to create a balance preventing the necessity of adjusting the PRAL/PRNL performance measures.

Adjustment of this measure would not be effective from a mathematical standpoint either. For example, no matter how much value one places on innings pitched, the PRAL of Scott Lewis would not drop below .01. As a result, adjusting his rating would at the most result in a difference of .19, hardly enough change to make a substantial change in the rankings. In fact, even if this were to occur, and assuming that all other PRAL values remained constant, the lowest ranking Lewis could have would be thirty-sixth of seventy-three, keeping him in the top 50%. Furthermore, even if the player who had pitched the most innings and possessed the worst rating had his score adjusted his PRAL would remain negative. Therefore, even with this scenario, the player with the negative rating would never be able to surpass Lewis. In conclusion, although evaluation of the performance of the pitchers does not involve as "neat and tidy" an approach as is the case with the non-pitching positions, this is still the best measure available. Moreover, the results presented in the following pages will document the explanatory value of PRAL/PRNL.

Control Variables

The control variables utilized in this chapter (YRS, SAL89, and SAL90) are conceptualized and empirically derived in a fashion similar to that exercised in chapter 2. Moreover, as per the discussion as to the utility of the MET variable, it was dropped from all of the analyses in this chapter.

RESEARCH FINDINGS

Pitcher Player Position: Starters

Table 4.1 reports the results of the equations prior to the testing of the old man and superstar hypotheses. When PRAL and the two-year salary lag (SAL89) were used in equation #1, two variables achieved statistical significance, SAL89 (t = 5.29, p < .001) and PRAL (t = 3.22, p < .005). Neither the RACE or YRS variables achieved statistical significance, whereas the amount of variance in SAL91 explained by equation #1 was 62%. In equation #2, when the one-year salary lag (SAL90) replaced SAL89, the results followed the patterns found in the analysis of the non-pitching positions. First, the amount of explained variance increased to 75%. Second, both the salary and performance variables maintained their statistical significance from equation #1 to #2. Moreover, the t-statistic of the salary variable when the more recent salary data was used in equation #2 increased dramatically from that of equation #1 (from t = 5.29 to t = 8.35), consistent with previous results. PRAL also followed the previously established pattern with regard to performance variables in that its t-statistic represented a slight decrease from equation #1 (it declined from t = 3.22 to t = 2.90). There was a new twist in the results for the starters, however, in that for the first time, the YRS variable was positive and statistically significant (t = 2.47, p < .05) in an equation where the old man and superstar hypotheses were not being tested. This result will be explored later in the section. Finally, the RACE variable was not statistically significant.

PRNL was used to evaluate the National League starters, and its results are presented in equations #3 and #4 in Table 4.1. When SAL89 was used as the salary variable in equation #3, the amount of variance explained was only 33%, whereas SAL89 was statistically significant (t = 3.13, p < .005). Although the salary variable was the only one to achieve a level of significance, the performance variable (PRNL) almost registered as statistically significant as it had a t-statistic of 1.97. The one-year salary lag (SAL90) replaced SAL89 in equation #4, with the result being a large increase in explained variance (72%). Moreover, both the salary and the performance variables achieved levels of statistical significance. The SAL90 variable ($t = 8.17$, $p < .001$) once again experienced a large increase in t-statistic, whereas PRNL also increased in statistical significance and t-statistic ($t = 2.82$, $p < .01$). Although the performance variable did not actually decline in t-statistic when SAL90 was used as has been the case in many other analyses, its increase was greatly outstripped by the leap in t-statistic of the salary variable from equation #3 to #4. In addition, although RACE was not a factor once again, the results of the National League starters differed from those of the American League starters in that when SAL90 was used in equation #4, the YRS variable did not become statistically significant.

When the starters were combined and ATPV replaced PRAL/PRNL as performance measures in equations #5 and #6, the results appeared to resemble the results achieved when the American League starters were being analyzed. In equation #5, with SAL89, the amount of variance explained (52%) was between the level of explanation procured in equations #1 and #3. Both the salary variable and the performance variable (ATPV) were statistically significant at .001, whereas neither the RACE or the YRS variable were statistically significant. SAL90 was used in equation #6 and results remained consistent with previous analysis. When the more recent salary data was employed, although statistical significance was maintained at .001, the t-statistic rose substantially (from 5.87 to 11.18). Furthermore, although the salary variable increased the explanatory value, the performance variable declined both in statistical significance and t-statistic ($t = 2.72$, $p < .01$), demonstrating that when performance is used in conjunction with the most recent salary data, the salary variable is usually a better explanatory variable. Moreover, the results mirrored those in equation #2 in an additional area as YRS became statistically significant again (YRS was almost statistically significant in equation #5 as well when its t-statistic was 1.92). RACE was statistically insignificant in equation #6 and explained variance with SAL90 in the equation increased to 72%.

The only result that differed from previous analyses and requires further exploration is the role of YRS within the starter pitcher position. When compared to other player positions with a similar sample size, many of the players with more than ten years of experience analyzed in equations #2 and #6 were also the most highly paid starters. For instance, when PRAL was used as the performance measure in equation #2, six of the ten highest starters were veterans. Also, when ATPV was used as the performance variable in equation #6, seven of the ten highest paid players were veterans. Moreover, YRS was not significant when PRNL was used in equation #4, a finding supported by the fact that only one veteran was among the ten highest paid starting pitchers. Figure 4.2 compares

Table 4.1
SAL91 Regressed on Variables for Starters

VARIABLE	EQ #1	EQ #2	EQ #3	EQ #4	EQ #5	EQ #6
SAL89	.60****		.47***		.52****	
	(5.29)		(3.13)		(5.87)	
SAL90		.69****		.82****		.72****
		(8.35)		(8.17)		(11.18)
RACE	-.00	-.01	-.09	-.05	-.05	-.02
	(-.04)	(-.09)	(-.66)	(-.69)	(-.74)	(-.48)
YRS	.16	.21*	.11	-.01	.17	-.14*
	(1.42)	(2.47)	(.72)	(-.09)	(1.92)	(2.20)
PRAL	.28***	.19***				
	(3.22)	(2.90)				
PRNL			.26	.20**		
			(1.97)	(2.82)		
ATPV					.26****	.14**
					(3.57)	(2.72)
Adjusted R^2	.62	.75	.33	.72	.52	.72
N	56	66	43	57	99	122

* $p < .05$.   ** $p < .01$.   *** $p < .005$.   **** $p < .001$.
Beta weights are reported. N equals sample size. T-statistics are in parentheses.
R^2 adjusted for number of independent variables and sample size.

Figure 4.2
Highly Paid Veterans

Player Position	Veterans in Top 10 Salary Ranking	Stat. Sign. $p < .05$	N
Starter (PRAL)	6 of 10	Yes	73
Starter (PRNL)	1 of 10	No	58
Catcher	4 of 10	No	62
Starter (ATPV)	7 of 10	Yes	131
Outfield	4 of 10	No	116

these findings with those from two other positions who had similar numbers of players.

The "Old Man" and "Superstar" Hypotheses Exposed

A comparison of Tables 4.1 and 4.2 reveals that although YRS was a positive and statistically significant variable in some of the regular equations, the exclusion of the veteran pitchers during the testing of the old man hypothesis only served to enhance the effect of experience.[8] This result is similar to those reported in other non-pitching position analyses. PRAL and SAL89 were used together in equation #1 and three of the four variables included became statistically significant. As is usually the case, both SAL89 (t = 3.09, p < .005) and PRAL (t = 2.40, p < .05) had substantial explanatory value. However, with the exclusion of the veterans, YRS (t = 3.54, p < .001) became the variable with the greatest explanatory power. Removing the veterans from the analysis, even though YRS was statistically significant in the regular equations, caused all traces of the old man bias to disappear, and consequently allowed the relationship between SAL91 and YRS to become almost perfectly linear. As has been explained in previous chapters, the removal of the old men results in the highest paid players also becoming the most experienced. Explanation of the variance in SAL91 increased from 63% in equation #1 to 88% in equation #2 when SAL90 replaced SAL89.[9] In addition, the salary variable once again increased in significance (from t = 3.09 to t = 11.30), and the performance variable also experienced an increase in significance and t-statistic, although not to the same degree (t = 3.67, p < .001). The YRS variable became statistically insignificant as the more recent salary data apparently crowded out its effect. Additionally, RACE was not statistically significant in either equation.

Analysis of the National League starters yielded similar results as YRS continued to play a large role in explaining the variance in SAL91. In equation #3, the two-year salary lag did not prove to be statistically significant for the first time in the analysis of the starters. YRS and PRNL, however, were statistically significant and were almost equivalent in terms of explanatory value. YRS (t = 2.73, p < .01) only became significant when the veterans were excluded as it did not register as statistically significant in either equation #3 or #4 of Table 4.1. Meanwhile, the performance variable (t = 2.69, p < .01) continued as a good predictor variable. Additionally, removal of the veterans also caused the explanation of variance to rise substantially compared to the results of the regular equation that used SAL89 (from 33% to 51%). Introduction of SAL90 resulted in its emergence (t = 5.19, p < .001) as the dominant predictor variable in equation #4 of Table 4.2. Moreover, similar to what occurred in equation #4 of Table 4.1, PRNL (t = 3.20, p < .005) experienced a rise both in level of significance and t-statistic when SAL90 replaced SAL89. Although YRS was not a factor when all National League starters were included in the analysis, removal of the old men had a similar effect in this situation as it did with the American League starters as it was statistically significant in both equations, but declined in both significance and t-statistic when SAL90 was used. RACE was not a statistically significant variable in either equation. Finally, use of SAL90 once again resulted in a higher explanation of variance (78%).

Replacing PRNL/PRAL with ATPV as the performance measure did little to change the complexion of the results as they generally followed the same patterns as the previous equations. In equation #5 both SAL89 (t = 3.68, p <

Table 4.2
SAL91 Regressed on Variables for Starters Incorporating the "Old Man"
Hypothesis

VARIABLE	EQ #1	EQ #2	EQ #3	EQ #4	EQ #5	EQ #6
SAL89	.40***		.27		.36****	
	(3.09)		(1.60)		(3.68)	
SAL90		.87****		.63****		.69****
		(11.30)		(5.19)		(9.05)
RACE	-.01	.08	.11	.07	.04	.04
	(-.14)	(1.53)	(.86)	(.92)	(.47)	(.87)
YRS	.46****	.10	.45**	.25*	.43****	.22***
	(3.54)	(1.28)	(2.73)	(2.04)	(4.46)	(2.94)
PRAL	.24*	.19****				
	(2.40)	(3.67)				
PRNL			.34**	.23***		
			(2.69)	(3.20)		
ATPV					.23***	.08
					(2.96)	(1.69)
Adjusted R^2						
N	.63	.88	.51	.78	.59	.75
	41	49	32	45	73	95

* $p < .05$.   ** $p < .01$.   *** $p < .005$.   **** $p < .001$.

Beta weights are reported. N equals sample size. T-statistics are in parentheses. R^2 adjusted for number of independent variables and sample size.

.001) and ATPV ($t = 2.96$, $p < .005$) were statistically significant. However, as in the other old man equations, YRS ($t = 4.46$, $p < .001$) was the most dominant variable. SAL90 replaced SAL89 in equation #6 and experienced a large increase in t-statistic (from 3.68 to 9.05), whereas the performance variable (ATPV) not only decreased in statistical significance, but became insignificant. Although YRS ($t = 2.94$, $p < .005$) was no longer the dominant variable in equation #6, it did maintain a high degree of statistical significance. Once again RACE was not statistically significant in either equation and the variance explained by the equations rose form 59% in equation #5 to 75% in equation #6.

The results of the testing of the old man hypothesis are interesting in that YRS became statistically significant in all but one of the equations and in many cases was the variable with the most explanatory value. Although YRS has appeared as positive and statistically significant with regard to other position analyses, this is the first instance in which the experience variable has become such a large factor. Indeed, a cursory look at the statistics in Figure 4.3 support these findings. Figure 4.3 demonstrates the role YRS played in salary determination by comparing the starters when the old men are included to the pool of starters when the old man hypothesis is tested and the veterans are excluded. This comparison is made for both of the leagues individually and as a whole. The forty highest paid pitchers in each group were extracted from the entire pool and divided into eight groups of five. Thus, along the horizontal axis of the graph, the number one includes the five highest paid players in that group, and its corresponding value on the vertical axis is the mean years experience for those five players. As the graph indicates, when the veterans are removed from the sample, and as salary declines, there is a general trend of decline in years experience as well. In contrast, there is no obvious decline in YRS that corresponds with decline in SAL91 when the old men are included with the rest of the starters. In conclusion, it appears that both the raw data and the regression results support the notion that the old man hypothesis plays a role in the explanatory value of the YRS variable.

Table 4.3 reports the results from the testing of the superstar hypothesis.[10] PRAL and SAL89 were used in equation #1 resulting in an explained variance of 56%. SAL89 was the only statistically significant variable at .001 as PRAL, YRS, and RACE failed to even come close to statistical significance. This trend continued when SAL90 was used in equation #2. Although explained variance increased markedly to 84%, the salary variable remained the only statistically significant variable. The use of SAL90 illustrated further the impact that more recent salary data can have on an equation as the t-statistic of SAL90 jumped to 12.92 from 5.92 when SAL89 was used.

PRNL was used as the performance variable in equations #3 and #4 when the National League starters were analyzed and the results were nearly identical to those of the American League starters with the exception of a lower explained variance. This has been a common occurrence thus far in the comparison of American and National League pitchers and perhaps should be monitored through the analysis of the rest of the pitcher positions. Once again, when the superstars were excluded and SAL89 was used, the only statistically significant variable was SAL89 ($t = 3.82$, $p < .001$). None of the other variables had a t-statistic above .70 and explained variance was a rather paltry (when compared with the other equations in the analysis) 38%. SAL90 replaced SAL89 in equation #4 and the only substantial change was the expected rise in t-statistic of the salary variable when SAL90 was used ($t = 8.52$, $p < .001$). All other variables were statistically insignificant. Explained variance continued to increase as well (from 38% to 77%) as more recent salary data is employed.

The results of equations #5 and #6 can perhaps shed some new light on the distinction between the performance variables utilized in the pitching position analysis. For the first time in the testing of the superstar hypothesis for the starting pitchers, the performance variable has become statistically significant. In equation #5, when SAL89 was used, ATPV was statistically significant at .01, although SAL89 attained a much higher t-statistic and level of statistical significance ($t = 6.17$, $p < .001$). When SAL90 was used, the t-statistic of the salary variable increased from 6.17 to 11.66, holding with previous findings. Moreover, ATPV remained statistically significant, although it dropped slightly

Table 4.3
SAL91 Regressed on Variables for Starters Incorporating the "Superstar" Hypothesis

VARIABLE	EQ #1	EQ #2	EQ #3	EQ #4	EQ #5	EQ #6
SAL89	.79****		.63****		.62****	
	(5.92)		(3.82)		(6.17)	
SAL90		.97****		.88****		.82****
		(12.92)		(8.52)		(11.66)
RACE	.08	.10	-.10	-.05	.02	.03
	(.79)	(1.66)	(-.68)	(-.72)	(.26)	(.52)
YRS	-.01	-.09	.09	.01	.09	.04
	(-.09)	(-1.08)	(.54)	(.14)	(.92)	(.58)
PRAL	.16	.07				
	(1.50)	(1.21)				
PRNL			.08	.04		
			(.55)	(.49)		
ATPV					.20**	.10*
					(2.55)	(1.97)
Adjusted R^2	.56	.84	.38	.77	.52	.74
N	43	49	32	46	80	99

* $p < .05$.   ** $p < .01$.   *** $p < .005$.   **** $p < .001$.

Beta weights are reported. N equals sample size. T-statistics are in parentheses. R^2 adjusted for number of independent variables and sample size.

Figure 4.3
Impact of YRS on Salary

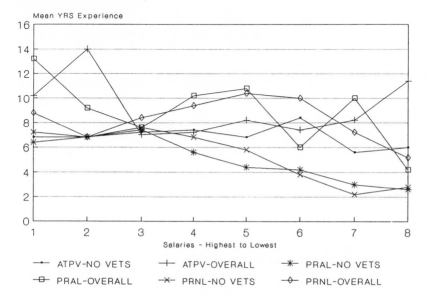

to $p < .05$. Neither equation identified RACE or YRS as significant, suggesting that race does not play a role in salary determination of the "underclass" as was hypothesized. In addition, explained variance continued to increase (from 52% to 74%) as more recent salary data was used.

With regard to the performance variable, the results from the testing of the superstar hypothesis in Figure 4.4, indicate that when ATPV is used in place of PRAL or PRNL, comparatively more of the highest paid pitchers are also among the highest performers (after the superstars are excluded). An examination of the raw data supports this view. When ATPV was used as the performance variable and the superstar hypothesis was tested, of the top ten performers remaining in the analysis, three of them are also among the ten highest paid starters.[11] In contrast, when PRAL and PRNL were used as performance variables, only one player in each of the analyses was in the top ten in both the salary and performance categories. In conclusion, the reason for this difference is that, as pointed out in the introduction, use of the ATPV variable at times allows pitchers with few innings pitched to be highly ranked in terms of performance, thereby pushing back what are arguably better performers. For instance, in this situation five players with fewer than eighty innings pitched were identified as superstars. However, all of the players identified as superstars by PRAL or PRNL were full-time starters. Consequently, a greater percentage of highly paid players, who also performed well, remained in the ATPV pool after the superstars were excluded.

Figure 4.4
Top Ten Starters by ATPV, PRAL/PRNL, and SAL91

Rank	ATPV Rating	PRAL/PRNL	SAL91 ($)
1	-2.64 Scott Lewis	3.34 Clemens	3,550,000 Langston
2	-3.48 Randy Tomlin	2.67 Dave Stewart	3,500,000 Stewart
3	-3.72 Ben McDonald	2.64 Chuck Finley	3,450,000 Welch
4	-3.76 Kevin J. Brown	2.07 Frank Viola	3,350,000 Drabek
5	-3.84 Nolan Ryan	2.01 Ed Whitson	3,333,000 Martinez
6	-3.88 Doug Drabek	1.97 Zane Smith	3,300,000 Ryan
7	-3.92 Dennis Martinez	1.76 Drabek	3,167,000 Boddicker
8	-3.92 Rich DeLucia	1.69 Bob Welch	3,167,000 Viola
9	-3.96 Chris Nabholz	1.59 Jose Rijo	3,000,000 Dave Stieb
10	-4.00 Roger Clemens	1.58 Kevin Appier	3,000,000 J. Morris

Pitcher Player Position: Relievers

Results from the analysis of relievers indicate that the same explanation used for the salary determinants of starters will not suffice for this player position. In Table 4.4, equation #1, which utilizes SAL89 as the salary variable and PRAL as the performance variable, explained only 29% of the variance in the 1991 salary measure. SAL89 was the only variable to register as statistically significant and qualified at the lowest possible level ($t = 2.29$, $p < .05$). The only other variable approaching statistical significance was RACE, a distinct change from the analysis of the starters where RACE was almost always the most insignificant variable. Neither PRAL nor YRS registered as statistically significant. Different results took shape when SAL90 was used in place of SAL89 in equation #2, as two variables became statistically significant. SAL90 ($t = 14.07$, $p < .001$) continued its dominance and following the trend, once again increased in t-statistic (and this time in significance as well) from equation #1 to #2. PRAL also became significant at .001, and its t-statistic increased five-fold from equation #1. This is contrary to other player position analyses in that the performance generally decreased or only increases slightly in t-statistic and statistical significance when SAL90 is used in place of SAL89. These findings do not completely contradict previous findings, however, in that the salary variable increased at an even faster rate than the performance variable from equation #1 to equation #2. Once again, neither the RACE nor YRS variables were statistically significant. Finally, despite some of the differences in these two equations compared to the others, the pattern of increased explanation of variance when more recent salary data is used continued as equation #2 explained 87% of the variance in SAL91.

The results of the analysis of the National League relievers are much more indicative of previous results. Although SAL89 in equation #3 was not statistically significant, it almost reached the .05 level as its t-statistic was 1.97. The only variable to achieve statistical significance was PRNL ($t = 3.91$, $p < .001$), continuing the pattern that performance has the edge in terms of explanatory value when it is used in conjunction with SAL89. The amount of explained variance in equation #3 was also a large increase over equation #1 when American League relievers were studied as 49% of the variance was explained when the National League relievers were examined. SAL90 replaced SAL89 in equation #4 and the results were predictable as the salary variable increased dramatically in t-statistic and statistical significance ($t = 7.32$, $p < .001$). The performance variable, however, also maintained its level of statistical significance and even raised its t-statistic from 3.91 to 5.36, although the rate of the salary variable's increase in t-statistic was much higher. Thus, the behavior of the two variables remained as expected. In addition, RACE did not become a statistically significant factor when the National League relievers were examined and YRS continued to be insignificant as well. Finally, the expected rise in the explanation of variance occurred as equation #4 explained 82% of the variance in the 1991 salary data.

When ATPV replaced PRAL/PRNL as the performance variable in order to compare both leagues, the results were not really a balance between the results of the two leagues when taken separately. None of the variables registered as statistically significant in equation #5 when SAL89 was used. Indeed, the only variable approaching significance was YRS, which had a t-statistic of 1.89. As

Table 4.4
SAL91 Regressed on Variables for Relievers

VARIABLE	EQ #1	EQ #2	EQ #3	EQ #4	EQ #5	EQ #6
SAL89	.52*		.40		.26	
	(2.29)		(1.97)		(1.63)	
SAL90		.99****		.94****		1.04****
		(14.01)		(7.32)		(13.21)
RACE	.26	.11	.02	.06	.16	.08
	(1.81)	(1.94)	(.14)	(.85)	(1.49)	(1.52)
YRS	.05	-.11	.33	-.11	.30	-.19**
	(.24)	(-1.61)	(1.75)	(-.83)	(1.89)	(-2.49)
PRAL	.12	.26****				
	(.81)	(4.74)				
PRNL			.55****	.37****		
			(3.91)	(5.36)		
ATPV					.05	.20****
					(.47)	(3.69)
Adjusted R^2	.29	.87	.49	.82	.24	.78
N	36	48	32	41	68	89

* $p < .05$.   ** $p < .01$.   *** $p < .005$.   **** $p < .001$.

Beta weights are reported. N equals sample size. T-statistics are in parentheses. R^2 adjusted for number of independent variables and sample size.

a result of the lack of explanatory value among any of the individual variables, the amount of variance explained by equation #5 was only 24%. Equation #6 was a different story, however, as the inclusion of SAL90 caused explained variance to increase to 78%. Moreover, three variables reached levels of statistical significance. SAL90 once again became the main predictor as its t-statistic climbed to 13.29, and it was statistically significant at .001. The performance variable (ATPV) was also statistically significant at .001, but in keeping with previous trends, its t-statistic did not escalate at the same rate as that of the salary variable. Perhaps the most confusing result involves the statistical significance of the YRS variable ($t = -2.55, p < .01$). The unusual thing about this variable is not only that it has a negative sign attached to it (indicating that players with fewer years experience are being paid higher salaries), but that in equation #5, when the SAL89 was used as the salary variable, YRS was almost significant as well with a *positive* sign. Thus, it appears that the use of the more recent salary data caused a 180 degree change in the direction of the YRS variable, a topic that will be addressed further.

The first thing that must be addressed regards the general lack of explanatory value of SAL89. A comparison of the highest paid players in 1989 to the highest paid players in 1991 reveals that in each league, seven of the ten highest paid pitchers in 1989 remained in the top ten in 1991. However, the players who dropped out of the list at times had substantial falls. In the American League, for example, the two highest paid relievers in 1989 were Jesse Orosco and John Candelaria, respectively, but in 1991, they had fallen into the thirteenth and fifteenth positions. Although both pitchers have had ten years or more experience in the major leagues and thus qualify as "old men," the fading superstar part of the old man effect does not apply here. Rather, this trend is the result of a condition unique to relievers. One must note that within the ranks of the pitchers, players can switch pitching positions more easily than non-pitchers can change player positions, because the skills required of all pitchers are essentially the same. Yet, pitchers are still paid according to their pitcher position even though the basic skills required are similar.

Couple this with the fact that the reliever position is often a position of demotion (and the lowest paying of the pitcher positions) for pitchers who have lost effectiveness as a starter or as a closer. The cumulative effect of this situation is that players who are moved to the reliever position from a closer or starter spot also bring their higher salaries with them; the salaries do not adjust immediately. However, within a year or two, the downward adjustment will take place and they will then be paid according to their effectiveness as a reliever. As Figure 4.5 illustrates, this is the case with Orosco, Candelaria, and three pitchers in the National League who also ranked in the top ten in salary in 1989 and then were transferred to the reliever position. As a result, the explanatory value of SAL89 suffered.[12]

Figure 4.5
Pitching Position Changes and Effect on Salary

Name (PPOS in 1989)	Rank (SAL89)	Rank (SAL91)
Candelaria (Starter)	2	15
Carman (Starter)	9	27
Mahler (Starter)	7	28
Orosco (Closer)	1	13
Show (Starter)	1	14

Another unusual result from the reliever analysis was the negative sign on the YRS variable in equation #6. Examination of the raw data reveals that ten of the nineteen players with ten years or more experience are ranked in the top twenty by salary in 1991. This would suggest that although the older players are not being paid much more than their younger counterparts, they are not being paid considerably less either. If one examines the salary rank of the other old men, however, it becomes apparent why the negative sign appeared. Figure 4.6 compares the average years experience of a reliever and their relative rank in SAL91 (grouping them by increments of five rank positions). Although the highest paid players do have the most years experience on average, as one moves down in the rankings, younger players are often being paid more than the more experienced relievers.

Figure 4.6
Trends in SAL91 Rank and Years Experience

SAL91	Mean YRS Experience	SAL91	Mean YRS Experience
Top 5	10.4	36-40	4.2
6-10	11.6	41-45	6.0
11-15	7.2	46-50	6.8
16-20	7.8	51-55	6.0
21-25	7.0	56-60	4.8
26-30	9.2	61-65	6.0
31-35	8.8		

The "Old Man" and "Superstar" Hypotheses Exposed

The results of application of the old man hypothesis in Table 4.5 appear to suggest answers to the abnormalities in the results reported above.[13] In equation #1, when SAL89 and PRAL are used, it appears that the exclusion of the veterans allowed for a better correlation between the salary and performance variables. This seems to suggest that perhaps the older players were being paid at higher rates than their performance indicated, an occurrence that must have been enough to throw the equation into disarray, leaving only SAL89 as statistically significant (refer to Table 4.4). Meanwhile in equation #1 of Table 4.5, both the salary ($t = 3.01$, $p < .01$) and performance ($t = 3.23$, $p < .005$) variables became statistically significant. Furthermore, as their t-statistics indicate, they are almost equal predictors of variance, although performance did attain a slightly higher level of statistical significance. In addition, the exclusion of the veterans also contributed to an increase in the amount of variance explained (from 29% in equation #1 of Table 4.4 to 55% explanation in equation #1 of Table 4.5). Movement from equation #1 to equation #2 did not produce any unexpected results as the same variables remained statistically significant. Both the salary and performance variables were statistically significant at .001 and the t-statistics for SAL90 ($t = 6.97$) and PRAL ($t = 5.12$) each represented a substantial increase from equation #1.

Although the performance variable increased in t-statistic and significance as well, this remains consistent with previous results in that the t-statistic of the salary variable increased at a faster rate. The exclusion of the veterans also did not lead to the statistical significance of the RACE or YRS variables in either equation. Finally, the amount of variance explained also improved to 78%.

When the equations involving the National League relievers were run, the exclusion of the veterans in equation #3 produced some dramatically different results. Equation #3 was insignificant as a whole, whereas SAL89 exhibited a negative relationship (although not statistically significant), for the first time in any of the analyses in this study. This appears to indicate that in some cases, those pitchers who were paid less in 1989 were paid the highest salaries in 1991. Perhaps the oddity of the results can be blamed on the fact that exclusion of the veterans reduced the number of relievers in the analysis by slightly more than one third. By virtue of an increase in the number of players in 1990, the veterans accounted for only one quarter of the pool of players in equation #4, and this, combined with the introduction of SAL90 instead of SAL89 apparently allowed statistical significance to be restored to the overall equation. In fact, equation #4 of Table 4.5 is almost an exact replica of its corresponding equation in Table 4.4. Similar to the equation in Table 4.4, this equation also identified the salary and performance variables as statistically significant at .001 and the t-statistic of the salary variable increased sharply from -.23 in equation #3 to 7.34 in equation #4. Neither the RACE nor the YRS variables were statistically significant in either equation. In conclusion, the amount of variance explained by equation #4 without the veterans (82%) was identical to that achieved when the veterans were included.

The results of equation #5 of Table 4.5 more or less mirrored the results of its companion equation in Table 4.4. In equation #5, the two-year salary lag and ATPV were used as the salary and performance variables, respectively. As was the case in Table 4.4, this equation did not cause any of the individual variables to become statistically significant, although the equation was significant as a whole. However, despite the statistical significance of the equation, the amount of variance explained was only 25%. Use of SAL90 in place of SAL89 led to an increase in explained variance to 73% in équation #6. Moreover, the salary and performance variables were both statistically significant. A comparison of the relative explanatory value of these two variables also indicate consistency with previously identified trends as the value of the salary variable (t = 9.57, p < .001) was higher than that of ATPV (t = 3.29, p < .005). However, the exclusion of the veterans led to an interesting result as the YRS variable, statistically significant and negative in equation #6 of Table 4.4, was insignificant in equation #6 of Table 4.5. This result would seem to suggest that the reason for the negative sign on the YRS variable was that the veteran relievers were being paid less than their younger counterparts and had become victims of the old man hypothesis. Finally, the RACE variable was not statistically significant in this equation.

As stated previously, the negative sign on the SAL89 variable was most likely the reason for the statistical insignificance of equation #3 of Table 4.5. When the players with ten years or more experience were excluded from analysis, the top ten salary rankings were compiled for SAL89 and SAL91. A comparison of the two lists reveals that only five of the top ten relievers by salary in 1989 remained among the highest paid relievers in 1991. Moreover, of those pitchers who fell

Table 4.5
SAL91 Regressed on Variables for Relievers Incorporating the "Old Man" Hypothesis

VARIABLE	EQ #1	EQ #2	EQ #3	EQ #4	EQ #5	EQ #6
SAL89	.48**		-.10		.35	
	(3.01)		(-.23)		(1.89)	
SAL90		.71****		.81****		.84****
		(6.99)		(7.34)		(9.59)
RACE	.09	.04	.08	-.04	.11	.00
	(.65)	(.47)	(.39)	(-.52)	(.84)	(.06)
YRS	.12	.10	.66	.16	.18	.04
	(.81)	(1.00)	(1.51)	(1.33)	(1.02)	(.41)
PRAL	.42***	.39****				
	(3.23)	(5.10)				
PRNL			.38	.31***		
			(1.80)	(3.74)		
ATPV					.14	.21***
					(1.15)	(3.29)
Adjusted R^2	.55	.78	.22	.82	.25	.73
N	29	40	21	31	50	71

* $p < .05$.   ** $p < .01$.   *** $p < .005$.   **** $p < .001$.

Beta weights are reported. N equals sample size. T-statistics are in parentheses. R^2 adjusted for number of independent variables and sample size.

off the list in that time period, four were among the top six paid relievers in 1989. An example of this dramatic change in salary structure involves Atlee Hammaker, a nine-year veteran with the San Francisco Giants who was a starter until 1989. In 1989, Hammaker had the second highest salary when ranked with the relievers. However, in 1991, after struggling with poor performances and injuries for a couple of years, his salary dropped to the lowest among National League relievers. Thus, it appears that the substantial salary decreases experienced by several of the highest paid relievers in 1989 resulted in the lack of explanatory value for the two-year salary lag.

The results of the analysis of the relievers within the context of the superstar hypothesis are reported in Table 4.6 and it appears that generally as the highest performing players were excluded from the analysis, previous salary became, comparatively speaking, a much more influential variable in salary determination.[14] In equation #1, SAL89 and PRAL were used as the salary and performance variables, respectively. Although the equation as a whole was statistically significant, none of the individual variables achieved this status and only 21% of the variance 1991 salaries was explained by the variables in the equation. Equation #2, however, produced expected results as SAL90 ($t = 7.09$,

p < .001) was statistically significant and became the dominant predictor of salary in 1991.[15] Moreover, neither the YRS nor the performance variable were statistically significant. In addition, RACE was not a statistically significant variable in either equation #1 or equation #2. Furthermore, an increase in the variance explained (78%) resulted once again as SAL90 replaced SAL89.

Exclusion of the superstars from the analysis of the National League relievers appeared to do little more than diminish the value of the performance variable (PRNL) in explaining 1991 salary variance. In equation #3 of Table 4.4, PRNL was the only statistically significant variable and explanation of variance of 49%. When the superstar hypothesis was tested, however, the performance variable was insignificant (none of the other variables registered as statistically significant either) and the amount of variance explained fell to 25%. A lack of superstars had less effect when SAL90 was used in equation #4. Although the salary variable decreased in t-statistic when compared to equation #4 of Table 4.4 (from t = 7.32 to t = 5.53), it did remain statistically significant at .001. Likewise, the performance variable remained statistically significant, although it decreased in significance from .001 to .05 when compared to the results in Table 4.4. In addition, the YRS and RACE variables were not identified as statistically significant, once again demonstrating that race does not apparently play a role in the salary determination of the lowest performing players. Finally, the amount of variance explained increased sharply to 72% when SAL90 replaced SAL89.

A study of all the non-superstar relievers regardless of league yielded results similar to those discovered in similar equations listed in Table 4.4. When SAL89 was used in equation #5 of Table 4.6, none of the variables were statistically significant by themselves even though the equation was statistically significant. Furthermore, the amount of variance explained was also very low at 19%. When SAL90 was introduced in place of SAL89 in equation #6, the salary variable (t = 11.86, p < .001) once again gained statistical significance and a higher t-statistic when the more recent salary data was used. Moreover, although the performance variable (ATPV) and RACE did not achieve statistical significance, the YRS variable exhibited a significant negative relationship (t = -2.52, p < .01). A nearly identical relationship was found in its corresponding equation in Table 4.4, suggesting that the superstars did not have any impact on the negative relationship regarding experience. Finally, use of SAL90 led to a substantial increase in the amount of variance explained (79%).

SAL89 continues to perform poorly even after the superstars are excluded. Apparently, the reason for this is that of the players identified as causing problems with the salary variable in equations #1, #3, and #5 in Table 4.4, none qualified as superstars. Thus, all of them remain in the analysis, although the size of the reliever population is decreased. As a result, the continued presence of the relievers with salary decreases from 1989 to 1991 only serves to exacerbate the difficulties with SAL89.

A problem similar to the one described above also contributed to the continued negative and statistically significant impact of YRS even after the

Table 4.6
SAL91 Regressed on Variables for Relievers Incorporating the "Superstar" Hypothesis

VARIABLE	EQ #1	EQ #2	EQ #3	EQ #4	EQ #5	EQ #6
SAL89	.52		.45		.21	
	(1.87)		(1.36)		(1.15)	
SAL90		1.07****		.99****		1.05****
		(7.09)		(5.53)		(11.86)
RACE	.29	.07	.01	.07	.12	.05
	(1.59)	(1.88)	(.06)	(.67)	(.91)	(.86)
YRS	.06	-.01	.21	-.09	.29	-.21**
	(.23)	(-.05)	(.65)	(-.50)	(1.60)	(-2.52)
PRAL	-.13	.37				
	(-.72)	(1.70)				
PRNL			.36	.23*		
			(1.80)	(2.26)		
ATPV					-.21	.07
					(-1.65)	(1.12)
Adjusted R^2	.21	.78	.25	.72	.19	.79
N	27	34	23	32	52	69

* $p < .05$.   ** $p < .01$.   *** $p < .005$.   **** $p < .001$.

Beta weights are reported. N equals sample size. T-statistics are in parentheses. R^2 adjusted for number of independent variables and sample size.

exclusion of the superstars. The continued negative significance suggests that none of the lower paid "old men" qualified as superstars. Indeed, once again all of the problematic elements of the analysis in Table 4.4 remained in the superstar analysis, although the reliever population decreased. Not only did this serve to perpetuate the negative significance of YRS, but five of the ten old men with salaries greater than $1 million were also excluded since they qualified as superstars, causing the influence of the remaining veterans to increase in magnitude.

Before the results of the analysis of the closers are presented, a final comment is necessary regarding the overall analysis of the relievers. If one examines the results of all of the pitcher position analyses, it becomes apparent that the reliever pitcher position is the only pitcher position that produces a very low explanation of the amount of variance in SAL91 when SAL89 is used. The root cause of this circumstance was alluded to earlier when the low status of the reliever when compared to the other two pitcher positions was discussed. Perhaps because of the nature of this position, salaries are much more volatile, causing the explanatory value of the salary variable to decline. Indeed, the raw data in Figure 4.7 demonstrates this volatility, which stems from the lower confidence of management in the relievers, therefore leading to fewer multi-year contracts and their accompanying stability in the salary structure.

Figure 4.7
Top Ten Relievers by ATPV, PRAL/PRNL, and SAL91

Rank	ATPV Rating	PRAL/PRNL	SAL91 ($)
1	-1.05 Steve Chitren	1.82 Steve Farr	3,625,000 Mark Davis
2	-1.67 Rob Dibble	1.49 Dibble	3,250,000 Darwin
3	-1.69 Gene Nelson	1.44 Bill Swift	2,400,000 Farr
4	-1.78 Danny Darwin	1.29 Greg Harris	2,000,000 Anderson
5	-1.84 J. Don Gleaton	1.28 Nelson	1,833,000 Ken Dayley
6	-1.84 Rick Honeycutt	1.20 Norm Charlton	1,725,000 Jim Gott
7	-1.84 Mark Williamson	1.07 Williamson	1,633,000 Bob Ojeda
8	-1.85 W. Whitehurst	.99 Edwin Nunez	1,350,000 Honeycutt
9	-1.89 Mark Lee	.99 L. Anderson	1,167,000 J. Agosto
10	-1.91 Duane Ward	.88 Barry Jones	1,150,000 Jim Clancy
10	-1.91 Mike Hartley		

Pitcher Player Position: Closer

The final group of players to be analyzed are the closers. As explained previously in this chapter, the closers are analyzed without regard to league, and ATPV is used as the performance variable. Analysis by league was not conducted because of the small number of pitchers in this category and the racial composition of the American League closers (there were no minorities). When the equation was run including all the closers, the results fit with patterns previously noted. In equation #1 of Table 4.7, SAL89 is used as the salary variable. Although the equation as a whole is statistically significant and explained variance is 51%, none of the individual variables were statistically significant. Two of the variables, however, achieved levels close to statistical significance as SAL89 had a t-statistic of 2.00 and ATPV registered a t-statistic of 1.84, both of which approached significance.

With the use of SAL90 in place of SAL89 in equation #2, two of the variables became statistically significant. Consistent with previous trends, the salary variable became highly significant and achieved a substantial increase in t-statistic when the more recent salary data was used (t = 4.82, p < .001). Performance was also statistically significant (t = 2.95, p < .01), although its advances were not at the same pace as that of the salary variable. Finally, although the RACE and YRS variable were not identified as statistically significant, the amount of explained variance increased to 73%.

Although on the surface, the results of Table 4.7 do not appear to be unusual, when Figure 4.9 is later examined, it will likely cause one to wonder why the

Table 4.7
SAL91 Regressed on Variables for Closers Incorporating the "Old Man" and "Superstar" Hypotheses

VARIABLE	OVERALL		OLD MAN		SUPERSTAR	
	EQ #1	EQ #2	EQ #1	EQ #2	EQ #1	EQ #2
SAL89	.73		.67***		.50	
	(2.00)		(3.66)		(.96)	
SAL90		.81****		.47*		.84****
		(4.82)		(2.26)		(5.24)
RACE	-.06	-.09	.11	.01	-.20	-.15
	(-.36)	(-.79)	(1.08)	(.05)	(-.92)	(-1.32)
YRS	-.10	-.07	.35	.50*	.18	.03
	(-.27)	(-.39)	(2.05)	(2.45)	(.37)	(.21)
ATPV	.40	.39**	.12	.16	.04	.16
	(1.84)	(2.95)	(1.23)	(1.15)	(.18)	(1.37)
Adjusted R^2	.51	.73	.87	.81	.47	.80
N	25	25	18	18	20	20

* $p < .05$.   ** $p < .01$.   *** $p < .005$.   **** $p < .001$.

Beta weights are reported. N equals sample size. T-statistics are in parentheses. R^2 adjusted for number of independent variables and sample size.

performance variable did not achieve a higher level of statistical significance. In fact, both the reliever and starter pitching position were able to achieve levels of statistical significance of equivalent or higher value than the closers, although an examination of Figure 4.9 demonstrates that within the closer pitcher position there is a higher correlation between performance and SAL91 than can be discovered within the other pitcher positions. Indeed, six of the closers with ATPVs in the top ten also have 1991 salaries ranking in the top ten.

However, because of the smaller number of closers when compared with the other positions, the four players ranking in the top ten of SAL91 who did not rank in the top ten as measured by ATPV had a greater influence on the statis-

Figure 4.8
Difference between SAL91 and ATPV Rank among Closers

Name	SAL91 Rank	ATPV Rank
Tim Burke	8	14
John Franco	4	16
Dan Plesac	9	22
Dave Righetti	6	21

tical significance of performance than they would have had within the other positions. Furthermore, as Figure 4.8 illustrates, there is a significant difference between the performance and salary rank of these players.

Figure 4.9
Top Ten Closers by ATPV, PRAL/PRNL, and SAL91

Rank	ATPV Rating	PRAL/PRNL	SAL91 ($)
1	-1.03 D. Eckersley	1.78 Eckersley	3,000,000 Eckersley
2	-1.75 Tom Henke	1.42 Jeff Brantley	2,967,000 Henke
3	-1.75 B. Thigpen	1.36 Thigpen	2,667,000 L. Smith
4	-1.79 Doug Jones	1.09 Myers	2,633,000 Franco
5	-1.81 Dave Smith	1.06 J. Montgomery	2,533,000 Reardon
6	-1.90 Lee Smith	.95 Henke	2,500,000 Righetti
7	-1.92 Mike Schooler	.85 L. Smith	2,417,000 Thigpen
8	-1.92 Jeff Reardon	.84 Jones	2,267,000 Tim Burke
9	-1.94 Craig Lefferts	.82 Gregg Olson	2,267,000 Dan Plesac
10	-1.94 Randy Myers	.79 Jack Howell	2,050,000 Jones

The "Old Man" and "Superstar" Hypotheses Exposed

A comparison of the old man hypothesis and the general examination of players in Table 4.7 indicates that once again the old man effect is present within a player position.[16] However, although some of the results can be treated as normal, given previous results, some of the results yielded are surprises and necessitate further investigation. Equation #1, which utilized SAL89, explained an astoundingly high 87% of the variance given the age of the salary data employed. Moreover, SAL89 was the only variable that was statistically significant ($t = 3.66$, $p < .005$). Although the ATPV and RACE variables were not close to a level of significance, YRS almost qualified as statistically significant as it had a t-statistic of 2.05. The fact that YRS has a t-statistic of this size is not unusual given the fact that the veterans with ten years or more experience have been removed from the analysis. Thus, since many veterans have lower salaries than some of the younger players, their removal increase the linearity of the relationship between experience and SAL91.

When SAL90 was used in equation #2, the YRS variable was able to break through and become statistically significant ($t = 2.45$, $p < .05$), lending more concrete support for the presence of the old man effect. However, some of the other results from this equation are troubling. First, although SAL90 is statistically significant, its level of significance and t-statistic declined ($t = 2.26$, $p < .05$) from the levels of the salary variable in equation #1. This result suggests that the older salary data had more explanatory value than SAL90, a proposition in direct contrast to every other equation involving pitcher positions.

Second, and finally, equation #2 yielded an explanation of variance of 81%, a value high in and of itself. Yet even this relatively high figure represents a slight decline from the amount of variance explained by equation #1 (87%). This finding is also in direct contrast with the findings of previous analyses.

Apparently, the greater explained variance by equation #1 of the old man hypothesis in Table 4.7 is the result of the higher statistical significance of SAL89 when compared with SAL90. Comparison of the salary rankings in 1989 and 1990 to those of 1991 demonstrate that salaries from 1989 do correspond better to SAL91 than do the salaries from 1990. Moreover, the primary differences among the rankings of SAL89 and SAL90 are the result of three closers. When the players with ten years or more experience are excluded, Tom Henke of the Toronto Blue Jays is the highest paid player according to SAL91. When this ranking is compared with the other two years, the SAL89 ranking appears to be more accurate as he ranked second in salary in 1989, whereas in 1990, he was only sixth. Similarly, Tim Burke of the Montreal Expos was ranked fourth in salary in 1991 and fifth in salary in 1989. However, he was the highest paid player in 1990 once the old men are removed from the analysis. The final closer to be considered is Bobby Thigpen of the Chicago White Sox, who was ranked third in salary in 1991 and seventh in 1989. Once again, Thigpen's salary ranking in 1990 (eleventh) was further removed from his ranking in 1991 than the SAL89 ranking.

The results of the superstar hypothesis, also found in Table 4.7, do not reveal any unexpected results.[17] Similar to the case when ATPV was used to analyze the effect of the superstar hypothesis with respect to relievers, equation #1, which used SAL89 as the salary variable, failed to produce any statistically significant variables even though the equation was significant itself. Moreover, the equation explained 47% of the variance in the 1991 salaries. The replacement of SAL89 with SAL90 in equation #2, however, allowed for an increase in the explanation of variance to 80%. Furthermore, SAL90 became statistically significant at .001 ($t = 5.24$). This finding is consistent with previous testing of the superstar hypothesis and provides further support for the notion that as the highest performing players are removed, performance declines in terms of explanatory value, whereas salary increases with respect to its explanatory value. Finally, in equation #2, RACE, YRS, and ATPV were all insignificant.

Lack of statistical significance of the performance variable can be readily explained on further analysis of the raw data. The exclusion of the superstars resulted in the removal of five closers from the analysis. As Figure 4.9 illustrates, four of the superstars were also among the ten highest paid closers in 1991. This is in contrast to an analysis of the next ten highest performers. In this group, only three players were among the top ten closers in terms of salary. Consequently, the exclusion of the superstars led to a reduced correlation between performance and salary.

NOTES

1. A pitcher is in a save situation when he enters the game with his team leading by three runs or fewer. He is credited with the save if he finishes the game while at the same time preserving the lead. An exception to the rule of entering with a lead of three runs or fewer occurs when a pitcher finishes a game by relieving for three innings or more, while preserving the lead. In this situation, the official scorer must make a judgment call when deciding whether to give credit for a save.

2. The only situation in which a strikeout is considered to be of greater value is when there is a runner on third with less than two outs. In this circumstance, if a batter hits the ball for an out, the runner on third may still be able to score. A strikeout, in contrast, generally does not allow the runner to score.

3. Recall that 10 is the constant used in the determination of ORS, because that is the number of runs necessary to add one victory to the average teams' win total. This relationship should also apply to the prevention of runs. Otherwise stated, every 10 runs that are prevented by an individual (whether it be a defensive non-pitcher or a pitcher) above the league average should result in one win. Since there are two components to the prevention of runs, defense and pitching, it follows that the components combined should have the equivalent value of offensive run production. Thus, each component should be valued at one half of offensive production. To accomplish this, a constant of 20 should be employed for both the defensive and pitching evaluations. However, it should be noted that 21% of all outs are strikeouts that are directly attributable to the pitcher. If this figure is subtracted from the other outs, approximately 79% of the outs remain to be shared between the pitcher and defensive players. Consequently, both the pitcher and the defensive players are directly responsible for 39.5% of the outs. In the end, the pitchers, theoretically, are responsible for 60.5% of the prevention of runs while the defensive players have responsibility for 39.5% of the prevention of runs. Therefore, the constant of 15 was selected for the measurement of the pitching runs, whereas 30 is used as the constant in the computation of fielding runs in order to approximate the ratio of runs prevented by the pitchers to runs prevented by the non-pitchers. Fifteen represents 67% of the responsibility for run prevention, whereas 30 represents 33%. Although these figures do not correspond exactly with the percentages described above, they are close approximations and were chosen as constants because they are nice, round figures. If the constants were chosen to mirror the exact theoretical percentages for the prevention of runs, the constant for pitcher would be 16.54 and 25.3 for defensive players.

4. The rules for determining the status of a run are more complex and further discussion is beyond the scope of this book. Complete rules regarding this matter can be found in most baseball rule books (e.g., *Thorn and Palmer, 1991*, Appendix 1, p. 2553).

5. A problem with the measure, however, is that unearned runs can also result from an error by the pitcher or a wild pitch meaning that some runs directly attributable to the pitcher are not accounted for by the ERA, the predominant measure of the pitcher's performance.

6. The divisional realignment that has been implemented for the 1994 season does not detract from the ability to generalize from the findings here as the two major leagues remain in tact while divisions have been broken down.

7. Tables reporting the results of the ATPV league-specific analyses have been compiled and are available on request from the authors.

8. Testing of the old man hypothesis led to the exclusion of the following number of

veterans in each equation: fifteen in equation #1, sixteen in equation #2, eleven in equation #3, twelve in equation #4, twenty-six in equation #5, and twenty-seven in equation #6.

9. When equation #2 was first run, Roger Clemens was identified as an outlier at .004. The equation was run again without Clemens and the results are reported above.

10. Testing of the superstar hypothesis led to the exclusion of the following number of pitchers in each equation: thirteen in equation #1, seventeen in equation #2, eleven in equations #3 and #4, nineteen in equation #5, and twenty-three in equation #6.

11. The rankings by SAL91 were also adjusted to account for the exclusion of the superstars as some of the superstars were also among the ten highest paid starters when all the starters were considered.

12. Orosco last qualified as a closer in 1988. All others listed in Figure 4.5 were in their former PPOS until 1989.

13. Testing of the old man hypothesis resulted in the exclusion of several veterans with ten years or more experience from the following equations: seven in equation #1, eight in equation #2, eleven in equation #3, ten in equation #4, and eighteen veterans in equations #5 and #6.

14. Testing of the superstar hypothesis resulted in the exclusion of the following number of relievers in each of the equations: nine in equation #1, thirteen in equation #2, nine in equation #3 and #4, sixteen in equation #5, and twenty in equation #6.

15. When equation #2 was first run, Mark Davis was identified as an outlier at .001. The equation was run again without Davis and the results are reported.

16. Testing of the old man hypothesis led to the exclusion of seven veterans from both equations #1 and #2.

17. Testing of the superstar hypothesis led to the exclusion of five closers from both equations #1 and #2.

Chapter 5

Conclusions and Implications

It has often been said that baseball is a game of chances. So too is multiple regression analysis. The present analysis has been primarily concerned with the use of multiple regression analysis (as it is meeting with even greater acceptance in court cases on salary determination discrimination) to ascertain the impact that race and performance have on the salary determination of professional baseball players in 1991. The implications that are associated with any of the present findings regarding these two aspects of salary determination may be great to the extent that professional baseball is a microcosm of the larger political and social culture of the United States. From the analysis in chapter 1, one can readily see that "what is good for the game of baseball is good for the United States." In a nutshell, this is a brief way of submitting the argument that indeed the relevance of race in professional baseball mirrors that of race in the larger context.

Those who have taken the time to involve themselves in the field of sport sociology and racial discrimination studies in professional sports will appreciate the fact that not only has this been a salary determination analysis, but also a positional analysis of sorts. Moreover, it has not been the typical "positional analysis," whereby one undertakes an investigation into whether blacks, hispanics, or whites are (statistically speaking) over- or underrepresented at any one position. Indeed, the research design utilized in this study has been constructed so as to conduct the analysis of salary determination via a positional breakdown. Consequently, this study has been able to increase the level of understanding as to what is known with respect to the key variables in the salary determination process as well as their relevance at varying player positions.

It is also important to note that, although this study has made great strides in terms of the development of performance measures and a more fully specified model, it also has it share of limitations. For example, the role of race (versus performance) has been tested for only at the "player" level of analysis. This study has in no way investigated the role of race with respect to other units of analysis (i.e., base coaches, managers, owners). That is not to suggest that these are not appropriate area's for further investigation. Rather, it is merely an indication of the limited scope of the current study.

Such studies, moreover, have a great deal of difficulty in determining appropriate indicators of racism and whether findings are suggestive of racism. For example, the 1990 census reports that the population of the United States was 80.3% white, 12.1% black, and so forth. Does this mean that "racism" exists if less than 12.1% of the managers of major league baseball teams are black? if less than 80.3% are white?

Relatively speaking, in 1993, professional baseball may not be indicted as racist against blacks and minorities in general if the basis for this statement is solely a cursory investigation as to the number of minority managers (as opposed to white) without any regard to qualifications, years experience, previous salary, good performance record (i.e., wins), and the like. Indeed, when the 1993 baseball season began there were six (21.4%) black or hispanic managers in major league baseball. That figure paralleled the six (22.2%) black head coaches in the National Basketball Association (NBA) and compared very favorably to the three (10.7%) minority head coaches in the National Football League (NFL).[1]

Regardless, however, professional baseball has come under attack for the relatively low number of minority players compared to other major league sports. In 1992, blacks made up approximately 18.0% of players listed on major league rosters. This compares poorly to the 75.0% of blacks in the NBA and 60.0% in the NFL. When looking at the lessening number of blacks in the minors (from an average of 40.0% in the 1970s to 15.0% in the 1990s) the situation is unlikely to get better any time soon. Zoss and Bowman (1989: 161) summarize it best: "Today black Americans are accepted mostly as players, mostly for certain positions, but still not as managers; and not in executive positions in any substantial numbers. . . . In fact, for these and other reasons, the number of blacks coming into baseball has declined steadily over the past decade." So troubling has this indictment become that professional baseball has implemented an ambitious program ironically called the "RBI" or Reviving Baseball In The Inner Cities, in order to more readily effect change.[2]

It is plausible that the aforementioned trends may be the result of aversive racism (what was referred to as symbolic or "modern day racism" in chapter 1). Perhaps it is the case that those who are in charge of player development are saying one thing with respect to minorities in "America's National Pastime," but then act (i.e., make decisions) in what are seemingly racist ways. Moreover, perhaps the aversive racist thesis can explain the indictment against major league baseball that remuneration to minorities is significantly lower than that of their white counterpart.

Alternatively, perhaps a racist attitude and behavior is a matter of perception and not born out of reality, but out of the conscious "rational" decision-making processes of managers and owners alike. Baseball, like other big league sports, is a business. Consequently, one might argue that these "team businesses" want to be successful and that salaries are determined on a merit basis in order to ensure the quality of the team that will (as conventional baseball wisdom holds) increase the likelihood of success (i.e., win the pennant and the series). What else could explain why any individual player, such as third baseman Bobby Bonilla of the New York Mets, would be paid an estimated $6.3 million for the 1994 season? From a rational perspective, one might more plausibly argue that this approximately $39,000 a game salary is based more on the Met's organization thinking that Bonilla is the best at what he does and not that the organization has chosen to more fully integrate their team regardless of the cost.

THE CONTROVERSY: RACE VERSUS PERFORMANCE

This study does not claim to have the definitive answer as to whether race or performance is more important in the salary determination of major league baseball players. The results of the analyses conducted at various player positions indicates a modicum of support for the thesis that race plays an important role in the determination of salary. The significance of this, however, will be qualified below. Moreover, the analyses conducted indicate an overwhelming amount of support for the role that performance (i.e., merit) has in the salary determination process.

With respect to the RACE variable, the most significant findings were at the first base position. Almost irrespective of the performance measure utilized, a significant positive relationship between being white and being paid relatively larger salaries exist. The significance of these findings was tempered considerably for first base when analyzing the "old man" and "superstar" hypotheses. In the latter cases the importance of the RACE variable declined to the point of insignificance. General insignificance also characterized the findings for the RACE variable at the positions of second base, third base, shortstop, outfield, designated hitter, and the pitching positions of starter, reliever, and closer.

Worthy of note are the findings that the RACE variable produced for the position of catcher and utility player. In both cases, significant negative findings were found indicating a "reverse discrimination" situation whereby the salaries of minorities in these positions were significantly greater than that of white players. In the case of the catcher position two significant findings were recorded. First, the overall evaluation of players at this position when utilizing ORS performance measure and SAL89 was negative and significant. Second, when the superstar hypothesis was tested and SAL89 and ORS were utilized the same finding was uncovered. This would suggest that even when the best performers were taken out that this "reverse discrimination" against whites continued among the more average talented players. This same type of negative finding was uncovered when the superstar hypothesis was tested for the utility players.

The performance variables (THV and ORS for the positions of first base, second base, third base, shortstop, and outfield; ORS for the positions of catcher, designated hitter, and utility; PRAL, PRNL, and ATPV for the pitching positions of starter, reliever, and closer) far and away exceeded expectations.

The THV variable was always positive and significant when SAL89 was utilized (regardless of whether one was testing the overall set of players at a position or evaluating the old man hypothesis), with the sole exception of when the old man hypothesis was evaluated for second baseman and shortstops. In these two cases, however, the direction of the relationship remained positive. When SAL90 was incorporated the significance of the THV variable declined dramatically. The significant positive findings remained only for the positions of third base and outfield whether evaluating the overall set of players at each position or when testing the old man hypothesis. Moreover, the position of shortstop remained significant in the overall analysis, but not when testing the old man hypothesis. What one may conclude from this is that as more recent salary data (SAL90 rather than SAL89) are utilized, it becomes a more important consideration in 1991 salary determination than did the performance of the player. This is especially the case for the positions of first base, second base, and shortstop.

When ORS is utilized as the performance measure, the results become even more supportive of the view that salary determination is primarily merit based and that race has little if any impact. In the overall analysis of the positions of first base, second base, third base, shortstop, and outfield, the ORS measure performed exceptionally well regardless if the small pool (i.e., those players who also had THV statistics) or large pool (i.e., those players who did not necessarily have THV statistics as well) was incorporated. In brief, the overall analysis of the aforementioned positions were always positive and significant regardless of whether they were used in conjunction with SAL89 or SAL90. The sole exception to this generalization is in the case of the ORS-small pool when used in conjunction with SAL90 for the position of shortstop. Even then, this finding remained positive and closely approximated statistical significance.

When the old man and superstar hypotheses were tested for these five positions the results again revealed significant positive findings. Only the position of shortstop (when run with SAL90) did not record a significant positive relationship when testing the old man hypothesis. When the superstars were removed from the analysis, however, the performance of the ORS measure for these positions lessened considerably. The results at first and second base remained intact regardless of whether SAL89 or SAL90 was used. A positive result was also recorded for outfielders when SAL89 was utilized. This finding, however, went away when more recent salary data (SAL90) was incorporated.

ORS was the primary performance measure for the positions of catcher, designated hitter, and utility as well. The results here again indicate a high degree of support for viewpoint of "performance-based salary determination." In the case of catchers, ORS was positive and significant regardless of whether SAL89 or SAL90 was used and regardless of whether the overall set of players was tested or if the old man or superstar hypotheses were examined. In the case of utility players, these results remained intact except that the investigation of the superstar hypothesis did not reveal any significant findings for the performance variable. The position of designated hitter (one might remember from the discussion in chapter 3) suffered from having to few number of cases for any meaningful and reliable results to be collected.

The performance measures for the pitching positions also produced a considerable amount of support for the viewpoint that salary determination is highly dependent on previous performance and not race. The results for the RACE variable were mentioned earlier and need not be repeated here. It will be remembered from chapter 3 that PRAL and PRNL ultimately measure the number of games that a team should add or subtract from its "average" 81-81 record. Thus, significant positive relationships would suggest that the performance of a pitcher (i.e., that number of games contributed to the overall win total of the team) goes a long way in the salary determination process.

The PRAL measure performed well for starters regardless of whether SAL89 or SAL90 was utilized when assessing the overall set of starters or those included when the old man hypothesis was tested. The PRNL measure met with similar results for the pitching position of starter. A similar set or results occurred when assessing PRAL and PRNL for the pitching position of reliever. Moreover, PRNL recorded a significant positive finding when the superstar hypothesis was tested and SAL90 was incorporated into the model.

Remember that the ATPV measure allowed for cross-league comparison. Although always positive, generally speaking, the results of this measure were at best limited in terms of significance. There were some instances, however, where this measure was of high utility. For example, the results for the starters, regardless of whether the old man or superstar hypothesis were being tested, were most always significant and always positive, indicating that, *ceteris paribus*, the best starters (regardless of league) were generally paid larger salaries. The utility of the measure, however, declined when evaluating relievers. Here, ATPV was significant only when SAL90 was used to evaluate the overall set of relievers as well as that set which had the "old men" removed. Moreover, the only significant finding for closers occurred when evaluating the overall set of closers with SAL90 in the equation.[3]

The impact that the control variable YRS had in the analysis is probably the least consistent in terms of results. With respect to first base, the YRS variable recorded its only significant finding in the overall analysis when in the equation with THV and SAL89 it produced a negative effect. Explained by the presence of a few quality "superstars," this effect was not found when the superstar hypothesis (in which superstars are excluded from the analysis) was tested. YRS was found to be insignificant with respect to the second and third base positions.

With respect to shortstop the negative findings returned and continued into the superstar analysis. Although an apparent anomaly this is easily enough explained with the "fading superstar" aspect of the "old man" hypothesis. In this case several of the "old men" who were among the highest paid shortstops were beginning to see their salaries decline as their performance dropped off. The fact that a significant negative finding occurred when testing the superstar hypothesis led to the recognition that only four of the seven highly paid shortstops (who were seeing their salaries in relative decline) were removed from the analysis.

With respect to the outfield position, the YRS variable recorded two significant positive results. One of these occurred when the old man hypothesis was tested and several players that fell victim to the "fading superstar" aspect of the hypothesis were eliminated. When these fading superstars were removed from the analysis a truer picture of the relationship emerged, indicating that more years experience does lead to higher salaries, but that there are what may best be referred to as diminishing marginal returns. The testing of the superstar hypothesis also revealed a significant positive finding as fifteen of the twenty-one veterans qualified as "superstars" and were removed from the analysis.[4]

In chapter 3, the inclusion of the YRS variable had little impact on the results. The only significant finding was with respect to the old man hypothesis of the designated hitters, which is a questionable result for reasons elaborated on in chapter 3. Perhaps the most significant impact that YRS had in the pitching positions, not surprisingly, was with respect to the starters. Although two of the six equations in the overall analysis of starters evinced significant positive findings, five of the six equations became significant when the old man hypothesis was tested. These findings were highly suggestive of the fact that many veterans were experiencing the "fading superstar" phenomenon. This same positive effect was found in the testing of the old man hypothesis for closers.

The only significant findings with respect to the YRS variable for relievers was that a negative association was found when testing the overall group and the superstar hypothesis when ATPV was utilized as the performance measure and SAL90 the previous salary measure. In summary, the YRS variable was crucial to specifying the model to be tested. Although not uniform (i.e., always a positive or negative relationship), the results of the YRS variable indicated the degree to which the testing of the old man and superstar hypotheses were very important aspects of uncovering what is perhaps a more accurate picture of the underlying relationships.

The previous salary variables, SAL89 and SAL90, also merit a few paragraphs. Given the extremely good performance of these variables, it has become obvious that any study of salary determination must include this factor. Whether a one- or two-year lag is the most appropriate is perhaps debatable. The consistent results here, however, indicate that both one- and two-year lags are crucial inputs in model building to more fully understand the complex determinants of salary determination.

To be brief, the inclusion of previous salary is not really a debatable proposition. What is uncertain is whether one should incorporate a one- or two-year lag in salary. Consistent throughout this entire study, as has been noted repeatedly when going through the positional analyses, is that the more recent salary data (SAL90 instead of SAL89 in this case) is most always a more significant explanatory variable. This is so much the case that often the inclusion of the more recent salary data (SAL90) will result in any of the performance measures in the same equation becoming less significant (although typically remaining statistically significant).

Implications Stemming from the Empirical Results

In chapter 1, it was suggested that professional baseball has come under attack for its "racist" tendencies. The results of this analysis would suggest that this is in large part an unwarranted perception that, although it may be held by many, does not stand up to empirical analysis. The fact that race was a significant factor primarily for the position of first base does not suggest that these perceptions can be justified. Coupled with this are the findings that a sort of "reverse discrimination" appears to be occurring with the positions of catcher and utility player.

A second related implication is that court cases that are brought claiming that discrimination actively exists within the area of salary determination in professional baseball may well be disadvantaged by the results of this study. As was noted in chapter 1, the courts are receptive to the use of multiple regression analysis in supporting a case (or lack thereof) of discrimination in the salary determination process. However, the courts have not accepted analyses that treat jobs as fungible (i.e., different jobs with different functions shouldn't be treated as one). Given the findings of this study it is quite possible that only minority first baseman and white catchers and utility players may well be able to capitalize on the findings. Professional baseball players at the other positions cannot really capitalize on findings that are only significant for positions in which they do not play and are not part of the cohort.

The third, and perhaps largest, implication of this study is that performance-related variables have suggested that professional baseball is not, in reality, a microcosm of the larger society when it comes to the primary issue of race versus performance as being more influential in the process of salary determination. This is not to suggest that a certain degree of racism does not exist within America's national pastime. It is quite conceivable that there will always be individuals that are so caught up with the dominant social culture that attitudes and beliefs (if not behaviors) will begin to get in the way of the sport. Perhaps this goes a ways in explaining the Campanis and Schott affairs noted in chapter 1.

What is of larger importance and perhaps more deservedly emphasized is that if the dominant political and social culture in the United States (for all the good that change has brought about over time with respect to issues of race) does harbor a symbolic or aversive racist attitude that baseball is increasingly growing more distant from this belief. One can point to the fact that fewer black players have resulted in the push by the commissioner's office to "recruit" more minorities through the aforementioned RBI program, but in reality, the key determinants of salary determination have not really served to "push" minorities out of the game.

The latter points to the need to explore further the reasons behind why the number of minorities is indeed shrinking in major league baseball. Perhaps the role of future studies in this area of sport sociology should be concerned with this question than with documenting the existence (or lack thereof) of discrimination in salary determination among major league baseball players.

NOTES

1. See "Imperfect Game," *The Economist*, April 3, 1993, p. 88.

2. See "What's Behind the Shrinking Number of African-American Players?" *Ebony*, June, 1992, p. 112.

3. Remember that PRAL and PRNL were not evaluated for the closers due to the exceptionally low numbers of closers in each league.

4. One should keep in mind that the testing of the old man and superstar hypotheses is in reality a way of eliminating some of the influential extreme cases (i.e., non-statistical outliers) that may mask the effects of any of the variables in the analysis when the determinants of salary determination is evaluated.

Appendix: Player Attributes and Data

The following is a complete listing of the variables included in the analysis as well as the complete data for each of the players involved in the study.

VARIABLE KEY

A = TEAM NAME

1 = CHICAGO CUBS	10 = LOS ANGELES	19 = TORONTO
2 = MONTREAL	11 = SAN DIEGO	20 = CALIFORNIA
3 = NEW YORK METS	12 = SAN FRANCISCO	21 = CHICAGO WHITE SOX
4 = PHILADELPHIA	13 = BALTIMORE	22 = KANSAS CITY
5 = PITTSBURGH	14 = BOSTON	23 = MINNESOTA
6 = ST. LOUIS	15 = CLEVELAND	24 = OAKLAND
7 = ATLANTA	16 = DETROIT	25 = SEATTLE
8 = CINCINNATI	17 = MILWAUKEE	26 = TEXAS
9 = HOUSTON	18 = NEW YORK YANKEES	

B = PLAYER POSITION

1 = PITCHER	4 = SECOND BASE	7 = OUTFIELD
2 = CATCHER	5 = THIRD BASE	8 = DESIGNATED HITTER
3 = FIRST BASE	6 = SHORTSTOP	9 = UTILITY

C = RACE

1 = US BLACK	4 = NON-US LATINO
2 = NON-US BLACK	5 = WHITE
3 = US LATINO	

D = TOTAL YEARS EXPERIENCE
E = TOTAL AT BATS
F = TOTAL HITS
G = TOTAL DOUBLES
H = TOTAL TRIPLES
I = TOTAL HOME RUNS
J = TOTAL WALKS

K = TOTAL STOLEN BASES
L = TOTAL TIMES CAUGHT STEALING
M = TOTAL PUT OUTS
N = TOTAL ASSISTS
O = TOTAL ERRORS
P = TOTAL SALARY IN 1989
Q = TOTAL SALARY IN 1990
R = TOTAL SALARY IN 1991
S = LEAGUE
    1 = AMERICAN LEAGUE
    2 = NATIONAL LEAGUE
T = POSITION OF PITCHER
    1 = STARTER
    2 = RELIEVER
    3 = CLOSER
U = INNINGS PITCHED
V = EARNED RUN AVERAGE
W = RATIO
X = METROPOLITAN SIZE

	A	B	C	D	E	F	G	H	I	J	K	L	M	N	O	P	Q	R	S	T	U	V	W	X
BELL-G	1	7	2	9	562	149	25	0	21	32	3	2	226	4	5	1900	2035	2100	2	9	999	999	999	8066
BERRYHIL	1	2	5	4	53	10	4	0	1	5	0	0	9999	999	99	115	9999	230	2	9	999	999	999	8066
DASCENZO	1	7	5	3	241	61	9	5	1	21	15	6	174	2	0	9999	112	165	2	9	999	999	999	8066
DAWSON	1	7	1	15	529	164	28	5	27	42	16	2	250	10	5	2100	2100	3300	2	9	999	999	999	8066
DUNSTON	1	6	1	6	545	143	22	8	17	15	25	5	255	392	20	550	1250	2100	2	9	999	999	999	8066
GIRARDI	1	2	5	2	419	113	24	2	1	17	8	3	9999	999	99	68	115	225	2	9	999	999	999	8066
GRACE	1	3	5	3	589	182	32	1	9	59	15	6	1324	180	12	140	325	1200	2	9	999	999	999	8066
SALAZA-L	1	9	4	11	410	104	13	3	12	19	3	1	55	136	10	400	580	575	2	9	999	999	999	8066
SANDBERG	1	4	5	10	615	188	30	3	40	50	25	7	278	469	8	925	1625	2650	2	9	999	999	999	8066
SMITH-DW	1	7	1	2	290	76	15	0	6	28	11	6	139	4	2	68	180	225	2	9	999	999	999	8066
VILLAN-H	1	9	4	1	114	31	4	1	7	4	1	0	268	7	7	9999	100	120	2	9	999	999	999	8066
VIZCAI-J	1	6	4	2	51	14	1	1	0	4	1	1	9999	999	99	9999	9999	114	2	9	999	999	999	8066
WALTON-J	1	7	1	2	392	103	16	2	2	50	14	7	247	3	6	68	185	210	2	9	999	999	999	8066
ASSENMAC	1	1	5	5	999	999	99	99	99	999	99	99	9999	999	99	226	475	1000	2	2	103	280	111	8066
BIELECKI	1	1	5	7	999	999	99	99	99	999	99	99	9999	999	99	122	675	810	2	1	168	493	141	8066
BOSKIE-S	1	1	5	1	999	999	99	99	99	999	99	99	9999	999	99	9999	100	130	2	1	97	369	121	8066
HARKEY-M	1	1	1	2	999	999	99	99	99	999	99	99	9999	999	99	9999	104	220	2	1	173	326	113	8066
JACKSO-D	1	1	5	8	999	999	99	99	99	999	99	99	9999	999	99	1150	1150	2625	2	1	117	361	123	8066
LANCASTE	1	1	5	4	999	999	99	99	99	999	99	99	9999	999	99	120	9999	550	2	2	109	462	134	8066
MADDUX-G	1	1	5	5	999	999	99	99	99	999	99	99	9999	999	99	275	437	2400	2	1	237	346	120	8066
MCELRO-C	1	1	1	2	999	999	99	99	99	999	99	99	9999	999	99	9999	9999	111	2	2	14	771	219	8066
SMITH-DA	1	1	5	11	999	999	99	99	99	999	99	99	9999	999	99	1100	1100	1900	2	3	60	239	97	8066
CALDERON	2	7	2	7	607	166	44	2	14	51	32	16	268	7	7	380	925	2200	2	9	999	999	999	4141
DESHIELD	2	4	1	1	499	144	28	6	4	66	42	22	9999	999	99	9999	100	215	2	9	999	999	999	4141
FITZGE-M	2	2	2	8	313	76	18	1	9	60	8	1	9999	999	99	335	551	700	2	9	999	999	999	4141
FOLEY-T	2	9	5	8	164	35	2	1	0	12	0	1	9999	999	99	320	335	350	2	9	999	999	999	4141
GALARRAG	2	3	4	6	579	148	29	0	20	40	10	1	1300	94	10	865	1960	2367	2	9	999	999	999	4141
GRISSOM	2	7	1	2	288	74	14	2	3	27	22	2	165	5	2	68	103	140	2	9	999	999	999	4141
HASSEY-R	2	2	5	13	254	54	7	0	5	27	0	0	9999	999	99	600	560	400	2	9	999	999	999	4141

	A	B	C	D	E	F	G	H	I	J	K	L	M	N	O	P	Q	R	S	T	U	V	W	X
MARTIN-D	2	7	3	5	392	109	13	5	11	24	13	11	257	6	3	185	410	805	2	9	999	999	999	4141
OWEN-S	2	6	5	8	453	106	24	5	5	70	8	6	216	340	6	565	980	1033	2	9	999	999	999	4141
SANTOVEN	2	2	4	4	163	31	3	1	6	8	0	3	9999	999	99	98	205	282	2	9	999	999	999	4141
WALKER-L	2	7	5	2	419	101	18	3	19	49	21	7	249	12	4	9999	103	185	2	9	999	999	999	4141
WALLACH	2	5	5	11	626	185	37	5	21	42	6	9	128	309	21	965	1316	1906	2	9	999	999	999	4141
BARNES	2	1	5	1	999	999	99	99	99	999	99	99	9999	999	99	9999	9999	103	2	1	28	289	103	4141
BOYD-D	2	1	1	9	999	999	99	99	99	999	99	99	9999	999	99	550	1575	1500	2	1	190	293	103	4141
BURKE-T	2	1	5	6	999	999	99	99	99	999	99	99	9999	999	99	755	1855	2267	2	3	75	252	113	4141
FREY-S	2	1	5	2	999	999	99	99	99	999	99	99	9999	999	99	9999	100	166	2	2	55	210	120	4141
GARDNE-M	2	1	5	2	999	999	99	99	99	999	99	99	9999	999	99	9999	103	185	2	1	152	342	117	4141
JONES-BA	2	1	5	5	999	999	99	99	99	999	99	99	9999	999	99	9999	250	875	1	2	74	231	117	4141
LONG-BIL	2	1	5	5	999	999	99	99	99	999	99	99	9999	999	99	265	344	130	2	2	55	437	142	4141
MAHLER-R	2	1	5	12	999	999	99	99	99	999	99	99	9999	999	99	790	790	200	2	2	134	428	118	4141
MARTI-DE	2	1	4	15	999	999	99	99	99	999	99	99	9999	999	99	735	1472	3333	2	1	226	295	98	4141
NABHOLZ	2	1	5	1	999	999	99	99	99	999	99	99	9999	999	99	9999	100	120	2	1	70	283	99	4141
ROJAS-ME	2	1	2	1	999	999	99	99	99	999	99	99	9999	999	99	9999	100	115	2	2	40	360	135	4141
RUSKIN-S	2	1	5	1	999	999	99	99	99	999	99	99	9999	999	99	9999	100	147	2	2	75	275	114	4141
SAMPEN-B	2	1	5	1	999	999	99	99	99	999	99	99	9999	999	99	9999	100	161	2	9	90	299	129	4141
BOSTON-D	3	7	1	7	367	100	21	2	12	28	19	7	203	3	3	210	350	750	2	9	999	999	999	18087
BROOKS-H	3	7	1	11	568	151	28	1	20	33	2	5	255	9	10	950	1367	2317	2	9	999	999	999	18087
CARREON	3	7	5	4	188	47	12	0	10	15	1	0	87	1	0	70	125	215	2	9	999	999	999	18087
CERONE-R	3	2	5	16	139	42	6	0	2	5	0	0	9999	999	99	445	600	100	2	9	999	999	999	18087
COLEMA-V	3	7	1	6	497	145	18	9	6	35	77	17	244	12	5	775	1012	3112	2	9	999	999	999	18087
ELSTER-K	3	6	5	5	314	65	20	1	9	30	2	0	159	251	17	140	260	625	2	9	999	999	999	18087
HERR-T	3	4	5	12	547	143	26	3	5	50	7	1	275	349	7	825	825	1400	2	9	999	999	999	18087
JEFFER-G	3	4	5	4	604	171	40	3	15	46	11	2	219	278	12	100	200	425	2	9	999	999	999	18087
JOHNSO-H	3	9	5	9	590	144	37	3	23	69	34	8	52	159	20	772	1667	2167	2	9	999	999	999	18087
MAGADAN	3	3	5	5	451	148	28	6	6	74	2	1	830	71	2	170	395	1250	2	9	999	999	999	18087
MCREYN-K	3	7	5	8	521	140	23	1	24	71	9	2	237	14	3	1967	1267	2267	2	9	999	999	999	18087

	A	B	C	D	E	F	G	H	I	J	K	L	M	N	O	P	Q	R	S	T	U	V	W	X
MILLER-K	3	9	5	4	233	60	8	0	1	23	16	3	9999	999	99	85	122	260	2	9	999	999	999	18087
O'BRIE-C	3	2	5	5	213	38	10	3	0	21	0	0	9999	999	99	90	165	300	2	9	999	999	999	18087
SASSER-M	3	2	5	4	270	83	14	0	6	15	0	0	9999	999	99	95	155	505	2	9	999	999	999	18087
CONE-D	3	1	5	5	999	999	99	99	99	999	99	99	9999	999	99	332	1300	2350	2	1	211	323	103	18087
DARLING	3	1	5	8	999	999	99	99	99	999	99	99	9999	999	99	1882	1567	1967	2	1	126	450	131	18087
FERNAN-S	3	1	3	8	999	999	99	99	99	999	99	99	9999	999	99	795	1667	2167	2	1	179	346	101	18087
FRANC-JO	3	1	3	7	999	999	99	99	99	999	99	99	9999	999	99	1117	1805	2633	2	3	67	253	116	18087
GOODEN-D	3	1	5	7	999	999	99	99	99	999	99	99	9999	999	99	2417	1917	2467	2	1	232	383	118	18087
INNIS-J	3	1	5	4	999	999	99	99	99	999	99	99	9999	999	99	78	9999	155	2	2	26	239	103	18087
PENA-A	3	1	2	10	999	999	99	99	99	999	99	99	9999	999	99	875	975	1000	2	2	76	320	111	18087
VIOLA-F	3	1	5	9	999	999	99	99	99	999	99	99	9999	999	99	2767	1967	3167	2	1	249	267	104	18087
WHITEHUR	3	1	5	2	999	999	99	99	99	999	99	99	9999	999	99	9999	101	155	2	2	65	329	99	18087
BACKMAN	4	5	5	11	315	92	21	3	2	42	6	3	34	104	12	750	600	650	2	9	999	999	999	5899
BOOKER-R	4	9	1	4	131	29	5	2	0	15	3	1	9999	999	99	9999	110	140	2	9	999	999	999	5899
CAMPUSAN	4	7	2	2	85	18	1	0	2	6	1	0	40	1	1	9999	100	125	2	9	999	999	999	5899
CHAMBERL	4	7	1	1	46	13	3	1	2	1	4	0	9999	999	99	9999	100	105	2	9	999	999	999	5899
DAULTO-D	4	2	5	7	459	123	30	1	12	72	7	1	9999	999	99	225	470	1917	2	9	999	999	999	5899
DYKSTRA	4	7	5	6	590	192	35	3	9	89	33	5	439	7	6	575	725	2217	2	9	999	999	999	5899
HAYES-C	4	5	1	3	561	145	20	0	10	28	4	4	121	324	20	68	150	280	2	9	999	999	999	5899
HAYES-V	4	7	5	10	467	122	14	3	17	87	16	7	272	8	6	1325	2000	2200	2	9	999	999	999	5899
HOLLINS	4	5	5	1	114	21	0	0	5	10	0	1	9999	999	99	9999	100	116	2	9	999	999	999	5899
JONES-R	4	7	1	3	58	16	2	0	3	9	2	0	9999	999	99	74	120	130	2	9	999	999	999	5899
JORDAN-R	4	3	1	3	324	78	21	0	5	13	10	5	743	37	4	95	9999	250	2	9	999	999	999	5899
KRUK-J	4	9	5	5	443	129	25	8	7	69	0	0	141	2	2	450	680	1175	2	9	999	999	999	5899
LAKE-S	4	2	5	8	80	20	2	0	0	3	3	0	9999	999	99	280	340	390	2	9	999	999	999	5899
MURPHY-D	4	7	5	15	563	138	23	1	24	61	9	3	321	7	5	2000	2100	2500	2	9	999	999	999	5899
READY-R	4	9	5	8	217	53	9	1	1	29	3	2	32	2	0	370	530	600	2	9	999	999	999	5899
THON-D	4	6	5	12	552	141	20	4	8	37	12	5	222	439	25	525	1100	1250	2	9	999	999	999	5899
AKERFELD	4	1	5	4	999	999	99	99	99	999	99	99	9999	999	99	9999	109	165	2	2	93	377	118	5899

	A	B	C	D	E	F	G	H	I	J	K	L	M	N	O	P	Q	R	S	T	U	V	W	X
BOEVER-J	4	1	5	6	999	999	99	99	99	999	99	99	9999	999	99	124	300	700	2	2	88	336	130	5899
COMBS-P	4	1	5	2	999	999	99	99	99	999	99	99	9999	999	99	9999	132	220	2	1	183	407	132	5899
GREENE-T	4	1	5	2	999	999	99	99	99	999	99	99	9999	999	99	9999	102	115	2	1	51	508	133	5899
GRIMSLEY	4	1	5	2	999	999	99	99	99	999	99	99	9999	999	99	9999	105	116	2	1	57	330	144	5899
HOWELL-K	4	1	1	7	999	999	99	99	99	999	99	99	9999	999	99	925	717	1700	2	1	106	464	133	5899
LAPOINT	4	1	5	11	999	999	99	99	99	999	99	99	9999	999	99	825	850	100	1	1	157	411	136	5899
MCDOWE-R	4	1	5	6	999	999	99	99	99	999	99	99	9999	999	99	762	1400	2000	2	3	86	386	134	5899
MULHOL-T	4	1	5	4	999	999	99	99	99	999	99	99	9999	999	99	95	175	475	2	1	180	334	108	5899
WILLIA-M	4	1	5	5	999	999	99	99	99	999	99	99	9999	999	99	425	1125	1500	2	3	66	393	151	5899
BELL-J	5	6	5	5	583	148	28	7	7	65	10	6	260	459	22	85	180	360	2	9	999	999	999	2243
BONDS-B	5	7	1	5	519	156	32	3	33	93	53	13	338	14	6	360	850	2300	2	9	999	999	999	2243
BONILL-B	5	7	1	5	625	175	39	7	32	45	4	3	289	8	12	740	1250	2400	2	9	999	999	999	2243
KING-J	5	5	5	2	371	91	17	1	14	21	3	3	58	215	18	68	112	215	2	9	999	999	999	2243
LAVALLIE	5	2	5	7	279	72	15	0	3	31	0	3	9999	999	99	482	655	925	2	9	999	999	999	2243
LIND-J	5	4	2	4	514	134	28	5	1	35	8	0	330	449	7	180	270	575	2	9	999	999	999	2243
MARTIN-C	5	9	4	8	217	52	9	0	10	30	2	1	340	28	2	490	825	925	2	9	999	999	999	2243
MCLEND-L	5	7	1	4	110	18	3	0	2	14	1	0	9999	999	99	91	9999	260	2	9	999	999	999	2243
REDUS-G	5	3	1	9	227	56	15	3	6	33	11	5	447	35	6	500	500	600	2	9	999	999	999	2243
SLAUGHT	5	2	5	9	230	69	18	3	4	27	0	1	9999	999	99	650	650	767	2	9	999	999	999	2243
VAN SLYK	5	7	5	8	493	140	26	6	17	66	14	4	326	6	8	2160	1210	2150	2	9	999	999	999	2243
VARSHO-G	5	7	5	3	48	12	4	0	0	1	2	0	9999	62	99	9999	115	155	2	9	999	999	999	2243
WILKERSO	5	5	1	8	186	41	5	1	0	7	2	2	25	999	11	500	400	450	2	9	999	999	999	2243
BELINDA	5	1	5	2	999	999	99	99	99	999	99	99	9999	999	99	9999	100	175	2	2	58	355	120	2243
DRABEK-D	5	1	5	5	999	999	99	99	99	999	99	99	9999	999	99	325	1100	3350	2	1	231	276	97	2243
HEATON-N	5	1	5	9	999	999	99	99	99	999	99	99	9999	999	99	650	800	1000	2	1	146	345	113	2243
KIPPER-B	5	1	5	6	999	999	99	99	99	999	99	99	9999	999	99	230	525	825	2	2	62	302	105	2243
LANDRU-B	5	1	5	5	999	999	99	99	99	999	99	99	9999	999	99	75	302	820	2	2	71	213	113	2243
PATTER-B	5	1	5	5	999	999	99	99	99	999	99	99	9999	999	99	9999	200	325	2	2	94	295	106	2243
SMILEY-J	5	1	5	5	999	999	99	99	99	999	99	99	9999	999	99	230	840	1050	2	1	149	464	120	2243

	A	B	C	D	E	F	G	H	I	J	K	L	M	N	O	P	Q	R	S	T	U	V	W	X
SMITH-Z	5	1	5	7	999	999	99	99	99	999	99	99	9999	999	99	525	660	2225	2	1	215	255	103	2243
TOMLIN-R	5	1	5	1	999	999	99	99	99	999	99	99	9999	999	99	9999	100	120	2	1	77	255	87	2243
WALK-B	5	1	5	11	999	999	99	99	99	999	99	99	9999	999	99	800	850	850	2	1	129	375	122	2243
GEDMAN-R	6	2	5	11	119	24	7	0	1	20	0	0	9999	999	99	1150	920	150	2	9	999	999	999	2444
GILKEY-B	6	7	1	1	64	19	5	2	1	8	6	1	9999	999	99	9999	9999	125	2	9	999	999	999	2444
GUERRE-P	6	3	2	13	498	140	31	1	13	44	1	1	1083	73	13	1848	2083	2283	2	9	999	999	999	2444
HUDLER-R	6	7	5	8	220	62	11	2	7	12	18	10	89	3	2	90	135	300	2	9	999	999	999	2444
JOSE-F	6	7	2	3	426	113	16	1	11	24	12	6	254	7	6	9999	112	160	2	9	999	999	999	2444
LANKFORD	6	7	1	1	126	36	10	3	3	13	8	2	9999	999	99	9999	100	125	2	9	999	999	999	2444
OQUENDO	6	4	2	7	469	118	17	5	1	74	1	1	285	393	3	500	600	800	2	9	999	999	999	2444
PAGNOZZI	6	2	5	4	220	61	15	0	2	14	1	1	9999	999	99	90	110	310	2	9	999	999	999	2444
PENA-G	6	4	4	1	45	11	2	0	0	4	1	1	9999	999	99	9999	9999	120	2	9	999	999	999	2444
PERRY-G	6	8	1	8	465	118	22	2	8	39	17	4	9999	999	99	662	702	1167	2	9	999	999	999	2444
SMITH-O	6	6	1	13	512	130	21	1	1	61	32	6	212	378	12	2340	1975	2225	2	9	999	999	999	2444
THOMPS-M	6	7	1	7	418	91	14	7	6	39	25	5	232	4	7	480	867	1517	2	9	999	999	999	2444
WILSON-C	6	5	5	2	121	30	2	0	0	8	0	2	9999	999	99	9999	100	130	2	9	999	999	999	2444
ZEILE-T	6	2	5	2	495	121	25	3	15	67	2	4	9999	999	99	68	100	160	2	9	999	999	999	2444
AGOSTO-J	6	1	4	10	999	999	99	99	99	999	99	99	9999	999	99	545	950	1167	2	2	92	429	134	2444
DELEON-J	6	1	4	8	999	999	99	99	99	999	99	99	9999	999	99	662	1667	2367	2	1	182	443	128	2444
DIPINO-F	6	1	5	10	999	999	99	99	99	999	99	99	9999	999	99	452	650	850	2	2	81	456	138	2444
HILL-K	6	1	1	3	999	999	99	99	99	999	99	99	9999	999	99	70	100	155	2	1	78	549	129	2444
MAGRAN-J	6	1	5	4	999	999	99	99	99	999	99	99	9999	999	99	185	315	1025	2	1	203	359	120	2444
MOYER-J	6	1	5	5	999	999	99	99	99	999	99	99	9999	999	99	205	340	200	1	2	102	466	139	2444
SMITH-BR	6	1	5	10	999	999	99	99	99	999	99	99	9999	999	99	592	1633	2133	2	1	141	427	124	2444
SMITH-LE	6	1	1	11	999	999	99	99	99	999	99	99	9999	999	99	1425	1250	2667	2	3	68	210	102	2444
TERRY-S	6	1	5	5	999	999	99	99	99	999	99	99	9999	999	99	105	385	350	2	2	72	475	133	2444
TEWKSBUR	6	1	5	5	999	999	99	99	99	999	99	99	9999	999	99	9999	100	160	2	1	145	347	105	2444
BELLIARD	7	9	2	9	54	11	3	0	0	5	1	2	23	16	0	225	380	400	2	9	999	999	999	2834
BLAUSER	7	6	5	4	386	104	24	3	8	35	3	5	141	257	16	82	180	280	2	9	999	999	999	2834

	A	B	C	D	E	F	G	H	I	J	K	L	M	N	O	P	Q	R	S	T	U	V	W	X
BREAM-S	7	3	5	8	389	105	23	2	15	48	8	4	971	104	8	510	635	1600	2	9	999	999	999	2834
CABRER-F	7	3	2	2	137	38	5	1	7	5	1	0	9999	999	99	9999	102	110	2	9	999	999	999	2834
GANT-R	7	7	1	4	575	174	34	3	32	50	33	16	357	7	8	9999	150	1195	2	9	999	999	999	2834
GREGG-T	7	3	5	4	239	63	13	1	5	20	4	3	9999	999	99	82	180	265	2	9	999	999	999	2834
HEATH-M	7	2	5	13	370	100	18	2	7	19	7	6	9999	999	99	425	500	950	2	9	999	999	999	2834
JUSTICE	7	7	1	2	439	124	23	2	28	64	11	6	9999	999	99	9999	102	296	2	9	999	999	999	2834
LEMKE-M	7	5	5	3	239	54	13	0	0	21	0	1	9999	999	99	9999	105	138	2	9	999	999	999	2834
NIXON-O	7	7	1	8	231	58	6	2	1	28	50	13	149	5	1	177	315	585	2	9	999	999	999	2834
OLSON-G	7	2	5	2	298	78	12	1	7	30	1	1	9999	999	99	9999	100	185	2	9	999	999	999	2834
PENDLETO	7	5	1	7	447	103	20	2	6	30	7	5	91	248	19	710	1850	1750	2	9	999	999	999	2834
SANDER-D	7	7	1	2	133	21	2	2	3	13	8	2	9999	999	99	9999	9999	660	2	9	999	999	999	2834
SMITH-L	7	7	1	13	466	142	27	9	9	58	10	10	254	6	12	400	1458	2042	2	9	999	999	999	2834
TREADWAY	7	4	5	4	474	134	20	2	11	25	3	4	241	360	15	95	250	770	2	9	999	999	999	2834
AVERY-S	7	1	5	1	999	999	99	99	99	999	99	99	9999	999	99	9999	100	110	2	1	99	564	153	2834
BERENG-J	7	1	4	13	999	999	99	99	99	999	99	99	9999	999	99	625	750	900	1	2	100	341	130	2834
FREEMA-M	7	1	1	4	999	999	99	99	99	999	99	99	9999	999	99	71	9999	190	2	2	48	431	113	2834
GLAVIN-T	7	1	5	4	999	999	99	99	99	999	99	99	9999	999	99	117	312	697	2	1	214	428	131	2834
GRANT-M	7	1	5	6	999	999	99	99	99	999	99	99	9999	999	99	155	400	540	2	2	91	473	144	2834
LEIBRA-C	7	1	5	11	999	999	99	99	99	999	99	99	9999	999	99	1250	1150	1833	2	1	162	316	113	2834
PARRETT	7	1	5	5	999	999	99	99	99	999	99	99	9999	999	99	212	675	855	2	2	108	464	145	2834
MERCKER	7	1	5	2	999	999	99	99	99	999	99	99	9999	999	99	9999	102	117	2	2	48	317	128	2834
SMITH-PE	7	1	5	4	999	999	99	99	99	999	99	99	9999	999	99	125	190	365	2	1	77	479	118	2834
SMOLTZ-J	7	1	5	3	999	999	99	99	99	999	99	99	9999	999	99	86	247	335	2	1	231	385	116	2834
BENZINGE	8	3	5	4	376	95	14	2	5	19	3	4	707	52	6	160	325	705	2	9	999	999	999	1744
BRAGGS-G	8	7	1	5	314	88	14	1	9	38	8	7	191	11	7	185	575	825	2	9	999	999	999	1744
DAVIS-E	8	7	1	7	453	118	26	2	24	60	21	3	257	11	2	1555	2100	3600	2	9	999	999	999	1744
DORAN-B	8	4	5	9	403	121	29	2	7	79	23	9	198	302	6	933	934	2833	2	9	999	999	999	1744
DUNCAN-M	8	4	2	5	435	133	22	11	10	24	13	7	245	287	15	200	375	925	2	9	999	999	999	1744
HATCHE-B	8	7	1	7	504	139	28	5	5	33	30	10	124	250	1	450	690	1200	2	9	999	999	999	1744

	A	B	C	D	E	F	G	H	I	J	K	L	M	N	O	P	Q	R	S	T	U	V	W	X
LARKIN-B	8	6	1	5	614	185	25	6	7	49	30	5	254	469	17	342	835	2100	2	9	999	999	999	1744
MORRIS-H	8	3	5	3	309	105	22	3	7	21	9	3	9999	999	99	9999	100	180	2	9	999	999	999	1744
OLIVER-J	8	2	5	3	364	84	23	0	8	37	1	1	9999	999	99	68	107	185	2	9	999	999	999	1744
ONEILL-P	8	7	5	6	503	136	28	0	16	53	13	11	271	12	2	215	692	975	2	9	999	999	999	1744
QUINON-L	8	9	4	6	145	35	7	0	2	13	1	0	12	41	1	85	150	300	2	9	999	999	999	1744
REED-JEF	8	2	5	7	175	44	8	1	3	24	0	0	9999	999	99	175	345	600	2	9	999	999	999	1744
SABO-C	8	5	5	3	567	153	38	2	25	61	25	10	70	273	12	155	260	1250	2	9	999	999	999	1744
WINNINGH	8	7	1	7	160	41	8	5	3	14	6	4	89	3	0	230	337	437	2	9	999	999	999	1744
ARMSTR-J	8	1	5	3	999	999	99	99	99	999	99	99	9999	999	99	9999	107	215	2	1	166	342	117	1744
BROWNING	8	1	5	7	999	999	99	99	99	999	99	99	9999	999	99	1025	2125	2650	2	1	227	380	115	1744
CARMAN-D	8	1	5	8	999	999	99	99	99	999	99	99	9999	999	99	575	540	300	2	2	86	415	115	1744
CHARLTON	8	1	5	3	999	999	99	99	99	999	99	99	9999	999	99	72	175	625	2	2	154	274	120	1744
DIBBLE-R	8	1	5	3	999	999	99	99	99	999	99	99	9999	999	99	85	200	475	2	2	98	174	89	1744
LAYANA-T	8	1	5	1	999	999	99	99	99	999	99	99	9999	999	99	9999	100	140	2	2	80	349	132	1744
MYERS-R	8	1	5	6	999	999	99	99	99	999	99	99	9999	999	99	300	875	2000	2	3	86	208	104	1744
POWER-T	8	1	5	10	999	999	99	99	99	999	99	99	9999	999	99	199	620	500	2	2	51	366	117	1744
RIJO-J	8	1	2	7	999	999	99	99	99	999	99	99	9999	999	99	457	700	2333	2	1	197	270	106	1744
SCUDDER	8	1	5	2	999	999	99	99	99	999	99	99	9999	999	99	68	107	140	2	2	71	490	134	1744
BIGGIO-C	9	2	5	3	555	153	24	2	4	53	25	11	9999	999	99	78	230	437	2	9	999	999	999	3711
CAMINITI	9	5	5	4	541	131	20	2	4	48	9	4	118	243	21	103	240	665	2	9	999	999	999	3711
CANDAELE	9	9	5	4	262	75	8	6	3	31	7	5	66	1	0	9999	112	350	2	9	999	999	999	3711
DAVIDS-M	9	7	5	5	130	38	5	1	1	10	0	3	103	1	2	9999	130	300	2	9	999	999	999	3711
FINLEY-S	9	7	5	2	464	119	16	4	3	32	22	9	298	4	7	68	125	260	2	9	999	999	999	3711
MCLEMORE	9	9	1	5	60	9	2	0	0	4	1	0	21	22	0	9999	9999	165	2	9	999	999	999	3711
NICHLOLS	9	2	1	5	49	10	3	0	0	8	0	0	9999	999	99	9999	100	123	2	9	999	999	999	3711
OBERKFEL	9	9	5	14	150	31	6	1	1	15	1	1	12	31	3	725	625	675	2	9	999	999	999	3711
RAMIREZ	9	6	2	11	445	116	19	3	2	24	10	5	190	321	25	1025	1012	1206	2	9	999	999	999	3711
ROHDE-D	9	4	5	1	98	18	4	0	0	9	0	0	9999	999	99	9999	100	118	2	9	999	999	999	3711
YELDING	9	7	1	2	511	130	9	5	1	39	64	25	230	5	7	68	110	260	2	9	999	999	999	3711

	A	B	C	D	E	F	G	H	I	J	K	L	M	N	O	P	Q	R	S	T	U	V	W	X
CLANCY-J	9	1	5	14	999	999	99	99	99	999	99	99	9999	999	99	1150	9999	1150	2	2	76	651	161	3711
DESHAISE	9	1	5	7	999	999	99	99	99	999	99	99	9999	999	99	470	1075	2100	2	1	209	378	120	3711
HARNISCH	9	1	5	3	999	999	99	99	99	999	99	99	9999	999	99	70	120	225	1	1	188	434	132	3711
HENRY-DW	9	1	1	7	999	999	99	99	99	999	99	99	9999	999	99	9999	120	140	2	2	38	563	155	3711
HERNAN-X	9	1	3	2	999	999	99	99	99	999	99	99	9999	999	99	9999	100	122	2	2	62	462	127	3711
JONES-JI	9	1	5	5	999	999	99	99	99	999	99	99	9999	999	99	9999	190	190	1	2	50	630	173	3711
PORTUGAL	9	1	3	6	999	999	99	99	99	999	99	99	9999	999	99	95	217	705	2	1	196	362	118	3711
SCHILLIN	9	1	5	3	999	999	99	99	99	999	99	99	9999	999	99	9999	103	125	1	2	46	254	112	3711
SCOTT-M	9	1	5	12	999	999	99	99	99	999	99	99	9999	999	99	1325	2187	2337	2	1	205	381	114	3711
BUTLER-B	10	7	5	10	622	192	20	9	3	90	51	19	420	4	6	900	1100	2833	2	9	999	999	999	14532
CARTER-G	10	2	5	17	244	62	10	0	9	25	1	1	9999	999	99	2199	1000	500	2	9	999	999	999	14532
DANIEL-K	10	7	1	5	450	133	23	1	27	68	4	3	207	13	3	325	600	2025	2	9	999	999	999	14532
GONZAL-J	10	7	4	6	99	23	5	3	2	6	3	1	62	1	0	90	150	260	2	9	999	999	999	14532
GRIFFI-A	10	6	2	15	461	97	11	3	1	29	6	3	221	382	26	1000	1000	900	2	9	999	999	999	14532
GWYNN-C	10	9	1	4	141	40	2	1	5	7	0	1	9999	999	99	80	125	260	2	9	999	999	999	14532
HARRIS-L	10	9	1	3	431	131	16	4	2	29	15	10	77	133	9	71	145	315	2	9	999	999	999	14532
LYONS-B	10	2	5	5	85	20	0	0	3	2	0	0	9999	999	99	115	9999	220	2	9	999	999	999	14532
MURRAY-E	10	3	1	14	558	184	22	3	26	82	8	5	1180	113	10	2331	2512	2562	2	9	999	999	999	14532
SAMUEL-J	10	4	2	8	492	119	24	3	13	51	38	20	194	258	13	1450	1350	1575	2	9	999	999	999	14532
SCIOSCIA	10	2	5	11	435	115	25	0	12	55	4	1	9999	999	99	1100	1233	2183	2	9	999	999	999	14532
SHARPERS	10	5	1	4	357	106	14	2	3	46	15	6	70	153	12	90	135	307	2	9	999	999	999	14532
STRAWBER	10	7	1	8	542	150	18	1	37	70	15	8	268	10	3	1445	1850	3800	2	9	999	999	999	14532
BELCHER	10	1	5	4	999	999	99	99	99	999	99	99	9999	999	99	225	450	900	2	1	153	400	109	14532
CANDELAR	10	1	3	16	999	999	99	99	99	999	99	99	9999	999	99	800	830	830	1	2	79	395	123	14532
CREWS-T	10	1	5	4	999	999	99	99	99	999	99	99	9999	999	99	130	215	670	2	2	107	277	103	14532
GOTT-JIM	10	1	5	9	999	999	99	99	99	999	99	99	9999	999	99	600	870	1725	2	2	62	290	135	14532
GROSS-KE	10	1	5	8	999	999	99	99	99	999	99	99	9999	999	99	890	997	2217	2	1	163	457	132	14532
HARTLEY	10	1	5	2	999	999	99	99	99	999	99	99	9999	999	99	9999	100	165	2	2	79	295	102	14532
HOWELL-J	10	1	5	11	999	999	99	99	99	999	99	99	9999	999	99	925	1025	1050	2	3	66	218	116	14532

	A	B	C	D	E	F	G	H	I	J	K	L	M	N	O	P	Q	R	S	T	U	V	W	X
MARTIN-R	10	1	4	3	999	999	99	99	99	999	99	99	9999	999	99	85	150	485	2	1	234	292	101	14532
MORGAN-M	10	1	5	10	999	999	99	99	99	999	99	99	9999	999	99	450	650	650	2	1	211	375	120	14532
OJEDA-B	10	1	5	11	999	999	99	99	99	999	99	99	9999	999	99	1058	1233	1633	2	2	118	366	126	14532
ABNER-S	11	7	5	4	184	45	9	0	1	9	2	3	108	1	1	77	105	180	2	9	999	999	999	2498
ALDRETE	11	9	5	5	161	39	7	1	1	37	1	2	51	4	1	202	297	250	2	9	999	999	999	2498
BARRET-M	11	4	5	9	159	36	4	0	0	15	4	0	90	147	2	775	1000	100	2	9	999	999	999	2498
CLARK-JE	11	3	1	3	101	27	4	1	5	5	0	0	9999	999	99	9999	100	127	2	9	999	999	999	2498
FARIES-P	11	4	5	1	37	7	1	0	0	4	0	19	9999	999	99	9999	999	100	2	9	999	999	999	2498
FERNAN-T	11	6	2	8	635	175	27	17	4	71	26	13	297	480	9	1400	1500	2100	2	9	999	999	999	2498
GWYNN-T	11	7	1	9	573	177	29	10	4	44	17	8	327	11	5	1132	1067	2325	2	9	999	999	999	2498
JACKSO-D	11	7	1	5	113	29	3	0	3	5	3	0	63	1	1	90	145	260	2	9	999	999	999	2498
HOWARD-T	11	7	1	1	44	12	2	0	0	0	0	1	9999	999	99	9999	9999	105	2	9	999	999	999	2498
LAMPKIN	11	2	5	2	63	14	0	1	1	4	0	1	9999	999	99	9999	9999	107	2	9	999	999	999	2498
MCGRIFF	11	3	1	5	557	167	21	1	35	94	5	3	1246	126	6	325	1450	2750	2	9	999	999	999	2498
PRESLEY	11	5	5	7	541	131	34	1	19	29	1	1	101	231	25	595	720	500	2	9	999	999	999	2498
ROBERT-B	11	9	1	4	556	172	36	3	9	55	46	12	160	8	3	74	195	875	2	9	999	999	999	2498
SANTIAGO	11	2	2	5	344	93	8	5	11	27	5	1	9999	999	99	345	1250	1650	2	9	999	999	999	2498
STEPHE-P	11	3	5	2	182	38	9	1	4	30	2	1	9999	999	99	9999	100	130	2	9	999	999	999	2498
TEMPLE-G	11	6	1	15	505	125	25	3	9	24	1	4	214	367	26	600	650	550	2	9	999	999	999	2498
ANDERSEN	11	1	5	13	999	999	99	99	99	999	99	99	9999	999	99	450	1065	2000	2	2	73	195	105	2498
BENES-A	11	1	5	2	999	999	99	99	99	999	99	99	9999	999	99	68	130	235	2	1	192	360	116	2498
GARDEN-W	11	1	5	7	999	999	99	99	99	999	99	99	9999	999	99	285	500	575	1	2	77	489	133	2498
HAMMAKER	11	1	5	9	999	999	99	99	99	999	99	99	9999	999	99	879	100	100	2	2	86	436	116	2498
HARRIS-G	11	1	5	3	999	999	99	99	99	999	99	99	9999	999	99	71	175	342	2	2	117	230	111	2498
HURST-B	11	1	5	11	999	999	99	99	99	999	99	99	9999	999	99	1733	1633	1883	2	1	223	314	101	2498
LEFFERTS	11	1	5	8	999	999	99	99	99	999	99	99	9999	999	99	600	1267	2042	2	3	78	252	104	2498
MADDUX-M	11	1	5	5	999	999	99	99	99	999	99	99	9999	999	99	9999	9999	110	2	2	20	653	126	2498
RASMUSSE	11	1	5	8	999	999	99	99	99	999	99	99	9999	999	99	802	802	805	2	1	187	451	135	2498
RODRIG-R	11	1	3	1	999	999	99	99	99	999	99	99	9999	999	99	9999	100	115	2	2	47	283	130	2498

	A	B	C	D	E	F	G	H	I	J	K	L	M	N	O	P	Q	R	S	T	U	V	W	X
WHITSON	11	1	5	14	999	999	99	99	99	999	99	99	9999	999	99	1050	1125	1325	2	1	228	260	104	2498
ANDERS-D	12	9	5	8	100	35	5	1	1	3	1	2	17	38	0	420	500	600	2	9	999	999	999	6253
BASS-K	12	7	1	9	214	54	9	1	7	14	2	2	88	2	3	940	1250	2000	2	9	999	999	999	6253
BENJAMIN	12	6	5	2	56	12	3	1	2	3	1	0	9999	999	99	9999	105	110	2	9	999	999	999	6253
CLARK-W	12	3	5	5	600	177	25	5	19	62	8	2	1456	119	12	1125	2275	3750	2	9	999	999	999	6253
DECKER-S	12	2	5	1	54	16	2	0	3	1	0	0	9999	999	99	9999	9999	100	2	9	999	999	999	6253
FELDER-M	12	7	1	6	237	65	7	2	3	22	20	9	165	8	5	107	275	200	2	9	999	999	999	6253
KENNED-T	12	2	5	13	303	84	22	0	2	31	1	2	9999	999	99	850	850	500	2	9	999	999	999	6253
KINGERY	12	9	5	5	207	61	7	1	0	12	6	1	126	7	3	9999	175	362	2	9	999	999	999	6253
LITTON-G	12	7	5	2	204	50	9	1	1	11	1	0	9999	999	99	68	122	165	2	9	999	999	999	6253
MCGEE-W	12	7	1	9	614	199	35	7	3	48	31	9	413	13	17	1400	1500	3562	2	9	999	999	999	6253
MITCHE-K	12	7	1	6	524	152	24	2	35	58	4	7	295	9	9	560	2108	3750	2	9	999	999	999	6253
PARKER-R	12	7	5	1	107	26	5	0	2	10	6	1	9999	999	99	9999	9999	115	2	9	999	999	999	6253
THOMPS-R	12	4	5	5	498	122	22	3	15	34	14	4	287	441	8	535	900	1500	2	9	999	999	999	6253
URIBE-J	12	6	2	7	415	103	8	6	1	29	5	9	182	373	20	687	983	1333	2	9	999	999	999	6253
WILLIA-M	12	5	5	4	617	171	27	2	33	33	7	4	140	306	19	95	215	600	2	9	999	999	999	6253
BLACK-B	12	1	5	10	999	999	99	99	99	999	99	99	9999	999	99	675	850	1750	1	1	206	357	106	6253
BRANTLEY	12	1	5	3	999	999	99	99	99	999	99	99	9999	999	99	78	195	425	2	3	86	156	117	6253
BURKETT	12	1	5	2	999	999	99	99	99	999	99	99	9999	999	99	9999	100	225	2	1	204	379	117	6253
DOWNS-K	12	1	5	5	999	999	99	99	99	999	99	99	9999	999	99	315	443	525	2	1	63	343	111	6253
GARRELTS	12	1	5	9	999	999	99	99	99	999	99	99	9999	999	99	705	1400	2400	2	1	182	415	130	6253
LACOSS-M	12	1	5	13	999	999	99	99	99	999	99	99	9999	999	99	800	1190	1450	2	1	77	394	132	6253
REUSCHEL	12	1	5	18	999	999	99	99	99	999	99	99	9999	999	99	987	1000	1350	2	1	87	393	139	6253
RIGHETTI	12	1	5	11	999	999	99	99	99	999	99	99	9999	999	99	1450	1550	2500	1	3	53	357	129	6253
ROBINS-D	12	1	5	13	999	999	99	99	99	999	99	99	9999	999	99	900	1086	1450	2	1	157	457	123	6253
WILSON-T	12	1	5	3	999	999	99	99	99	999	99	99	9999	999	99	9999	122	205	2	1	110	400	112	6253
ANDERS-B	13	7	5	3	234	54	5	2	3	31	15	2	149	3	2	9999	120	165	1	9	999	999	999	2382
DEVEREAU	13	7	1	4	367	88	18	1	12	28	13	12	281	4	5	80	145	210	1	9	999	999	999	2382
EVANS-D	13	8	5	19	445	111	18	3	13	67	3	4	9999	999	99	1100	1500	860	1	9	999	999	999	2382

	A	B	C	D	E	F	G	H	I	J	K	L	M	N	O	P	Q	R	S	T	U	V	W	X
GOMEZ-L	13	5	4	1	39	9	0	0	0	8	0	0	9999	999	99	9999	9999	102	1	9	999	999	999	2382
HOILES-C	13	2	5	2	67	12	3	0	1	5	0	0	9999	999	99	9999	9999	107	1	9	999	999	999	2382
HORN-S	13	8	1	4	246	61	13	0	14	32	0	0	9999	999	99	9999	120	175	1	9	999	999	999	2382
HULETT-T	13	9	5	7	153	39	7	1	3	15	1	0	17	56	3	150	207	327	1	9	999	999	999	2382
MELVIN-B	13	2	5	6	301	73	14	1	5	11	0	1	9999	999	99	230	350	650	1	9	999	999	999	2382
MILLIGAN	13	3	1	4	362	96	20	1	20	88	6	3	846	87	9	75	155	330	1	9	999	999	999	2382
ORSULAK	13	3	5	7	413	111	14	3	11	46	6	8	267	5	3	260	610	1100	1	9	999	999	999	2382
RIPKEN-B	13	7	5	4	406	118	28	1	3	28	5	2	250	366	8	100	215	700	1	9	999	999	999	2382
RIPKEN-C	13	4	5	10	600	150	28	4	21	82	3	1	242	435	3	2467	1367	2333	1	9	999	999	999	2382
WHITT-E	13	6	5	14	180	31	8	0	2	23	0	2	9999	999	99	800	1200	300	1	9	999	999	999	2382
WORTHING	13	5	1	3	425	96	17	0	8	63	1	2	90	218	18	68	207	207	1	9	999	999	999	2382
BALLAR-J	13	1	5	4	999	999	99	99	99	999	99	99	9999	999	99	97	290	465	1	2	133	493	133	2382
BAUTISTA	13	1	2	3	999	999	99	99	99	999	99	99	9999	999	99	120	120	138	1	2	26	405	118	2382
DUBOIS-B	13	1	5	2	999	999	99	99	99	999	99	99	9999	999	99	68	9999	100	1	1	58	509	143	2382
JOHNSO-D	13	1	5	3	999	999	99	99	99	999	99	99	9999	999	99	70	113	200	1	1	180	410	121	2382
KILGUS-P	13	1	5	4	999	999	99	99	99	999	99	99	9999	999	99	130	9999	160	1	2	16	606	149	2382
MCDONA-B	13	1	5	2	999	999	99	99	99	999	99	99	9999	999	99	9999	262	442	1	1	118	243	93	2382
MESA-J0	13	1	2	2	999	999	99	99	99	999	99	99	9999	999	99	9999	100	107	1	1	46	386	125	2382
OLSON-G	13	1	5	3	999	999	99	99	99	999	99	99	9999	999	99	70	305	505	1	3	74	242	110	2382
ROBIN-JM	13	1	5	4	999	999	99	99	99	999	99	99	9999	999	99	175	410	575	1	1	145	596	146	2382
WILLIA-M	13	1	5	4	999	999	99	99	99	999	99	99	9999	999	99	120	285	685	1	2	85	221	98	2382
BOGGS-W	14	5	5	9	619	187	44	5	6	87	0	0	108	241	20	1775	1900	2700	1	9	999	999	999	4172
BRUNANSK	14	7	5	10	518	132	27	5	16	66	5	10	304	8	7	1240	1500	2500	1	9	999	999	999	4172
BURKS-E	14	7	1	4	588	174	33	8	21	48	9	11	324	7	2	275	670	1825	1	9	999	999	999	4172
CLARK-JA	14	3	5	16	334	89	12	1	25	104	4	3	855	69	6	2000	2000	2900	1	9	999	999	999	4172
GREENWEL	14	7	5	6	610	181	30	6	14	65	8	7	287	13	7	550	1225	2550	1	9	999	999	999	4172
KUTCHER	14	9	5	5	74	17	4	1	1	13	3	3	41	0	0	90	185	250	1	9	999	999	999	4172
MARSHALL	14	9	5	10	275	71	14	2	10	11	0	2	319	31	2	1100	1100	1300	1	9	999	999	999	4172
MARZANO	14	2	5	4	83	20	4	0	0	5	0	1	9999	999	99	9999	125	190	1	9	999	999	999	4172

	A	B	C	D	E	F	G	H	I	J	K	L	M	N	O	P	Q	R	S	T	U	V	W	X
NAEHRING	14	6	5	1	85	23	6	0	2	8	0	0	9999	999	99	9999	100	125	1	9	999	999	999	4172
PENA-TO	14	2	4	11	491	129	19	1	7	43	8	6	9999	999	99	1175	1700	2300	1	9	999	999	999	4172
QUINTANA	14	3	2	3	512	147	28	0	7	52	1	2	1188	137	17	71	160	285	1	9	999	999	999	4172
REED-JOD	14	9	5	4	598	173	45	0	5	75	4	4	215	374	6	175	350	800	1	9	999	999	999	4172
RIVERA-L	14	6	4	5	346	78	20	0	7	25	4	3	186	310	18	105	310	565	1	9	999	999	999	4172
ROMINE-K	14	7	5	6	136	37	7	0	2	12	4	0	81	0	2	150	260	355	1	9	999	999	999	4172
BOLTON-T	14	1	1	4	999	999	99	99	99	999	99	99	9999	999	99	9999	135	270	1	1	119	338	121	4172
CLEMENS	14	1	1	7	999	999	99	99	99	999	99	99	9999	999	99	2300	2700	2600	1	1	228	193	100	4172
DARWIN-D	14	1	1	13	999	999	99	99	99	999	99	99	9999	999	99	815	1325	3250	2	2	162	221	95	4172
FOSSAS-T	14	1	1	3	999	999	99	99	99	999	99	99	9999	999	99	68	9999	125	1	2	29	644	166	4172
GRAY-JEF	14	1	1	2	999	999	99	99	99	999	99	99	9999	999	99	325	100	155	1	2	50	444	123	4172
HARRI-GA	14	1	1	10	999	999	99	99	99	999	99	99	9999	999	99	417	615	1300	1	1	184	400	131	4172
HESKETH	14	1	1	7	999	999	99	99	99	999	99	99	9999	999	99	9999	110	465	2	2	34	529	124	4172
KIECKER	14	1	1	1	999	999	99	99	99	999	99	99	9999	999	99	387	100	167	1	1	152	397	123	4172
LAMP-D	14	1	1	14	999	999	99	99	99	999	99	99	9999	999	99	1275	725	750	1	2	105	468	125	4172
REARDON	14	1	1	12	999	999	99	99	99	999	99	99	9999	999	99	250	1633	2533	1	3	51	316	103	4172
YOUNG-MA	14	1	1	7	999	999	99	99	99	999	99	99	9999	999	99	9999	1037	2267	1	1	225	351	124	4172
ALOMAR-S	15	2	2	3	445	129	26	2	9	25	4	1	9999	999	99	9999	115	345	1	9	999	999	999	2760
BAERGA-C	15	5	5	1	312	81	17	2	7	16	0	2	286	382	10	9999	100	165	1	9	999	999	999	2760
BROWNE-J	15	4	4	5	513	137	26	5	6	72	12	7	9999	999	99	147	310	800	1	9	999	999	999	2760
COLE-ALE	15	7	1	1	227	68	5	4	0	28	40	9	9999	999	99	9999	100	155	1	9	999	999	999	2760
FERMIN-F	15	6	4	4	414	106	13	2	1	26	3	3	213	421	16	85	205	575	1	9	999	999	999	2760
HERNAN-K	15	3	5	17	130	26	2	0	1	14	0	0	340	20	2	2000	1750	1750	1	9	999	999	999	2760
JACOBY-B	15	5	5	9	553	162	24	4	14	63	1	4	44	158	4	962	1012	1150	1	9	999	999	999	2760
JAMES-CH	15	8	5	5	528	158	32	4	12	31	4	3	9999	999	99	400	620	1367	1	9	999	999	999	2760
MANTO-JE	15	3	5	1	76	17	5	1	2	21	0	1	9999	999	99	9999	9999	110	1	9	999	999	999	2760
SKINNER	15	2	5	8	139	35	4	1	2	7	0	0	9999	999	99	200	280	550	1	9	999	999	999	2760
WARD-TU	15	7	5	1	46	16	2	1	1	3	3	0	9999	999	99	9999	100	100	1	9	999	999	999	2760
WEBSTER	15	7	5	8	437	110	20	6	12	20	22	6	330	1	3	550	645	750	1	9	999	999	999	2760

	A	B	C	D	E	F	G	H	I	J	K	L	M	N	O	P	Q	R	S	T	U	V	W	X
CANDIOTT	15	1	5	7	999	999	99	99	99	999	99	99	9999	999	99	512	1062	2500	1	1	202	365	119	2760
FARRELL	15	1	5	4	999	999	99	99	99	999	99	99	9999	999	99	175	320	410	1	1	96	428	132	2760
JONES-D	15	1	5	6	999	999	99	99	99	999	99	99	9999	999	99	307	950	2050	1	3	84	256	96	2760
KING-ER	15	1	5	5	999	999	99	99	99	999	99	99	9999	999	99	165	455	1450	1	1	151	328	108	2760
NAGY-CH	15	1	5	1	999	999	99	99	99	999	99	99	9999	999	99	9999	100	115	1	1	45	591	158	2760
NICHOLS	15	1	5	3	999	999	99	99	99	999	99	99	9999	999	99	73	9999	125	1	1	16	788	180	2760
OLIN-ST	15	1	5	2	999	999	99	99	99	999	99	99	9999	999	99	9999	116	175	1	2	92	341	125	2760
OROSCO-J	15	1	3	11	999	999	99	99	99	999	99	99	9999	999	99	975	940	850	1	2	64	390	134	2760
SEANEZ-R	15	1	4	2	999	999	99	99	99	999	99	99	9999	999	99	9999	9999	106	1	2	27	560	158	2760
SWINDELL	15	1	5	5	999	999	99	99	99	999	99	99	9999	999	99	295	890	2025	1	1	214	440	123	2760
BERGMA-D	16	8	5	15	205	57	10	1	2	33	3	2	9999	999	99	437	525	575	1	9	999	999	999	4665
CUYLER-M	16	7	1	1	51	13	3	1	0	5	1	2	243	14	8	9999	9999	100	1	9	999	999	999	4665
DEER-R	16	7	5	7	440	92	15	1	27	64	2	3	1190	14	14	760	885	1967	1	9	999	999	999	4665
FIELDER	16	3	1	5	573	159	25	1	51	90	0	1	9999	111	99	9999	1250	1750	1	9	999	999	999	4665
FRYMAN-T	16	5	5	1	232	69	11	1	9	17	3	3	290	999	8	9999	100	150	1	9	999	999	999	4665
INCAVIGL	16	7	3	5	529	123	27	0	24	45	3	4	288	12	5	475	825	500	1	9	999	999	999	4665
MOSEBY-L	16	7	1	11	431	107	16	5	14	48	17	5	69	9	20	1300	1400	1600	1	9	999	999	999	4665
PHILLIPS	16	9	1	9	573	144	23	5	8	99	19	9	9999	200	99	375	867	1567	1	9	999	999	999	4665
SALAS-M	16	2	5	7	164	38	3	0	9	21	0	0	146	999	4	9999	225	450	1	9	999	999	999	4665
SHELBY-J	16	7	1	10	246	61	10	3	4	10	4	5	9999	5	99	550	100	525	1	9	999	999	999	4665
TETTLETO	16	2	5	7	444	99	21	2	15	106	2	4	232	999	14	300	825	1600	1	9	999	999	999	4665
TRAMMELL	16	6	5	14	559	170	37	1	14	68	12	10	286	409	6	1300	1800	2200	1	9	999	999	999	4665
WHITAKER	16	4	1	14	472	112	22	2	18	74	8	2	9999	372	99	1025	1800	2000	1	9	999	999	999	4665
CERUTTI	16	1	5	6	999	999	99	99	99	999	99	99	9999	999	99	417	762	800	1	1	140	476	138	4665
GIBSON-P	16	1	5	3	999	999	99	99	99	999	99	99	9999	999	99	92	150	565	1	2	97	305	133	4665
GLEATON	16	1	5	10	999	999	99	99	99	999	99	99	9999	999	99	9999	176	510	1	2	82	294	98	4665
GULLICKS	16	1	5	10	999	999	99	99	99	999	99	99	9999	999	99	9999	1826	1825	2	1	193	382	132	4665
HENNEMAN	16	1	5	4	999	999	99	99	99	999	99	99	9999	999	99	195	335	1100	1	3	94	305	120	4665
PETRY-D	16	1	5	12	999	999	99	99	99	999	99	99	9999	999	99	785	475	650	1	1	149	445	136	4665

	A	B	C	D	E	F	G	H	I	J	K	L	M	N	O	P	Q	R	S	T	U	V	W	X
TANANA-F	16	1	5	18	999	999	99	99	99	999	99	99	9999	999	99	925	1100	1900	1	1	176	531	135	4665
BICHETTE	17	7	5	3	349	89	15	1	15	16	5	2	183	12	7	9999	120	185	1	9	999	999	999	1607
BROCK-G	17	3	5	9	367	91	23	0	7	43	4	2	885	63	5	700	787	937	1	9	999	999	999	1607
DEMPSEY	17	2	5	22	128	25	5	0	0	23	1	0	9999	999	99	420	500	150	1	9	999	999	999	1607
GANTNER	17	4	5	15	323	85	8	5	0	29	18	3	164	220	7	850	700	1000	1	9	999	999	999	1607
HAMILT-D	17	7	1	2	156	46	5	0	1	9	10	3	120	1	1	9999	100	168	1	9	999	999	999	1607
MALDONAD	17	7	2	10	590	161	32	2	22	49	3	5	293	9	2	900	1005	825	1	9	999	999	999	1607
MOLITOR	17	9	5	13	418	119	27	6	12	37	18	3	136	190	4	1750	2433	3233	1	9	999	999	999	1607
RANDOLPH	17	4	1	16	388	101	13	3	2	45	7	1	198	313	11	875	875	500	1	9	999	999	999	1607
SHEFFIEL	17	5	1	3	487	143	30	1	10	44	25	10	98	254	25	85	135	400	1	9	999	999	999	1607
SPIERS-B	17	6	5	2	363	88	15	3	3	16	11	6	159	326	12	68	135	250	1	9	999	999	999	1607
STUBBS-F	17	9	1	7	448	117	23	2	23	48	19	6	497	42	5	345	450	1867	1	9	999	999	999	1607
SURHOFF	17	2	5	4	474	131	21	4	6	41	18	7	9999	999	99	180	587	1085	1	9	999	999	999	1607
SVEUM-D	17	9	5	4	117	23	7	0	1	12	0	1	17	28	4	225	9999	275	1	9	999	999	999	1607
VAUGHN-G	17	7	1	2	382	84	26	2	17	33	7	4	195	8	7	68	107	190	1	9	999	999	999	1607
YOUNT-R	17	7	5	17	587	145	17	5	17	78	15	8	422	3	4	1150	3200	3200	1	9	999	999	999	1607
BOSIO-C	17	1	5	5	999	999	99	99	99	999	99	99	9999	999	99	200	710	875	1	1	132	400	117	1607
BROWN-KJ	17	1	1	1	999	999	99	99	99	999	99	99	9999	999	99	9999	9999	107	1	1	23	257	94	1607
CRIM-C	17	1	5	4	999	999	99	99	99	999	99	99	9999	999	99	225	600	860	1	2	85	347	119	1607
HIGUERA	17	1	4	6	999	999	99	99	99	999	99	99	9999	999	99	1525	2125	2750	1	1	170	376	116	1607
KNUDSON	17	1	5	6	999	999	99	99	99	999	99	99	9999	999	99	85	170	485	1	1	168	412	123	1607
LEE-M	17	1	2	2	999	999	99	99	99	999	99	99	9999	999	99	9999	100	110	1	2	21	211	101	1607
NAVARRO	17	1	4	2	999	999	99	99	99	999	99	99	9999	999	99	68	120	190	1	1	149	446	133	1607
NUNEZ-ED	17	1	2	9	999	999	99	99	99	999	99	99	9999	999	99	175	400	825	1	2	80	224	117	1607
PLESAC-D	17	1	5	5	999	999	99	99	99	999	99	99	9999	999	99	770	1517	2267	1	3	69	443	132	1607
BARFIELD	18	7	1	10	476	117	21	2	25	82	4	3	305	16	9	1300	1267	1967	1	9	999	999	999	18087
BLOWERS	18	5	5	2	144	27	4	0	5	12	1	0	9999	999	99	68	9999	130	1	9	999	999	999	18087
ESPINOZA	18	6	4	6	438	98	12	2	2	16	1	2	268	447	17	68	285	610	1	9	999	999	999	18087
GEREN-B	18	2	5	3	277	59	7	0	8	13	0	0	9999	999	99	70	170	230	1	9	999	999	999	18087

148

	A	B	C	D	E	F	G	H	I	J	K	L	M	N	O	P	Q	R	S	T	U	V	W	X
HALL-M	18	8	1	10	360	93	23	2	12	6	0	0	9999	999	99	875	1100	1100	1	9	999	999	999	18087
KELLY-RO	18	7	2	4	641	183	32	4	15	33	42	17	420	5	5	80	295	900	1	9	999	999	999	18087
LEYRITZ	18	5	5	1	303	78	13	1	5	27	2	3	9999	999	99	9999	100	135	1	9	999	999	999	18087
LOVULLO	18	3	5	2	87	10	2	0	1	14	0	0	9999	999	99	9999	9999	100	1	9	999	999	999	18087
LUSADER	18	7	5	4	87	21	2	0	2	12	0	0	53	1	1	9999	9999	125	1	9	999	999	999	18087
MAAS-K	18	3	5	1	254	64	9	0	21	43	1	2	9999	999	99	9999	100	250	1	9	999	999	999	18087
MATTINGL	18	3	5	9	394	101	16	0	5	28	1	0	800	78	3	2200	2500	3420	1	9	999	999	999	18087
MEULENS	18	7	2	2	83	20	7	0	3	9	1	0	9999	999	99	68	9999	120	1	9	999	999	999	18087
NOKES-M	18	2	5	6	351	87	9	1	11	24	2	2	9999	999	99	195	650	887	1	9	999	999	999	18087
SAX-S	18	4	5	10	615	160	24	2	4	49	43	9	292	457	10	1267	1067	1667	1	9	999	999	999	18087
VELARDE	18	5	5	4	229	48	6	2	5	20	0	3	43	128	10	72	136	145	1	2	121	415	137	18087
CADARET	18	1	5	4	999	999	99	99	99	999	99	99	9999	999	99	169	305	620	1	2	156	419	121	18087
CARY-C	18	1	5	6	999	999	99	99	99	999	99	99	9999	999	99	90	285	570	1	1	30	356	107	18087
EILAND-D	18	1	5	3	999	999	99	99	99	999	99	99	9999	999	99	9999	9999	110	1	1	127	198	108	18087
FARR-S	18	1	5	7	999	999	99	99	99	999	99	99	9999	999	99	605	775	2400	1	2	93	339	103	18087
GUETTERM	18	1	5	6	999	999	99	99	99	999	99	99	9999	999	99	137	500	1050	1	2	93	339	103	18087
HABYAN-J	18	1	5	5	999	999	99	99	99	999	99	99	9999	999	99	9999	9999	105	1	2	8	208	135	18087
HAWKINS	18	1	5	9	999	999	99	99	99	999	99	99	9999	999	99	933	1133	1533	1	2	157	537	137	18087
LEARY-T	18	1	5	9	999	999	99	99	99	999	99	99	9999	999	99	670	825	1975	1	1	208	411	124	18087
PLUNK-E	18	1	5	5	999	999	99	99	99	999	99	99	9999	999	99	226	514	950	1	2	72	272	128	18087
SANDERSO	18	1	5	3	999	999	99	99	99	999	99	99	9999	999	99	500	850	2125	1	1	206	388	120	18087
WITT-M	18	1	5	0	999	999	99	99	99	999	99	99	9999	999	99	1400	1310	2417	1	1	117	400	121	18087
ALOMAR-R	19	4	2	3	586	168	27	5	6	48	24	7	311	392	17	150	400	1250	1	9	999	999	999	4466
BORDERS	19	2	5	3	346	99	24	2	15	18	0	1	9999	999	99	101	180	700	1	9	999	999	999	4466
CARTER-J	19	7	1	8	634	147	27	1	24	48	22	6	385	13	5	1630	1867	3667	1	9	999	999	999	4466
GONZAL-R	19	4	3	6	103	22	3	1	1	12	1	1	61	94	1	95	206	306	1	9	999	999	999	4466
GRUBER-K	19	5	5	7	592	162	36	6	31	48	14	2	123	280	19	487	1250	3033	1	9	999	999	999	4466
HILL-GL	19	8	1	2	260	60	11	3	12	18	8	3	9999	999	99	9999	100	170	1	9	999	999	999	4466
LEE-MAN	19	4	2	6	391	95	12	4	6	26	3	1	259	286	4	160	380	712	1	9	999	999	999	4466

	A	B	C	D	E	F	G	H	I	J	K	L	M	N	O	P	Q	R	S	T	U	V	W	X
MULLINIK	19	9	5	14	97	28	4	0	2	22	2	1	12	25	2	650	550	725	1	9	999	999	999	4466
MYERS-G	19	2	5	3	250	59	7	1	5	22	0	1	9999	999	99	9999	105	160	1	9	999	999	999	4466
OLERUD-J	19	8	5	2	358	95	15	1	14	57	0	2	9999	999	99	9999	292	292	1	9	999	999	999	4466
TABLER-P	19	7	5	10	238	65	15	1	2	23	0	2	88	5	1	825	725	700	1	9	999	999	999	4466
WHITE-DE	19	7	2	6	443	96	17	3	11	44	21	6	302	11	9	380	580	750	1	9	999	999	999	4466
WHITEN-M	19	7	1	1	88	24	1	1	2	7	2	0	9999	999	99	9999	100	115	1	9	999	999	999	4466
WILSON-M	19	7	1	11	588	156	36	4	3	31	23	4	370	5	3	1000	1125	1625	1	9	999	999	999	4466
ACKER-J	19	1	5	8	999	999	99	99	99	999	99	99	9999	999	99	469	700	1050	1	2	91	383	134	4466
DAYLEY-K	19	1	5	9	999	999	99	99	99	999	99	99	9999	999	99	925	925	1833	2	2	73	356	114	4466
HENKE-T	19	1	5	9	999	999	99	99	99	999	99	99	9999	999	99	975	1167	2967	1	3	74	217	94	4466
KEY-J	19	1	5	7	999	999	99	99	99	999	99	99	9999	999	99	1767	1467	2167	1	1	154	425	112	4466
STIEB-D	19	1	5	12	999	999	99	99	99	999	99	99	9999	999	99	1500	1850	3000	1	1	208	293	109	4466
STOTTL-T	19	1	5	3	999	999	99	99	99	999	99	99	9999	999	99	85	168	315	1	1	203	434	129	4466
WARD-D	19	1	5	5	999	999	99	99	99	999	99	99	9999	999	99	168	300	800	1	2	127	345	102	4466
WELLS-D	19	1	5	4	999	999	99	99	99	999	99	99	9999	999	99	107	275	800	1	1	189	314	101	4466
WILLS-F	19	1	5	8	999	999	99	99	99	999	99	99	9999	999	99	9999	242	435	1	2	99	473	127	4466
FELIX-J	20	7	4	2	463	122	23	7	15	45	13	8	244	11	9	68	155	310	1	9	999	999	999	14532
GAETTI-G	20	5	5	10	577	132	27	5	16	36	6	1	102	318	18	1517	1167	2700	1	9	999	999	999	14532
GALLAG-D	20	7	5	4	126	32	4	1	0	7	1	2	96	3	2	80	100	357	1	9	999	999	999	14532
HILL-D	20	4	5	7	352	93	18	2	3	29	1	2	128	173	3	9999	225	500	1	9	999	999	999	14532
HOWELL-J	20	5	5	6	316	72	19	1	8	46	3	0	70	193	17	470	652	652	1	9	999	999	999	14532
ORTON-J	20	2	5	2	84	16	5	0	1	5	0	1	9999	999	99	9999	9999	120	1	9	999	999	999	14532
PARKER-D	20	8	1	18	610	176	30	3	21	41	4	7	9999	999	99	975	1475	1825	1	9	999	999	999	14532
PARRISH	20	2	5	14	470	126	14	0	24	46	2	2	9999	999	99	1210	1991	2417	1	9	999	999	999	14532
POLONIA	20	7	2	4	403	135	7	9	2	25	21	14	142	3	3	165	220	770	1	9	999	999	999	14532
SCHOFIEL	20	6	5	8	310	79	8	1	1	52	3	4	170	318	17	908	983	1483	1	9	999	999	999	14532
SOJO-L	20	4	4	1	80	18	3	0	1	5	1	1	9999	999	99	9999	9999	110	1	9	999	999	999	14532
VENABLE	20	7	1	11	189	49	9	3	4	24	5	1	112	3	3	1959	235	425	1	9	999	999	999	14532
WINFIELD	20	7	1	17	475	127	21	2	21	52	0	1	177	7	2		2148	3300	1	9	999	999	999	14532

	A	B	C	D	E	F	G	H	I	J	K	L	M	N	O	P	Q	R	S	T	U	V	W	X
ABBOT-J	20	1	5	2	999	999	99	99	99	999	99	99	9999	999	99	68	185	312	1	1	211	451	137	14532
BAILES-S	20	1	5	5	999	999	99	99	99	999	99	99	9999	999	99	300	9999	425	1	2	35	637	171	14532
BLYLEVEN	20	1	5	21	999	999	99	99	99	999	99	99	9999	999	99	1225	1175	1750	1	1	134	524	131	14532
EICHORN	20	1	5	6	999	999	99	99	99	999	99	99	9999	999	99	272	272	625	1	2	84	308	135	14532
FINLEY-C	20	1	5	5	999	999	99	99	99	999	99	99	9999	999	99	180	800	2500	1	1	236	240	112	14532
HARVEY-B	20	1	5	4	999	999	99	99	99	999	99	99	9999	999	99	170	332	1040	1	3	64	322	112	14532
LANGSTON	20	1	5	7	999	999	99	99	99	999	99	99	9999	999	99	1400	1800	3550	1	1	223	440	131	14532
LEWIS-S	20	1	5	1	999	999	99	99	99	999	99	99	9999	999	99	9999	9999	102	1	1	16	220	66	14532
MCCASKIL	20	1	5	6	999	999	99	99	99	999	99	99	9999	999	99	430	967	2100	1	1	174	325	121	14532
ROBIN-JD	20	1	5	7	999	999	99	99	99	999	99	99	9999	999	99	750	925	1000	1	2	88	345	119	14532
YOUNG-C	20	1	1	1	999	999	99	99	99	999	99	99	9999	999	99	9999	100	105	1	2	30	352	141	14532
CORA-J	21	6	2	3	100	27	3	0	0	6	8	3	9999	999	99	77	9999	120	1	9	999	999	999	8066
FISK-C	21	2	5	21	452	129	21	0	18	61	7	2	9999	999	99	1220	2360	1250	1	9	999	999	999	8066
FLETCHER	21	4	5	10	509	123	18	3	4	5	1	3	305	436	9	1200	1000	1300	1	9	999	999	999	8066
GREBECK	21	5	5	1	119	20	3	1	1	8	0	0	9999	999	99	9999	100	125	1	9	999	999	999	8066
GUILLEN	21	6	2	6	516	144	21	4	1	26	13	17	252	474	17	800	1000	1600	1	9	999	999	999	8066
JACKSO-B	21	7	1	5	405	110	16	1	28	44	15	9	230	8	12	610	1000	700	1	9	999	999	999	8066
JOHNSO-L	21	7	1	4	541	154	18	9	1	33	36	22	353	5	10	77	100	330	1	9	999	999	999	8066
KARKOVIC	21	2	5	5	183	45	10	0	6	16	2	0	9999	999	99	106	108	123	1	9	999	999	999	8066
LYONS-S	21	9	5	6	146	28	6	1	1	10	1	0	206	19	2	325	525	650	1	9	999	999	999	8066
MERULLO	21	2	5	1	81	18	1	0	1	6	0	1	9999	999	99	9999	9999	108	1	9	999	999	999	8066
PASQUA-D	21	8	5	6	325	89	27	3	13	37	1	1	9999	999	99	240	375	800	1	9	999	999	999	8066
RAINES-T	21	7	1	12	457	131	11	5	9	70	49	16	239	3	6	2105	2177	3500	1	9	999	999	999	8066
SNYDER-C	21	7	5	5	438	102	27	3	14	21	1	4	224	11	6	340	700	800	1	9	999	999	999	8066
SOSA-S	21	7	2	2	532	124	26	10	15	33	32	16	315	14	13	68	100	170	1	9	999	999	999	8066
THOMAS-F	21	3	1	1	191	63	11	3	7	44	0	1	9999	999	99	9999	100	120	1	9	999	999	999	8066
VENTURA	21	5	5	2	493	123	17	1	5	55	1	4	116	268	25	9999	100	150	1	9	999	999	999	8066
EDWARD-W	21	1	1	2	999	999	99	99	99	999	99	99	9999	999	99	9999	100	140	1	2	95	322	118	8066
FERNAN-A	21	1	4	1	999	999	99	99	99	999	99	99	9999	999	99	9999	100	120	1	1	87	380	129	8066

	A	B	C	D	E	F	G	H	I	J	K	L	M	N	O	P	Q	R	S	T	U	V	W	X
HIBBAR-G	21	1	5	2	999	999	99	99	99	999	99	99	9999	999	99	68	100	150	1	1	211	316	112	8066
HOUGH-C	21	1	5	21	999	999	99	99	99	999	99	99	9999	999	99	900	1025	800	1	1	218	407	132	8066
MCDOWE-J	21	1	5	3	999	999	99	99	99	999	99	99	9999	999	99	9999	125	175	1	1	205	382	120	8066
PALL-D	21	1	5	3	999	999	99	99	99	999	99	99	9999	999	99	72	100	448	2	2	76	332	108	8066
PATTER-K	21	1	5	3	999	999	99	99	99	999	99	99	9999	999	99	72	125	150	1	2	66	339	128	8066
PEREZ-M	21	1	2	4	999	999	99	99	99	999	99	99	9999	999	99	288	323	218	1	1	197	461	121	8066
RADINSKY	21	1	5	1	999	999	99	99	99	999	99	99	9999	999	99	9999	100	130	1	2	52	482	146	8066
THIGPEN	21	1	5	5	999	999	99	99	99	999	99	99	9999	999	99	570	535	2417	2	3	88	183	94	8066
BRETT-G	22	9	5	18	544	179	45	7	14	56	9	2	865	66	7	1948	2009	2075	1	9	999	999	999	1566
EISENREI	22	7	5	7	496	139	29	7	5	42	12	14	261	6	1	120	475	950	1	9	999	999	999	1566
GIBSON-K	22	7	5	12	315	82	20	0	8	39	26	2	191	4	1	1333	1333	1700	1	9	999	999	999	1566
MACFARLA	22	2	5	4	400	102	24	4	6	25	1	0	9999	999	99	71	105	260	1	9	999	999	999	1566
MAYNE-B	22	2	5	1	13	3	0	0	0	3	0	1	9999	999	99	9999	9999	100	1	9	999	999	999	1566
MCRAE-B	22	7	5	1	168	48	8	3	2	9	4	3	9999	999	99	9999	100	124	1	9	999	999	999	1566
MORMAN	22	9	5	4	37	10	4	2	1	3	0	0	8	1	0	68	9999	115	1	9	999	999	999	1566
PECOTA-B	22	9	5	5	240	58	15	2	5	33	8	5	82	122	3	85	115	307	1	9	999	999	999	1566
SEITZER	22	5	5	5	622	171	31	5	6	67	7	5	100	262	18	340	1001	1625	1	9	999	999	999	1566
SHUMPERT	22	4	1	1	91	25	6	1	0	2	3	3	9999	999	99	9999	100	110	1	9	999	999	999	1566
STILLWEL	22	6	5	5	506	126	35	4	3	39	0	2	181	350	24	460	795	1280	1	9	999	999	999	1566
THURMAN	22	7	1	4	60	14	3	0	0	2	1	1	32	0	0	68	9999	127	1	9	999	999	999	1566
APPIER	22	1	5	2	999	999	99	99	99	999	99	99	9999	999	99	9999	100	215	1	1	185	276	116	1566
AQUINO-L	22	1	4	4	999	999	99	99	99	999	99	99	9999	999	99	68	108	120	1	2	68	316	119	1566
BODDICKE	22	1	5	11	999	999	99	99	99	999	99	99	9999	999	99	1375	675	3167	1	1	228	336	120	1566
CRAWFORD	22	1	5	9	999	999	99	99	99	999	99	99	9999	999	99	150	375	500	1	2	80	416	118	1566
DAVIS-M	22	1	5	10	999	999	99	99	99	999	99	99	9999	999	99	600	2125	3625	1	2	68	511	166	1566
DAVIS-S	22	1	5	9	999	999	99	99	99	999	99	99	9999	999	99	587	1167	2367	1	1	112	474	132	1566
GORDON-T	22	1	1	3	999	999	99	99	99	999	99	99	9999	999	99	68	185	325	1	1	195	373	135	1566
MONTGOME	22	1	5	4	999	999	99	99	99	999	99	99	9999	999	99	95	300	1085	1	3	94	239	114	1566
SCHATZED	22	1	5	1	999	999	99	99	99	999	99	99	9999	999	99	245	562	700	2	2	69	220	115	1566

	A	B	C	D	E	F	G	H	I	J	K	L	M	N	O	P	Q	R	S	T	U	V	W	X
BUSH-R	23	9	5	9	181	44	8	0	6	21	0	3	52	1	0	550	350	500	1	9	999	999	999	2464
CASTIL-C	23	8	4	9	137	30	4	0	0	3	0	1	9999	999	99	432	550	600	1	9	999	999	999	2464
DAVIS-C	23	8	2	10	412	109	17	1	12	61	1	2	9999	999	99	1375	1375	1700	1	9	999	999	999	2464
GAGNE-G	23	6	5	8	388	91	22	3	7	24	8	8	184	377	14	570	833	1733	1	9	999	999	999	2464
GLADDEN	23	7	5	8	534	147	27	6	5	26	25	9	286	12	6	610	700	1100	1	9	999	999	999	2464
HARPER-B	23	2	5	11	479	141	42	3	6	19	3	2	9999	999	99	147	500	737	1	9	999	999	999	2464
HRBEK-K	23	3	5	10	492	141	26	0	22	69	5	2	1057	81	3	1560	2100	2600	1	9	999	999	999	2464
LARKIN-G	23	8	5	4	401	108	26	4	5	42	5	3	9999	999	99	145	228	725	1	9	999	999	999	2464
LEIUS-S	23	6	5	1	25	6	1	0	2	2	0	0	9999	999	99	9999	9999	105	1	9	999	999	999	2464
MACK-S	23	7	1	3	313	102	10	4	8	29	13	4	230	8	3	9999	100	270	1	9	999	999	999	2464
NEWMAN-A	23	9	1	6	388	94	14	0	0	33	13	6	118	173	2	180	350	450	1	9	999	999	999	2464
ORTIZ-J	23	2	2	9	170	57	7	1	0	12	0	4	9999	999	99	300	350	450	1	9	999	999	999	2464
PAGLIRUL	23	5	5	7	398	101	23	2	7	39	1	3	79	200	13	575	605	605	1	9	999	999	999	2464
PUCKETT	23	7	1	7	551	164	40	3	12	57	5	4	354	9	4	2050	2700	3167	1	3	999	999	999	2464
AGUILERA	23	1	5	6	999	999	99	99	99	999	99	99	9999	999	99	295	663	1533	1	3	65	276	107	2464
ANDERS-A	23	1	5	5	999	999	99	99	99	999	99	99	9999	999	99	200	341	785	1	1	188	453	123	2464
BEDROSIA	23	1	5	10	999	999	99	99	99	999	99	99	9999	999	99	1650	1450	1450	2	3	79	420	134	2464
ERICKS-S	23	1	5	1	999	999	99	99	99	999	99	99	9999	999	99	9999	100	143	1	1	113	287	131	2464
GUTHRIE	23	1	5	2	999	999	99	99	99	999	99	99	9999	999	99	68	100	160	1	1	144	379	121	2464
LEACH-T	23	1	5	8	999	999	99	99	99	999	99	99	9999	999	99	425	370	500	1	2	81	320	117	2464
MORRIS-J	23	1	5	14	999	999	99	99	99	999	99	99	9999	999	99	1989	2100	3000	1	1	249	451	120	2464
TAPANI-K	23	1	5	2	999	999	99	99	99	999	99	99	9999	999	99	9999	100	197	1	1	159	407	110	2464
WEST-DAV	23	1	5	3	999	999	99	99	99	999	99	99	9999	999	99	68	100	160	1	1	146	510	138	2464
BAINES-H	24	8	1	11	415	118	15	1	16	67	0	3	9999	999	99	1285	1333	1333	1	9	999	999	999	6253
BLANKE-L	24	5	5	3	136	26	3	0	0	20	3	1	9999	999	99	68	107	125	1	9	999	999	999	6253
CANSEC-J	24	7	4	6	481	132	14	2	37	72	19	10	182	7	1	1600	2010	3500	1	9	999	999	999	6253
GALLEGO	24	4	3	6	389	80	13	2	3	35	5	5	153	258	4	207	500	565	1	9	999	999	999	6253
HENDER-D	24	7	1	10	450	122	28	0	20	40	3	1	319	5	4	850	850	2600	1	9	999	999	999	6253
HENDER-R	24	7	1	12	489	159	33	3	28	97	65	10	289	5	5	2120	2350	3250	1	9	999	999	999	6253

	A	B	C	D	E	F	G	H	I	J	K	L	M	N	O	P	Q	R	S	T	U	V	W	X
LANSFORD	24	5	1	3	507	136	15	1	3	45	16	14	100	194	9	1375	1325	1275	1	9	999	999	999	6253
MCGWIRE	24	3	5	5	523	23	16	0	39	110	2	1	1329	95	5	455	1545	2850	1	9	999	999	999	6253
QUIRK-J	24	2	5	16	121	34	5	1	1	14	0	0	9999	999	99	68	227	500	1	9	999	999	999	6253
RILES-E	24	9	1	6	155	31	2	1	8	26	0	1	21	49	1	470	735	792	1	9	999	999	999	6253
STEINBAC	24	2	5	5	379	95	15	2	9	19	0	1	9999	999	99	280	750	1050	1	9	999	999	999	6253
WEISS-W	24	6	5	4	445	118	17	1	2	46	9	3	194	373	12	190	275	780	1	9	999	999	999	6253
WILSON-W	24	7	1	15	307	89	13	3	2	30	24	6	187	2	0	2150	800	1000	1	9	999	999	999	6253
BURNS-T	24	1	5	3	999	999	99	99	99	999	99	99	9999	999	99	100	235	325	2	1	78	297	126	6253
CHITREN	24	1	5	1	999	999	99	99	99	999	99	99	9999	999	99	9999	9999	105	2	2	17	102	56	6253
ECKERSLE	24	1	5	16	999	999	99	99	99	999	99	99	9999	999	99	937	1579	3000	1	3	73	61	55	6253
HONEYCUT	24	1	5	14	999	999	99	99	99	999	99	99	9999	999	99	650	750	1350	2	1	63	270	98	6253
KLINK-J	24	1	5	2	999	999	99	99	99	999	99	99	9999	999	99	9999	100	140	2	1	39	204	118	6253
MOORE-M	24	1	5	9	999	999	99	99	99	999	99	99	9999	999	99	1242	1192	1567	1	1	199	465	131	6253
NELSON-G	24	1	5	10	999	999	99	99	99	999	99	99	9999	999	99	607	658	1100	1	2	74	157	90	6253
SHOW-E	24	1	5	10	999	999	99	99	99	999	99	99	9999	999	99	1450	1050	800	2	2	106	576	149	6253
STEWAR-D	24	1	1	11	999	999	99	99	99	999	99	99	9999	999	99	1075	1100	3500	1	1	267	256	106	6253
WELCH-B	24	1	5	13	999	999	99	99	99	999	99	99	9999	999	99	1133	1358	3450	1	1	238	295	112	6253
YOUNG-C	24	1	5	8	999	999	99	99	99	999	99	99	9999	999	99	572	675	775	1	1	124	485	130	6253
BRADLE-S	25	2	5	7	233	52	9	0	1	15	0	1	9999	999	99	310	495	612	1	9	999	999	999	2559
BRILEY-G	25	7	1	3	337	83	18	2	5	37	16	4	177	4	2	68	150	265	1	9	999	999	999	2559
BUHNER-J	25	7	5	4	163	45	12	0	7	17	2	2	55	1	2	80	160	247	1	9	999	999	999	2559
COTTO-H	25	7	1	7	355	92	14	3	4	22	21	3	194	4	2	250	440	600	1	9	999	999	999	2559
DAVIS-A	25	8	1	7	494	140	21	0	17	85	0	2	9999	999	99	1325	1550	1725	1	9	999	999	999	2559
GRIFF-JR	25	7	1	2	597	179	28	7	22	63	16	11	330	8	7	68	210	535	1	9	999	999	999	2559
GRIFF-SR	25	9	1	18	140	42	4	0	4	12	2	1	37	1	1	320	100	700	1	9	999	999	999	2559
JONES-T	25	7	5	5	204	53	8	1	6	9	1	2	68	3	2	300	375	525	1	9	999	999	999	2559
MARTIN-E	25	5	2	4	487	147	27	2	11	74	1	4	89	259	27	9999	123	350	1	9	999	999	999	2559
OBRIEN-P	25	3	5	9	366	82	18	0	5	44	0	0	850	76	5	700	1187	2037	1	9	999	999	999	2559
REYNOL-H	25	4	1	8	642	162	36	5	5	81	31	16	330	499	19	635	967	1867	1	9	999	999	999	2559

	A	B	C	D	E	F	G	H	I	J	K	L	M	N	O	P	Q	R	S	T	U	V	W	X
SCHAEFER	25	5	5	2	107	22	3	0	0	3	4	1	9999	99	99	9999	100	110	1	9	999	999	999	2559
SINATRO	25	2	5	8	50	15	1	0	0	4	1	0	9999	99	99	9999	114	140	1	9	999	999	999	2559
VALLE-D	25	2	3	7	308	66	15	0	7	45	1	2	9999	99	99	317	510	667	1	9	999	999	999	2559
VIZQUEL	25	6	4	2	255	63	3	2	2	18	4	1	103	239	7	68	135	180	1	9	999	999	999	2559
DELUCIA	25	1	3	1	999	999	99	99	99	999	99	99	9999	99	99	9999	9999	100	1	1	36	200	98	2559
HANSON-E	25	1	5	3	999	999	99	99	99	999	99	99	9999	99	99	68	190	400	1	1	236	324	105	2559
HARRI-GE	25	1	1	2	999	999	99	99	99	999	99	99	9999	99	99	68	108	132	1	2	38	474	147	2559
HOLMAN-B	25	1	5	3	999	999	99	99	99	999	99	99	9999	99	99	82	193	300	1	1	189	403	123	2559
JACKSO-M	25	1	1	5	999	999	99	99	99	999	99	99	9999	99	99	210	430	700	1	2	77	454	128	2559
JOHNSO-R	25	1	5	3	999	999	99	99	99	999	99	99	9999	99	99	70	185	350	1	1	219	365	123	2559
KRUEGER	25	1	5	8	999	999	99	99	99	999	99	99	9999	99	99	150	335	400	1	1	129	398	135	2559
MURPHY-R	25	1	5	6	999	999	99	99	99	999	99	99	9999	99	99	295	825	950	1	2	57	632	186	2559
SCHOOLER	25	1	5	3	999	999	99	99	99	999	99	99	9999	99	99	115	265	490	1	3	56	225	103	2559
SWAN-R	25	1	5	2	999	999	99	99	99	999	99	99	9999	99	99	9999	100	108	1	1	47	364	115	2559
SWIFT-B	25	1	5	5	999	999	99	99	99	999	99	99	9999	99	99	165	405	850	1	2	128	239	115	2559
DAUGHT-J	26	7	5	3	310	93	20	2	6	22	0	0	9999	99	99	68	115	205	1	9	999	999	999	3885
DIAZ-M	26	6	4	4	22	3	1	0	0	0	0	0	9999	99	99	75	9999	120	1	9	999	999	999	3885
FRANCO-J	26	4	2	9	582	172	27	1	11	82	31	10	310	444	19	1275	1462	2287	1	9	999	999	999	3885
GONZA-JU	26	7	2	2	90	26	7	1	4	2	0	1	9999	99	99	9999	100	120	1	9	999	999	999	3885
GREEN-G	26	6	5	3	88	19	3	0	0	6	1	1	9999	99	99	9999	115	125	1	9	999	999	999	3885
HUSON-J	26	6	5	3	396	95	12	2	0	46	12	4	157	254	17	9999	103	160	1	9	999	999	999	3885
KREUTER	26	2	5	3	22	1	1	0	0	8	0	0	9999	99	99	72	9999	110	1	9	999	999	999	3885
KUNKEL-J	26	9	5	7	200	34	11	1	3	11	2	1	77	126	9	80	140	200	1	9	999	999	999	3885
PALMEIRO	26	3	4	5	598	191	35	6	14	40	3	3	1215	91	7	212	345	1475	1	9	999	999	999	3885
PARENT-M	26	2	5	5	189	42	11	0	3	16	1	0	9999	99	99	100	190	280	1	9	999	999	999	3885
PETRALLI	26	2	5	9	325	83	13	1	0	50	0	2	9999	99	99	325	537	562	1	9	999	999	999	3885
PETTIS-G	26	7	1	9	423	101	16	8	3	57	38	15	285	10	2	440	753	903	1	9	999	999	999	3885
REIMER-K	26	8	5	3	100	26	9	1	2	10	0	1	9999	99	99	9999	100	115	1	9	999	999	999	3885
RUSSEL-J	26	2	5	7	128	35	4	0	2	11	1	0	9999	99	99	450	155	165	1	9	999	999	999	3885

	A	B	C	D	E	F	G	H	I	J	K	L	M	N	O	P	Q	R	S	T	U	V	W	X
SIERRA-R	26	7	2	5	608	170	37	2	16	49	9	0	283	7	10	357	1625	2625	1	9	999	999	999	3885
STANLE-M	26	2	5	5	189	47	8	1	2	30	1	0	9999	999	99	95	120	145	1	9	999	999	999	3885
WALLING	26	9	5	16	127	28	5	0	1	8	0	0	86	6	0	625	500	275	1	9	999	999	999	3885
ARNSBERG	26	1	5	4	999	999	99	99	99	999	99	99	9999	999	99	9999	120	287	1	2	62	215	131	3885
BARFI-JO	26	1	5	2	999	999	99	99	99	999	99	99	9999	999	99	9999	100	110	1	2	44	467	114	3885
BOHANON	26	1	5	1	999	999	99	99	99	999	99	99	9999	999	99	9999	9999	105	1	1	34	662	159	3885
BROWN-K	26	1	5	4	999	999	99	99	99	999	99	99	9999	999	99	72	233	320	1	1	180	360	119	3885
CHIAMPAR	26	1	5	1	999	999	99	99	99	999	99	99	9999	999	99	9999	9999	110	1	1	37	263	119	3885
JEFFCOAT	26	1	5	7	999	999	99	99	99	999	99	99	9999	999	99	83	195	390	1	2	110	447	124	3885
ROGERS-K	26	1	5	2	999	999	99	99	99	999	99	99	9999	999	99	68	157	287	1	3	97	313	125	3885
RYAN-N	26	1	5	24	999	999	99	99	99	999	99	99	9999	999	99	1850	1400	3300	1	1	204	344	96	3885
WITT-B	26	1	5	5	999	999	99	99	99	999	99	99	9999	999	99	200	445	1383	1	1	222	336	126	3885

References

Barrett, Gerald V., and Donna M. Sansonetti. "Issues Concerning the Use of Regression Analysis in Salary Discrimination Cases." *Personnel Psychology* 41 (Autumn, 1988): 503-16.

Berry, William, and Stanley Feldman. *Multiple Regression in Practice*. Beverly Hills: Sage Publications, 1985.

Chadwick, Bruce. *When the Game Was Black and White: The Illustrated History of Baseball's Negro Leagues*. New York: Abbeville Press, 1992.

Christiano, Kevin J. "Salary Discrimination in Major League Baseball: The Effect of Race." *Sociology of Sport Journal* 3 (June 1986): 144-53.

_____. "Salaries and Race in Professional Baseball: Discrimination 10 Years Later." *Sociology of Sports Journal* 5 (June 1988): 136-49.

Dovidio, John. "The Subtlety of Racism." *Training and Development* 47 (April 1993): 51-7.

Frantzich, Stephen E., and Stephen L. Percy. *American Government: The Political Game*. Dubuque: Brown and Benchmark, 1994.

Gwartney, James, and Charles Haworth. "Employer Costs and Discrimination: The Case of Baseball." *Journal of Political Economy* 82 (July/August 1974): 873-81.

Hill, James Richard, and William Spellman. "Pay Discrimination in Baseball: Data from the Seventies." *Industrial Relations* 23 (Winter 1984): 103-12.

Howard, Larry W., and Janis L. Miller. "Fair Pay for Fair Play: Estimating Pay Equity in Professional Baseball with Data Envelopment Analysis." *Academy of Management Journal* 36 (August 1993): 882-94.

James, Bill. *The Bill James Baseball Abstract*. New York: Ballantine Books, 1988.

Jiobu, Robert M. "Racial Inequality in a Public Arena: The Case of Professional Baseball." *Social Forces* 67 (December 1988): 524-34.

Johnson, Bruce K. "Team Racial Compositions and Players' Salaries." In *Diamonds are Forever: The Business of Baseball*, ed. Paul Sommers, 189-202. Washington, D.C.: The Brookings Institution, 1992.

Kahn, Lawrence M. "Discrimination in Professional Sports: A Survey of the Literature." *Industrial and Labor Relations Review* 44 (April 1991): 395-418.

Lachmann, Richard. *The Encyclopedic Dictionary of Sociology*. Guilford: The Dushkin
    Publishing Group, 1991.
Lewis-Beck, Michael. *Applied Regression: An Introduction*. Beverly Hills: Sage Publi-
    cations, 1980.
Mann, Steve. *The Baseball Superstats 1989*. New York: McGraw-Hill Publishing Com-
    pany, 1989.
Medoff, Marshall. "A Reappraisal of Racial Discrimination Against Blacks in Professional
    Baseball." *Review of Black Political Economy* 5 (Spring 1975): 259-68.
Mogull, Robert. "Salary Discrimination in Major League Baseball." *Review of Black
    Political Economy* 5 (Spring 1975): 269-79.
Norusis, Marija. *SPSSX: Advanced Statistics Guide*. New York: McGraw-Hill Book
    Company, 1985.
Pascal, Anthony H., and Leonard A. Rapping. "The Economics of Racial Discrimination
    in Organized Baseball." In *Racial Discrimination in Economic Life*, ed. Anthony
    H. Pascal, 119-56. Lexington: D.C. Heath and Co., 1972.
Pattnayak, Satya R., and John Leonard. "Racial Segregation in Major League Baseball,
    1989." *Sociology and Social Research* 6 (October 1991): 3-9.
Scully, Gerald W. "Pay and Performance in Major League Baseball." *American Economic
    Review* 165 (December 1974a): 915-30.
Scully, Gerald W. "Discrimination: The Case of Baseball." In *Government and the Sports
    Business*, ed. Roger G. Hall, 221-273. Washington, D.C.: The Brookings Insti-
    tution, 1974b.
Sears, David O. "Symbolic Racism." In *Eliminating Racism: Profiles in Controversy*, eds.,
    Phyllis A. Katz and Dalmus A. Taylor, 53-84. New York: Plenum, 1988.
Singell, Larry D., Jr. "Baseball-specific Human Capital: Why Good but not Great Players
    are more Likely to Coach in the Major Leagues." *Southern Economic Journal*
    58 (July 1991): 77-86.
Sloan, Dave, ed. *Official Baseball Guide - 1985 Edition*. St. Louis: The Sporting News,
    1985.
_____. *Official Baseball Guide - 1986 Edition*. St. Louis: The Sporting News, 1986.
Smith, Tom. "Changing Racial Labels: From `Colored' to `Negro' to `Black' to `African
    American.'" *Public Opinion Quarterly* 56 (1992): 496-514.
Sommers, Paul M. "An Empirical Note on Salaries in Major League Baseball." *Social
    Science Quarterly* 71 (December 1990): 861-67.
Thorn, John, and Pete Palmer, eds. *Total Baseball*. New York: Warner Books, Inc., 1991.
Voigt, David Q. "America's Game: A Brief History of Baseball." In *The Baseball Ency-
    clopedia: The Complete and Definitive Record of Major League Baseball*, 3-61.
    New York: Macmillan Publishing Company, 1993.
Weigel, Russell H., and Paul W. Howes. "Conceptions of Racial Prejudice: Symbolic-
    Racism Reconsidered." *Journal of Social Issues* 41 (1985): 117-38.
World Almanac and Book of Facts, 1993, ed., Mark S. Hoffman. New York: Pharos
    Books, 1993.
Zoss, Joel, and John Bowman. *Diamonds in the Rough: The Untold History of Baseball*.
    New York: Macmillan Publishing Company, 1989.

Index

About the Authors

BRET L. BILLET is an Associate Professor of Political Science at Wartburg College in Iowa. He is the author of two books, including *Modernization Theory and Economic Development* (Praeger, 1993).

LANCE J. FORMWALT is a law student at the University of Iowa.

ISBN 0-275-95193-6

90000>

EAN

9 780275 951931

HARDCOVER BAR CODE